Please renew/return this item by the last date shown.

So that your telephone call is charged at local rate,
please call the numbers as set out below:

	From Area codes 01923 or 0208:	From the rest of Herts:
Renewals:	01923 471373	01438 737373
Enquiries:	01923 471333	01438 737333
Minicom:	01923 471599	01438 737599

L32b

INT

D1389042

THE
EMPRESS BROWN
The Story of a Royal
Friendship

TOM CULLEN

THE
EMPRESS
BROWN

The Story of
a Royal Friendship

THE BODLEY HEAD
LONDON SYDNEY
TORONTO

© Tom Cullen 1969
SBN 370 00323 3
Printed and bound in Great Britain for
The Bodley Head Ltd
9 Bow Street, London, WC2
by C. Tinling & Co. Ltd., Prescot
Set in Monotype Scotch Roman
First published 1969

CONTENTS

ILLUSTRATIONS

'She belongs to this nation, and not to any individual in it. What she did and said affected profoundly the lives of vast multitudes of men and women, and it is absurd that any effort to increase our knowledge of her should be frustrated . . .'

ST JOHN ERVINE, 1937

'But the Queen is much more than a symbol: she stands peculiarly for the idea that the ultimate reality in corporate life . . . is not an abstraction, but a human being of like passions with ourselves.'

DERMOT MORRAH, *The Work of the Queen*, 1958

'The Queen will talk as if she were Mrs Jones and might live just where she liked.'

SIR THOMAS BIDDULPH,
Keeper of the Privy Purse, 1871

'The more circumstantial stories respecting the Queen's relations with John Brown deserve to be the subject of serious historical criticism.'

ROYDON HARRISON, *Before Socialism*, 1965

'Jesus, I had to laugh at the way he came out with the one about the winkers on her blind drunk in her royal palace every night of God, old Vic, with her jorum of mountain dew and her coachman carting her up body and bones to roll into bed and she pulling him by the whiskers and singing him old bits of songs about *Ehren on the Rhine* and come where the booze is cheaper.'

JAMES JOYCE, *Ulysses*, 1922

Although John Brown has been dead for eighty-six years, his bones still rattle in the Royal closet at Windsor, where, as a subject for scandal, he is regarded as second to the Abdication. (I am told that right up to World War II it was considered bad form to mention Brown's name in certain London clubs.) Therefore, anyone who attempts to elucidate the 'Brown question' faces a daunting task. An account is given later of Edward VII's attempts to wipe out every last trace of Brown by destroying all the memorials which Queen Victoria erected to him. No less thorough, if gentler in her method, was Princess Beatrice, the Queen's youngest daughter. In going through her mother's journals, for example, and copying out those extracts which she thought relevant, before consigning the originals to the flames, Princess Beatrice excised almost every mention of Brown, though we know from those entries which escaped the *auto-da-fé* that the Highlander figured prominently in the Queen's daily jottings.

Brown had one friend at Court, however. Sir Henry Ponsonby, the Queen's private secretary from 1870, was not only amused by Brown, whom he called 'Child of Nature', but respected him and saw his usefulness. Ponsonby's letters to his wife constitute an important source of information concerning not only Brown, but Queen Victoria's life at Balmoral, and I am grateful to his grandson, Lord Ponsonby of Shulbrede, for allowing me to quote from them. The extracts from Queen Victoria's published letters and journals are quoted by gracious permission of Her Majesty the Queen. I am indebted to the present Lord Derby for giving me access to the papers of his ancestor, the 14th Earl of

Derby, who was thrice Queen Victoria's Prime Minister, and permitting me to quote from them.

I would also like to thank for their help Mr Hugh W. Lamond, of Torphins, Aberdeenshire, and his sister, Mrs Hilda Harris, of Stockport, Cheshire, who are John Brown's great-nephew and great-niece, respectively. In particular, Mrs Harris has been most kind in making available to me the mementoes she inherited from Hugh Brown, her grandfather and brother to John. These include important holograph letters written by Queen Victoria.

Of others who have helped to make this book possible I would like to single out Mr Norman Williams, who assisted with research at the British Museum's Newspaper Library; Mr Tom Van Dycke and his wife Elizabeth, who have read the book in manuscript and made important suggestions; Dr Hal Yarrow, for expert medical opinion concerning Brown's illnesses; Mr David Duff, of Weybread, Diss, Norfolk, and Dr George F. Pinne, of Omaha, Nebraska.

Anyone who writes about Queen Victoria today must place himself under debt to the Countess of Longford, whose recent study of the Queen throws new light on her character. I am grateful to Weidenfeld and Nicolson for permission to quote from Lady Longford's *Victoria R.I.*, and to the following authors, editors and publishers for permission to quote from their books: John Murray for *The Life of Benjamin Disraeli* by Monypenny and Buckle and *The Letters of Queen Victoria;* Eyre and Spottiswoode for *Recollections of Three Reigns* by Sir Frederick Ponsonby; William Kimber for *The Work of the Queen* by Dermot Morrah; Stanley Paul for *Queen Victoria's John Brown* by E. E. P. Tisdall; Evans Brothers for *Dearest Child* edited by Roger Fulford; Hodder and Stoughton for *The Queen and Mr. Gladstone* by Philip Guedalla; Macmillan for *Henry Ponsonby* by Arthur Ponsonby; and the Earl of Antrim for *Recollections* by the Countess of Antrim (privately printed).

My thanks are due also to the staffs of the British Museum

Reading Room, the British Museum Newspaper Library, the Public Record Office, the London Library, the War Office Library, and the Central Public Library, Aberdeen.

The numbers to be found in the text refer to the sources quoted, which are listed alphabetically in the Selected Bibliography at the back of the book.

1

PENNY PLAIN
TUPPENNY COLOURED

'THE Queen will not be dictated to . . .' How often in the
course of her lifetime Queen Victoria was to use these words,
or similar ones, in order to impose her will upon others—
that dreadful Mr Gladstone, for example, whom she accused
of trying to run her as Bismarck ran the German Empire.
'The Queen will not be dictated to . . .' the words had the
finality of that other much quoted phrase, 'We are not
amused'. They meant that Queen Victoria had made up her
mind, that nothing could dissuade her from her course, that
the discussion was, in fact, closed. But when 'the poor,
nervous, shaken Queen', as she described herself in June,
1867, accused her Prime Minister, the 14th Earl of Derby, of
trying to dictate to her, it was as much in sorrow as in anger.

Queen Victoria was angry, to be sure—for Lord Derby
had dared to suggest that she leave John Brown, the
Queen's personal attendant, at home when she went to
review troops in Hyde Park on July 5, 1867. The mere sight
of Brown perched on the box of the Queen's carriage might
lead to incidents of an 'unpleasant nature', the Prime
Minister had hinted. Hissing and booing were the least part
of it; there might even be objects hurled. The Queen's anger
melted to sadness when she reflected that there were souls
so wicked. How could people so misjudge her good, faithful
Brown? How could anyone wish to harm this Highlander,
who had entered her service as a stable hand, and who, by
dint of his intelligence and devotion, had risen to become
her permanent attendant? Overriding her other emotions,
however, was annoyance with herself for having, in a
moment of weakness, given in to Lord Derby. For rather

15

than expose Brown to public humiliation she had consented reluctantly to leave him behind, only to regret her decision immediately afterwards.

What made matters worse was that Queen Victoria had been looking forward to the July 5th Review in Hyde Park, which she had ordered her Cousin George, the Duke of Cambridge, and Commander-in-Chief of the British Armed Forces, to make 'as imposing as possible'. The Queen was proud of being a soldier's daughter,* as she often boasted, and her interest in things military ranged from approving the appointments of all officers above the rank of colonel to deciding such knotty questions as whether brown gaiters should be worn by the Guards when in marching order (emphatically not, she informed those in charge). Her Majesty knew the unit histories of all the troops she was scheduled to inspect on July 5, from the dashing King's Hussars who, with their fur-trimmed capes, looked as though they might dismount and dance a csardas at any moment, to the 17th Lancers with their ominous skull-and-crossbones badge. She knew why the Royal Horse Artillery had adopted as its motto '*Ubique*' and why the 72nd Highlanders, the Duke of Albany's Own, had the word 'Hindoostan' emblazoned on their standards, and wore trews instead of the traditional kilt. In the past on an occasion such as a military review Queen Victoria had been in the habit of imparting these bits of information to Brown as he sat behind her in her open landau, the two often carrying on a running conversation. But now Lord Derby had gone and spoiled it all by decreeing that Brown should be sacrificed. In her bewilderment the Queen poured out her heart to a favourite equerry, Lord Charles Fitzroy.

'. . . she is much astonished and shocked,' the Queen wrote, 'at an attempt being made by some people to

---

* Her father was Colonel of the 1st Royal Scots, also known as 'Pontius Pilate's Guard', because they claimed to be older than any regiment.

prevent her faithful servant going with her to the Review in Hyde Park, thereby making the poor, nervous, shaken Queen, who is so accustomed to his watchful care and intelligence, terribly nervous and uncomfortable . . . what it all means she does not know . . .'[148]

'My dear Grey:—I think you ought to have the earliest information of a danger which we have long apprehended, but which seems imminent,' was the way Lord Derby began his letter, marked 'Secret', to the Queen's secretary setting forth details of the hostile reception planned for Brown in Hyde Park. Lord Derby's informant was Lord Portman, wealthy clubman and one-time Liberal Member of Parliament. 'Lord Portman', the Prime Minister continued, 'has heard from three different and independent quarters that there is an organization getting up to hoot J.B.'[33] The 'hooting', of course would come from the Reform League, otherwise known as 'Mr Beales and his Roughs', who were at that moment busy trampling the flowerbeds in furtherance of their campaign for free speech in Hyde Park, and who would stop at nothing to embarrass the Queen.* It required no imagination on Lord Derby's part to visualize the impact that an anti-Brown demonstration would have upon the diplomats and the titled guests assembled in the viewing stands, not to mention the 10,000 troops, including seven cavalry regiments, that were scheduled to pass in review. 'How this danger is to be averted I do not know,' Lord Derby confessed to Grey, adding, almost as a conditioned reflex, 'nothing can be said to the Queen'. The only solution the Prime Minister could could come up with was that Brown should develop 'some slight ailment which would induce him to wish to be excused' (Derby's underlining).

---

* Edmond Beales, President of the Reform League, had organized the so-called Hyde Park riots of July, 1866, in the course of which park railings had been torn down. However, far from being a firebrand, Beales later became a judge, Gladstone appointing him to the County Court bench in 1870. Marx called him 'that silly ass Beales'.

'Whether you can trust him so far I do not know', he concluded.

General Sir Charles Grey, whose dundrearies added to his appearance as a Victorian worthy, knew better than to ask John Brown to play possum. In the first place, there was no love lost between the two, Grey having exerted subtle pressure on the Queen to get rid of her Highland servant for appearance's sake. Secondly, Brown would be sure to take umbrage at the suggestion, and go running to the Queen. The best course was to brave the Queen's wrath by telling her all, which Grey did. It was thus that Queen Victoria learned of the anti-Brown plot on the same day as her secretary.

In acceding to her Prime Minister's wish that she should leave John Brown at home on the day of the review, Queen Victoria was undoubtedly acting out of genuine concern for the Highlander. She was abnormally sensitive where Brown's feelings were concerned, and went to great lengths to avoid exposing him to snubs of any kind. Perhaps she remembered her own humiliation when in 1839, during a wave of unpopularity, she had been greeted with hisses and cries of 'Mrs Melbourne' at Ascot, where she had appeared accompanied by Lord Melbourne. Or again, she may have been thinking of another episode which was reported at about this time. A gentleman in Highland dress on his way to a Buckingham Palace drawing-room was waylaid by street urchins, who surrounded his carriage shouting, ' 'Ooray! 'Ere's John Brown!' according to *The World*. In high dudgeon the gentleman lowered a window to splutter, 'I'm no John Brown, I'm Cameron o' Lochiel!' So saying, he tore off his bonnet with its eagle feather signifying chieftainship and brandished this out the window as though it were proof of his identity.

But, to return to Queen Victoria, as June drew to a close she was having furious second thoughts about her decision to jettison Brown. Instinct warned her never to yield under pressure, for it was thus that dangerous precedent was established—in this case, to deprive her of Brown's company on some future occasion. And in the two years since he had become her personal attendant, she had learned to depend upon Brown, to find his presence on the box more reassuring than a score of outriders. The more she thought about it the more Lord Derby's intervention took on the aspect of a plot to get rid of Brown, the rumours of a park 'incident' being the pretext. It was in this spirit that the Queen wrote to her equerry, the sympathetic Lord Charles Fitzroy.

'. . . she would be very glad', she wrote from Windsor, 'if Lord Charles could come down tomorrow morning any time before luncheon, that she might have some conversation with him . . . as to what can be done for the future to prevent her being teased and plagued with the interference of others . . . The Queen will not be dictated to, or made to alter what she has found to answer for her comfort . . .'[148]

Had Lord Derby, her tormentor, been present one fancies that Queen Victoria would have stamped her foot, or swept everything from the top of her writing table, as she had been known to do in fits of rage. As it was, the Queen, judging from the tone of her letter, was headed for one of her emotional crises which usually ended in nervous prostration. Would Her Majesty at the last moment have pleaded 'nerves' as her excuse for boycotting the Hyde Park review? Or would she have defied her Prime Minister and taken Brown with her, as she had done in the past? Would Lord Derby, in turn, have been forced to retire from the scene in confusion, as had Sir Robert Peel at the time of the so-called 'Bedchamber Plot'?

The answers to these posers will never be known. The crisis was resolved not in London or Windsor, but six thousand miles away in the dusty, sun-baked town of Queretaro, where the Mexican rebel Juarez had ordered the execution of the Emperor Maximilian, who was distantly related to Queen Victoria by marriage. Lord Derby quickly seized upon this assassination as a pretext for cancelling the Review, while Queen Victoria ordered the Court into deep mourning. ('Too horrid!' read the entry in the Queen's journal.)

For Lord Derby to have braved Queen Victoria's wrath on the 'Brown question' meant that gossip concerning the Queen and her gillie was widespread, for none of her Prime Ministers would willingly have approached the Queen on so delicate and personal a matter. Certainly Gladstone and Disraeli would have thought twice before broaching such a subject. (Gladstone earlier had funked the mission of urging the Queen to appear more in public, freely confessing to his wife, 'I was a coward'.) But then the Earl of Derby, who was serving Her Majesty for the third time as Premier, was part of the old landed aristocracy, imperious, blunt in his speech, with none of the tortured complexities of his lieutenant, Disraeli. Then, too, crippled with gout, he may have sensed that he was nearing the end of his career, and that he had nothing to lose from reminding the Queen of the scandalous rumours that were circulating about her.

Some ideas of what these rumours were may be gleaned from the jottings of an anonymous American observer published in *Tinsley's Magazine* in its issue of October, 1868. The American confessed himself horrified to find that 'Englishmen do not scruple to sully the fair name of their Queen'.

'Soon after my arrival in England', he reported, 'at a table where all the company were gentlemen by rank or position, there were constant references to and jokes about "Mrs Brown" . . . I lost the point of all the witty sayings, and should have remained in blissful ignorance throughout the dinner had not my host kindly informed me that "Mrs Brown" was an English synonym for the Queen.

I have been told that the Queen was not allowed to hold
a review in Hyde Park, because Lord Derby and the
Duke of Cambridge objected to John Brown's presence;
... that the Queen was insane, and John Brown her
keeper; that the Queen was a spiritualist, and John
Brown was her medium—in a word, a hundred stories,
each more absurd than the other, and all vouched for by
men of considerable station and authority.'

The English were not a chivalrous race, the visitor concluded, for if Englishmen did not hesitate to spatter with
mud the name of their own Sovereign they could 'scarcely
be expected to spare that of any other woman'.

Queen Victoria was, of course, aware of the rumours concerning herself and Brown, as was clear from the letter to
Lord Charles Fitzroy already cited, in which she spoke of
'those wicked and idle lies about poor, good Brown'.[148]
Nor was she at a loss where to lay the blame, for in this same
letter she referred to 'ill-natured gossip in the higher classes,
caused by dissatisfaction at not forcing the Queen out' (by
which she meant, of course, forcing her out of retirement).
In reality, Queen Victoria had only herself to blame. There
would have been no 'Empress Brown' scandal had she not,
after Prince Albert's death, shut herself off from the rest of
her subjects, thereby neglecting her duties and depriving
society of its figurehead. 'Empress Brown', incidentally, was
the invention of the pre-Raphaelites—William Morris and
William de Morgan, the potter, disputed the credit for first
having thought up the title. 'What a rage the Empress
Brown will be in!' declared Morris, in commenting upon an
unsuccessful police attempt to break up a Trafalgar Square
rally in 1877.[137]

Walter Bagehot in his classic on *The English Constitution*,
has defined monarchy as 'government in which the attention
of the nation is concentrated on one person doing interesting
actions', a consideration which in countries where 'the

genius of the people was untheatrical' would be trifling, Bagehot admitted. But in England 'the outward show of life', as Bagehot called it, mattered very much indeed. The English people loved pageantry, and they expected their Sovereign to supply them the occasions for it.

Queen Victoria's visits to the Royal Mausoleum at Frogmore where Prince Albert's remains were interred could by no stretch of the imagination qualify as 'interesting actions'. Nor could her officiating at various unveiling ceremonies, as England began to be dotted with little Albert Memorials (as early as March, 1862, Lord Torrington had warned J. T. Delane, editor of *The Times*, 'If this goes on every town in England will have some miserable work of art').[131] Meanwhile, at the opening of Parliament each year the sight of the vacant throne with the Sovereign's purple robes draped over it like a discarded grapeskin was an affront to all those brought up in the tradition that the Royal show must go on.* On those rare occasions when she did open Parliament in person, the Queen wore what Lord Derby called her 'quandry' face, meaning that she looked cross, and her widow's weeds were like a rebuke to the glittering assembly.

Not only did the Queen refuse to function as the head of society, she refused to allow her son, Albert Edward, to deputize for her. As a result, Buckingham Palace during the greater part of her reign resembled the cobweb-festooned Court of the Princess Aurora in the second act of *Sleeping Beauty*. Debutantes came of age and failed to 'come out' at formal Court presentations. Their mothers were, if anything, more irate than they at this opportunity missed to curtsey to the Queen. In these circumstances it is not surprising that 'society' should turn on the Queen and seek to get revenge by means of gossip and innuendo. Nor was the revolt confined to the 'frivolous classes', as Queen Victoria called them. 'It matters less what Society thinks . . . but the mass of the

* During the last 39 years of her reign Queen Victoria opened Parliament in person on only seven occasions, and each time her speech was read by the Lord Chancellor.

people expect a King or a Queen to look and play the part', Viscount Halifax confided to the Queen's secretary, Sir Henry Ponsonby. 'They want to see a Crown and a Sceptre and all that sort of thing. They want the gilding for their money.'

Gilding for their money—the average taxpayer minded less shelling out £100,000 a year for the maintenance of two Royal yachts, or £48,000 for the upkeep of the Royal palaces, than he did that the palaces were never lived in, the yachts seldom used. Sir Henry Ponsonby summed it up admirably in an epigram: 'The poor people who are starving for want of a shilling will be furious to read that the Queen spends £3,000 a year on foreign cooks, while the middle classes . . . will be furious that no better use is made of those cooks'.[110]

All of this accumulated ill-will could find no outlet in a direct attack upon the Queen—that was not the English way. But her discontented subjects could get at Her Majesty through her attendant, John Brown, who, in addition to being inseparable from the Queen, was an 'outlandish Scot' (there was much anti-Gaelic prejudice mixed up in the attacks upon him). And so the 'wicked and idle lies', as Queen Victoria called them, were invented, each more outrageous than the other, until *The Sunday Times* felt constrained to cry halt to the 'sinister mendacity' and 'disgusting scandal', while warning, 'The mendacity is not without meaning—the scandal is not without significance.' 'Unpleasant lies', this influential newspaper concluded, 'are invented . . . because there is a strong inducement of dissatisfaction which is too earnest for silence and yet too timid for utterance.'

The scandal, though muted, remains. The passage of years has done nothing to lessen the mystery of Queen Victoria's friendship for John Brown, the mere mention of whose name is still enough to provoke sniggers. Nor can 'too timid for utterance' be pleaded as an excuse for silence today, when the reputation of 'the other Victorians' is undergoing a rigorous scrutiny.* Perhaps it is time to take another look at the received truths concerning the Queen and her gillie.

Undoubtedly one of the greatest of the penny-plain, tuppenny-coloured images that have been handed down is that of John Brown fussing over Queen Victoria, while she submits docilely to his far-from-gentle ministrations. While out walking near Balmoral in the mid-seventies John Berry Torr, an eminent barrister and editor of the *Court Gazette*, once came upon the Queen's carriage empty at the side of the road. Beside it stood Her Majesty trying hard not to fidget while Brown pinned a plaid around her shoulders. Perhaps startled by Torr's cough, the Queen suddenly jerked her head. There was a sharp outcry of pain as the pin grazed the Royal chin, followed by Brown's expostulation, 'Hoots, wumman, canna ye hold yer head still!'[139]

There have been too many eye-witnesses to domestic scenes of this sort for us to doubt that something very like them took place frequently when the Queen and her Highland attendant were out driving. Or again, take those almost military inspections which, we are told, Brown frequently held before the two of them even started out on their drive. Was the Queen's bonnet on crooked? Brown would set it straight, or order Her Majesty to do so in his best drill sergeant manner. Had she worn the same black silk dress twice running? In reminding her of this Brown would describe the dress as 'green moulded', and without a murmur the Queen would hurry indoors to change.

The many accounts of such scenes have, as I say, the force of cumulative evidence. The scenes, themselves, rank among the great comic valentines of modern history, and like most historic clichés reveal more than a little truth about the persons concerned. Queen Victoria's submission to Brown, the degree of intimacy between them thus unconsciously laid bare, become all the more astonishing when one

---

* See Steven Marcus's book of this title which deals with sexuality and pornography in mid-nineteenth century England.

remembers how hypersensitive the Queen was about anyone touching her person. (She described it as a 'dreadful mis-adventure' when at a Drawing-room her lace veil was inadvertently twitched off by her Mistress of Robes, the Duchess of Buccleuch, in arranging the veil.)[93] As for that peremptory 'wumman' which Brown habitually used in addressing the Queen, surely it deserves a niche all of its own among nineteenth-century curiosities, taking its place along-side the more arcane 'Faery', invented by Disraeli to describe the same Royal mistress.

What are we to make of that other image that has been handed down—John Brown initiating the Queen to the delights of his native *usquebaugh*? Intercepted on his way to the Queen's carriage with a picnic hamper, Brown was asked by one of the Maids of Honour if it was tea things that they took with them on their drives. 'Wall, no', Brown replied, 'Her Mad-jesty don't much like tea. We take out biscuits and sperrits.'[110] Actually, Queen Victoria's intro-duction to 'sperrits' had come on one of her early Highland expeditions when she was persuaded to mix whisky with the mountain spring water 'as the people declared pure water would be too chilling', she tells us in her journal.[145] Soon it was not only water that the Queen mixed whisky with; Gladstone, while on a visit to Balmoral, was shocked to find that 'she drinks her claret strengthened, I should have thought spoiled, with whiskey.'[52] News of Queen Victoria's fondness for whisky travelled quickly to the Courts of Europe. Thus we find the Empress of Russia, whose daughter Marie had married Prince Alfred, the Duke of Edinburgh, writing in 1874, 'Marie has discovered that the Queen drinks whiskey, sometimes with water but generally without . . .' The Russian Empress, who had no love for Queen Victoria, added, 'She is afraid of Brown, who treats her like a small child and seems to regard her with a sort of condescension.'[25]

'Afraid of Brown . . . ' this is the impression retained by others who observed Queen Victoria and the Highlander together. But what could she possibly be afraid of, this Queen who would never permit a Prime Minister, however gouty, to sit in her presence, whose own son, the Prince of Wales, went in such awe of her that as a middle-aged man he would cower behind a pillar while trying to nerve himself to appear late at his mother's dinner table? Why did she allow herself to be bossed by this man, submit to his rough ministrations so meekly?

John Brown was Rasputin in a sporran and kilt, if D. B. Wyndham Lewis is to be believed. Lewis, in an entertaining essay in *The Saturday Book*, found that the two men had much in common:

> 'Both were uncouth peasants dominating an obstinate, neurotic, and though strictly virtuous, infatuated Sovereign by a skilful mixture of roughness and charm . . . Both Rasputin and Brown were credited by the mob with occult powers; in Rasputin's case accurately. Both were insolent fanatics addicted to fire-water, both were flattered and detested, both were a gift to scandal-mongers and enemies of the Crown at home and abroad. . . . If, the sinister moujik from Tobolsk brought a throne down, the virtuous moujik from Aberdeenshire certainly endangered one.'[74]*

E. E. P. Tisdall eagerly goes along with the thesis that Brown was the Rasputin behind the mid-Victorian throne, describing the Highlander as 'one of the best hated and most powerful men in Great Britain . . . the figure-head of the most astonishing Royal scandal that ever rolled through

---

* David Duff, in his *Hessian Tapestry*, suggests that the Empress Alexandra Feodorovna may have been predisposed towards Rasputin by having been exposed as a child to John Brown while on visits to her grandmother, Queen Victoria. 'When "Alicky" visited her grandmother, as she often did,' Duff writes, 'she saw, through the eyes of a child, that a peasant was the most important person in the Household. If one wanted anything one asked John Brown.'

the avenues and back alleys of any nation'.[139] Another who subscribes to this theory is Clare Jerrold, who adds that Brown 'knew too many secrets, and ... was charged occasionally by the Queen with delicate and secret missions.'[71]

The trouble with these writers is that they have got hold of the wrong servant. It was Brown's successor, Abdul Karim, better known as the Munshi, who was the Russian monk's match as far as ambition and low cunning were concerned. Karim, who entered the Queen's employ in 1887 as an ordinary serving boy, had all photographs of himself handing dishes to the Queen destroyed when he later became her Indian secretary. Whereas Brown was content with a gold Devoted Service Medal, the Munshi held out for a C.I.E. (Companion of the Indian Empire) and got it, plus a pension for his father and jobs for his brothers-in-law. Brown deemed himself lucky to be given a house at Balmoral, but the Munshi got not only Karim Cottage at Balmoral, but the title deed to a free gift of land at Agra which yielded 600 rupees a year in rents. (In contrast a hero of the Indian Mutiny could expect to receive less than half this amount in rents upon his retirement from service.) Perhaps the difference between the two men can be made clear by a homely illustration. Whereas Brown was glad to assist the Queen by drying her signature, it would never have occurred to him later to hold the blotting paper up to a mirror. Yet this is just the sort of under-handed practice of which the Munshi would have been capable, according to those who knew him best. To sum up, neither by ambition, nor education and training, was Brown qualified for the spy role.

If Brown's hold on Queen Victoria was not political, then it must have been a physical attraction, according to Tisdall, who scoffs at the idea that the Queen's attachment to her gillie was of 'a purely platonic nature—such as might exist between the Mother Superior of a Convent and the regular visiting priest'.[140] Queen Victoria was subject to the well-known Hanoverian itch, Tisdall hints. The blood that flowed in her veins was that of her dissolute uncles, George IV and William IV, the latter having peopled Windsor Castle with his illegitimate offspring. Indeed, he even argues the case for the Queen having contracted a morganatic marriage with Brown. In conclusion he states that the Queen was 'ill-balanced, hysterical, fantastically selfish and self-confessedly of a passionate nature.'[140]

Here we are on familiar ground, and it must be admitted at once that a convincing case can be made that the Queen's relationship with Brown was more than Platonic. It was not just a question of the degree of familiarity between the two as attested by eye-witnesses, nor of the Queen's persistence in advancing her favourite's interests in the face of combined opposition from her family and advisers, although these betokened a deep emotional attachment. The fact was that Queen Victoria was a full-blooded, passionate woman widowed in her prime, and the Hanoverian heritage did count for something. After re-living scenes where Queen Victoria gave someone "toko" for incurring her wrath, or swept everything from her dressing table in a fit of towering rage, who can doubt that the Queen was hot-blooded (she, herself, speaks of 'my very violent feelings of affection')?[151] Given the Queen's peculiar 'nervous' temperament, which will be dealt with at length later, surely those violent feelings must have sought some physical expression, or so it has been argued by those who have been puzzled by Her Majesty's devotion to Brown.

In examining these arguments strong weight will be given to the testimony of those who were close to the Queen, and hence in a position to judge her actions—witnesses such as Randall Davidson, the future Archbishop of Canterbury, who threatened to resign as Dean of Windsor if the Queen carried out her project of writing a memoir of John Brown after the Highlander's death. Again, particular attention will be paid to the views of the Prince of Wales (later King

Edward VII), who was in a unique position to know the extent of his mother's attachment.

Of all the qualities that could be ascribed to Brown, the Queen singled out for praise the one in which he was probably the most deficient—his 'discretion'—in a letter to her daughter, the Princess Royal, in 1865. She, of course, used 'discretion', a favourite word with her, in a variety of meanings, some of them peculiarly her own. To Her Majesty a 'discreet' person was one who was instinctively agreeable to herself, as well as one who was prudent, modest, or circumspect. Thus, if she took a dislike to a person at first sight she was apt to say, 'I chose to have a headache last night. I was not sure that So-and-So was discreet.'[120] In the letter referred to above Queen Victoria assured her daughter that John Brown possessed discretion to a degree 'which the highest Prince might be proud of. And in this House', she continued, 'where there are so many people, and often so much indiscretion and *no Male head* now—such a person is invaluable.'[79] (My italics.) To compare Brown to a blooded Prince must have been galling enough for Queen Victoria's family, but to single him out in such a marked fashion in preference to her own son, the Prince of Wales, as the male head of the house—this must have been intolerable. This aspect of the Brown affair was perhaps *the* crying scandal, as far as the Queen's family were concerned, though not so apparent to the public. (The public, for example, had no way of knowing that Victoria invariably sided with Brown in his quarrels with her own son.)

It was certainly a source of deep humiliation to the Prince of Wales, and explains the thoroughness with which, immediately after his mother's death, he sought to wipe out every vestige of Brown. The Queen was hardly cold in her grave before busts of Brown were smashed, photographs of him were burned, and, crowning insult, Brown's apartment at Windsor Castle was converted into a billiard-room, all on Edward VII's orders. 'Alas, during my absence Bertie has had all your beloved Mother's rooms dismantled

and all her precious things removed,' Queen Alexandra informed the Empress Frederick.[90] Some writers have sought
to explain away this irrational outburst by suggesting that,
as a child, Edward VII was spanked over Brown's knee, on
the Queen's orders, for some misdemeanour. But the
memory of some childhood slight would hardly account for
the fury of the King, then nearing his sixtieth birthday. The
destruction of the Brown memorials is more the work of an
aged Hamlet still smarting from Gertrude's neglect.

'What a coarse animal that Brown is', Lord Cairns
observed, after watching John Brown officiate at a Balmoral
gillies' ball. 'Of course, the ball couldn't go on without him',
his lordship admitted. 'Still, I did not conceive it possible
that anyone could behave so roughly as he does to the
Queen.' Lord Cairns was not alone in marvelling at the off-
hand, almost cavalier manner in which Brown treated his
Royal mistress on these occasions, but then everything
about a gillies' ball was remarkable.

To begin with, nowhere else was Her Majesty to be seen
in such an unguarded mood, the gillies' dances being the
informal occasions that the Badminton Horse Trials are
now to her great-great-granddaughter, Elizabeth II. At a
Buckingham Palace ball the Queen was expected to be animated, to converse, to make herself generally agreeable to
her guests; but here at Balmoral, seated on a low dais in the
centre of the canvas marquee, she spoke to no one, except
for an occasional aside to the Duchess of Athole, her usual
companion. Instead, she had eyes only for the dancers,
whom she watched with the expertise which the present
monarch brings to the judging of horseflesh at the Badminton Trials. She knew the peculiarities of each dancer, who
excelled at the schottische and who at the 'perpetual jig'.

The other prominent figure at the gillies' ball was, of
course, John Brown, who was the undisputed Master of the
Queen's Revels. Standing at the foot of her dais, Brown
would mop his brow and demand, 'Now what's your

Mad-jesty's pleasure?' Usually, in deference to the company, it was a Caledonian. On those occasions when the Queen, to please an English guest, requested a country dance, Brown turned angrily on his heel in ordering the company to form up for a Roger de Coverley.

There was something faintly decadent about this Royal invasion of what was intended to be primarily a servants' entertainment. It was as though the Royal family had grown too effete to invent amusements of its own, but must descend to the servants' hall to find them. One is reminded of Marie Antoinette and her Court who got themselves up as shepherds and shepherdesses when the insipid pleasures of Versailles began to pall. It was symptomatic that in time the Queen's sons put the gillies to shame in dancing the wild indigenous Caledonian reels. As for the gillies, they came to be looked upon as mere figurants, like those walk-ons in colourful tartans in the wedding scene of *Lucia di Lammermoor*.

But Balmoral was no Petit Trianon; the gillies refused to content themselves with a walk-on role at a *fête champetre*. As the whisky took effect, there were loud shrieks as the couples pranced in the 'hoolichan', a noisy form of reel. Inevitably there were mishaps. On one occasion Lord Cowley, Master of the Queen's Household, was tripped by a groom and sent sprawling across the floor. On this same occasion another groom, while executing a *haut pas*, fell across the legs of Prince Leopold, the Queen's youngest son, whose haemophiliac condition caused his mother anxiety lest he sustain the slightest bruise. 'Even Brown saw that this was unseemly and ordered the music to stop', Ponsonby noted.[110]

As the gillies' ball started at seven those who waited at table were often unsteady when it came to serving the Queen's dinner at nine. But Victoria had schooled herself to look upon the ball as a sort of *Walpurgisnacht* during which all was permitted to the servants, and she entered whole-heartedly into the spirit of the occasion. Wine spilt on a guest's trousers was to be ignored, stewards who lurched too noticeably were quietly replaced, and the Queen herself kept up an animated conversation to cover the crash of falling crockery in distant corridors. She could be very amusing on these occasions, reaching back in her memory to the time of her uncle, George IV, to tell how badly things were done then. Some of the stories she related were at her own expense, such as the time she had absent-mindedly snatched a fork from a banquet table and walked with it into the ballroom thinking that it was her fan.

'I have seen the head of the Church of England dancing', the Spanish Ambassador is said to have marvelled after watching Elizabeth I tread a lively measure at Richmond Palace. What, one wonders, would have been the reaction of His Most Catholic Excellency had he been set down three centuries later at Balmoral in the midst of a gillies' ball, and witnessed that other female Defender of the Faith dancing, not with one of her courtiers, but with a gillie? For Queen Victoria, when she resumed dancing after a mourning interval of thirteen years, was regularly partnered by John Brown. Surely the nineteenth century can offer few daguerreotypes stranger than that of this ill-assorted couple, the short, stout, but graceful Queen being led through the intricacies of 'The Flowers of Edinburgh' by the grizzled giant in the flapping tartans.

Queen Victoria grew so fond of Balmoral that after Prince Albert's death she added a spring visit to her regular autumn sojourn there, thus passing four months in every year at this 'Summer Palace', as Disraeli called it. They were four months during which she was carefully hidden from view, leading a life that was little suspected by her subjects; and they were the months every year when John Brown came into his own, acting as her unofficial Lord Chamberlain, so to speak. It is with this hidden life that this book deals. 'Yes, this is a very curious place', Lord John Manners remarked upon visiting Balmoral for the first time.

'More curious things go on here than I should have dreamt of', he added with masterly understatement.[110] As time went on they grew curiouser and curiouser. But there was no hint of this in store when on September 8, 1848, Queen Victoria and Prince Albert drove up to Balmoral and cast their eyes upon it for the first time.

2

TAMING THE HIGHLANDS

'WE arrived at Balmoral at a quarter to three', reads the
matter-of-fact entry in Queen Victoria's journal for September 8, 1848. 'It is a pretty little castle in the old Scottish
style. There is a picturesque tower and garden in front, with
a high wooded hill; at the back there is a wood down to the
Dee . . .'145

Although Queen Victoria did not know it, her arrival was
something of an historic occasion, for this Highland retreat
was to remain her favoured abode during more than half a
century, the spot in her realm where her happiest days were
spent. Now she was seeing it for the first time. But even on
that first day she seemed to have some intimation of the
deep attachment she would form for the Highlands, for she
hurried through lunch so that she and Albert could admire
the view from the top of the wooded hill opposite their
windows. To the left rose snow-capped Lochnager, whose
praises Byron had sung, while below the sparkling Dee
rushed through the glen. The scenery was wild without
being desolate, the young Victoria noted. 'It was so calm,
and so solitary . . . and the pure mountain air was most
refreshing.' Yes, decidedly, it 'did one good'. Besides, the
wooded hills reminded dearest Albert of his beloved
Thüringerwald.

It was in search of health that the Royal couple had come
to Deeside, the dryness of its climate and its pure mountain
air being ideally suited to their 'peculiar constitutions'
according to their physician, Sir James Clark. Although
they were both only in their thirtieth year, in his opinion
Queen Victoria and Prince Albert were already marked as
the victims of the 'Coburg temperament', whose symptoms

included everything from headaches and attacks of nerves to the occasional fits of depression from which these highly-strung cousins suffered.

Balmoral held another attraction for the young couple— its remoteness, the castle being located 567½ miles from London and twenty from the nearest railhead. When they first set foot on Deeside Victoria and Albert had already been married eight years, and six of their eventual nine children had arrived, making their appearance with an eye-popping regularity that delighted the British public and the cartoonists of *Punch*. Thanks to their growing progeny, the Royal couple began to need privacy in which to enjoy their children free from prying eyes and lead something like a normal family life. The need had been borne in upon Queen Victoria earlier in 1848 when, while awaiting the arrival of her sixth child, Princess Louise, she had lain awake in Buckingham Palace listening to a Chartist mob smash the street lamps outside the palace gates ('our little riots', as she ruefully dismissed them in a letter to Uncle Leopold). But by April 10 the 'little riots' had grown so alarming that Queen Victoria and her three-week-old baby were evacuated to Osborne, in the Isle of Wight.

Fortunately for them, the small Deeside castle at Balmoral was available in the autumn of 1848 when they needed it most, its former occupant, Sir Robert Gordon, having died suddenly the previous year. So it was that without ever having seen the castle, acting entirely on the say-so of Sir James Clark, that the Royal couple negotiated for the property, which was then held by the Earl of Aberdeen on a twenty-seven year lease. They were to have no regrets. Even that first day the recent troublesome events which had come to England as the backwash of revolution on the Continent seemed to recede. 'All seemed to breathe freedom and peace, and to make one forget the world and its sad turmoils,' the young Queen entered in her journal.

No, Queen Victoria was not one to be put down by

political events for long. She was still the young matron very much in love with Prince Albert and revelling in the freedom that marriage had brought her, even though she rebelled at being put in the family way at such close intervals. ('Men never think, at least seldom think, what a hard task it is for us women to go through this very often,' she had chided her Uncle Leopold.) Her own childhood had been a lonely one spent with her dolls amid the austerities of Kensington Palace, where, as she once told Disraeli, 'I never had a room to myself; I never had a sofa, nor an easy chair; and there was not a single carpet that was not threadbare'.[34] With her accession had come the cold formalities of Buckingham Palace and Windsor, both of which she detested. But now, at Balmoral, the Queen was free from surveillance for the first time. (Charles Greville, the diarist, was horrified to discover, upon visiting Balmoral in 1849, that 'the whole guard of the Sovereign . . . is a single policeman'.)[56] Balmoral also gave her the opportunity to mingle with ordinary people, as distinguished from courtiers, for the first time in her life, and she took full advantage of it. 'The Queen is running in and out of the house all day long,' Greville wrote of those early days. 'Often [she] goes about alone, and walks into cottages, sits down, and chats with the old women.'[56]

Queen Victoria's advent on Deeside had a greater impact on the Highlands than any event since Bonnie Prince Charles had landed at Moidart and proceeded to rally the clans to his cause. In the first place, the Queen was the first British sovereign to venture that far north since the Union of Scotland and England. In the second, like the Bonnie Prince, she gloried in the drop of Stuart blood in her veins, vaunting her Jacobite connections at the expense of her Hanoverian ancestors. Lastly, her presence at Balmoral for four months in the year was to set a vogue that would change the face of this part of Scotland. Soon would begin the trek north of the factory-owners from the Midlands, who would shoot up the deer forests and build houses in the style known as 'Albert baronial', small-scale replicas of Balmoral even to the pepper-pot turrets. The taming of the Highlands had begun with the clearance of cottars from the land to make way for sheep, those 'four-footed clansmen', as they were bitterly referred to. The process would be greatly hastened by the 'civilizing' presence of the Queen.

The irony was that the Highlanders among whom the Queen and the unco guid Albert settled were, in origin, a wild, cateran lot who had eked out their living with stag-poaching and whisky-smuggling. (The district still abounds in drove roads which were used by the smugglers in their moonlight flits.) Indeed, illegal distilling was so common that at one time an excise man, or 'gauger', was staked out at Balmoral to keep an eye on things. Finding himself with a lawless population on his hands, Sir Robert Gordon, when he leased the Balmoral estate, very wisely made no effort to invoke the law. Instead, he hired the most expert of the poachers and smugglers as gillies and encouraged the remainder to emigrate to the colonies. The contrabandists, thus transformed, proved to be trustworthy dependants, whom Queen Victoria, in turn, acquired when she took over Balmoral. As Sir Robert had done before her, the Queen completely ignored the cateran origin of her new retainers and pronounced the gillies 'gentlemen', one and all. ('They are independent and free . . . but have a higher sense of real respect, and of what is gentlemanlike, than the most over-polished English servant', she declared.)[83] As for the gillies themselves, they did their best to live up to the confidence their new *ceanncinnidh*, or chieftain, had reposed in them, and in time many of them acquired a patina of respectability.

In other ways Queen Victoria's 'civilizing' influence can be seen at work in the Highlands during those early years. 'Civilizing' in this context is not meant to carry imperialist connotations, but rather represents an effort, largely unconscious, on the Queen's part to reduce the nature to manageable proportions, to mould it, as it were, with her plump hands. Had she not been Queen she might have made her living as a painter of miniatures, or, again, had tree-dwarfing then been in vogue, she might easily have been one of its foremost exponents, bending and twisting twigs to stunt growth in approved *bonzai* fashion. As it is, the art of the miniaturist can best be seen in her prose, in the 'dear littles' and 'pretty littles' with which she peppers the pages of her Highland journals, for example. That adjective 'little', with its various modifiers, is used to describe everything from Lochnagar, which rose to a majestic height of 3,800 feet, to the head of a deer that Albert had just shot, and that the Queen sketched on the spot before its blood had had time to congeal. The habit seems to have been catching, for Greville, after observing the Royal couple at Balmoral, declared that 'they live not merely like private gentle-folks, but like very small gentle-folks, small house, small rooms, small establishment.'[56]

Another early visitor, the Earl of Malmesbury, wrote amusingly about the cramped quarters of the old castle, where the billiard-room served as library and drawing-room as well. When the men played billiards after dinner, the Queen and her mother, the Duchess of Kent, were 'constantly obliged to get up from their chairs to be out of the way of the cues'. However, 'nothing could be more cheerful and evidently perfectly happy than the Queen and the Prince', he claimed.

With the birth of Prince Arthur in 1850, and of Prince Leopold three years later, it became evident to all that the old castle, which was little more than a laird's manse, was too small for Royal needs. Rather than seek more commodious accommodation elsewhere, the Queen and Albert, both of whom had by this time become attached to Balmoral, discussed purchasing the estate outright, pulling down the old castle and replacing it with a larger one. In 1852 an unexpected bequest from a Scottish eccentric enabled them to do just this.* His head full of schemes, Prince Albert immediately devoted himself to the task of designing their new Scottish abode.

From the start, the re-building of the castle seemed to be dogged by bad luck. To begin with, the skilled masons, who were imported from a distance, did not share Queen Victoria's love of solitude or relish being cooped up together in wooden barracks. By September, 1853, work had already been held up by several strikes, 'now quite the fashion all over the country', as Prince Albert assured Baron Stock-mar.[95] (Albert thought that the newly-opened labour markets in Australia, China and California had something to do with the workers' independent attitude.) To relieve the tedium the artisans bought whisky from one Charlie Stewart, nicknamed 'Princie', and this may have contributed in-directly to the second disaster which overtook the building of the new castle. In September, 1853, a fire of mysterious origin broke out and destroyed nearly everything that had been erected to date. It was manfully fought, the Prince himself joining the bucket brigade that passed water up from the river, but in the end the wooden barracks were burned down, and with them went the workmen's tools and their savings from their wages. The workmen were paid £400 by way of compensation, though the fire was 'clearly their fault' according to Sir Theodore Martin, Prince Albert's biographer, who saw in the Royal generosity 'a practical rebuke to the theory that wages are the sole tie between employer and employed, to which the leaders of the insane strikes of this period were quite insensible.'[95]

Thus, preoccupied with improving the estate and with family concerns, the Royal couple found that their annual sojourns at Balmoral slipped by only too quickly. They

* James Camden Neild left a personal fortune amounting to £250,000 to Queen Victoria when he died in September, 1852. Balmoral was purchased for £31,400, and the Queen used part of the legacy to carry out extensive improvements on the estate. In her lifetime the estate was expanded from its original 17,400 acres to more than 40,000, including the Ballochbuie Forest, reputedly the oldest in Scotland.

arrived usually towards the end of August when the birch leaves had begun to yellow and the heather to take on a purple hue, but the last of the scarlet rowan berries had long disappeared by the time they left, late in November. And each year Queen Victoria found it harder to leave 'this dear Paradise'. Already steeped in Scottish lore from her reading of Sir Walter Scott, the Queen began to think of herself as *ceanncinnidh*, or founder of the clan, as she moved about her estate, visiting the cottar women and making them presents of flannel petticoats and warm shawls.

But if Victoria viewed the Highlands through the pages of the *Waverley* novels, Albert saw them with the eyes of a homesick Coburger, who had grown up in the midst of scenic grandeur. While at Balmoral the Prince Consort seemed to be trying to recapture something. His youth? The memory of carefree days spent in the Thüringerwald?

Whatever it was, the ladies at Court were quicker to detect the depths of the Prince's nostalgia than was his wife. Mary Bulteel (later Lady Ponsonby) described the Prince's expression as 'sad and thoughtful', discerning a 'poetic feeling' of which even the Prince was unaware, but which showed itself in his appreciation for music.[115] Sarah, Lady Lyttleton, was another to remark the Prince's soulful expression when he played the organ ('Such a modulation! Minor, and solemn, and ever-changing . . . and still the same fine vein of melancholy . . . How strange he is!').[95] Prince Albert's melancholia rose partly from the fact that, despite his wife's adoration and the growing confidence reposed in him by her Ministers, he was a stranger in a strange land. The aristocracy still regarded him as a German interloper who preferred sanitary reform to fox-hunting, the study of social statistics to whist, and who was incurably addicted to 'good works'.

But there may have been another reason why the Prince Consort was sad. Those in a position to observe him closely seem agreed that the Prince did not return the Queen's love with anything like the ardour she expressed for him. Kindness, yes; affection, certainly—when Victoria was expecting her first child, the Prince, who was not then twenty-one, showed himself capable of extraordinary tenderness— but passion seemed to be lacking. The Queen on more than one occasion described her husband's attentions to her as being 'motherly', a curious adjective to use in the circumstances.

Lord Melbourne put his finger on a symptom, if not the cause, of the Prince's unhappiness, when, less than a year after the marriage, he commented, 'The Prince is bored with the sameness of his chess every evening. He would like to bring literary and scientific people about the Court.' Queen Victoria, however, had 'no fancy to encourage such people', Melbourne continued. 'This arises from a feeling on her part that her education has not fitted her to take part in such conversation.'[147] Nor did the Prince take delight in his children when they were young, as his wife was the first to admit. 'After a certain age', she wrote to her eldest daughter, the Princess Royal 'if they are nice (and not like Bertie and Leopold are) he is very fond of playing with them.'[151]

Thus from the beginning it was not the pure mountain air alone that drew Prince Albert to the Highlands, but the opportunity to slip away from his family occasionally and to 'rough it' on his own. Balmoral he looked upon as a *Jägersrühe*, or hunting-lodge, and when not occupied with the plans for the new castle he threw himself whole-heartedly into deer-stalking, which he described to Prince Leiningen as 'that most fatiguing' of sports. 'There is not a tree, or a bush behind which you can hide yourself', he wrote. 'One has . . . to keep under the hill out of their wind, crawling on hands and knees, and dressed entirely in grey.'[145]

On these occasions the Prince wore a grey tartan of his own design, but his appearance in a kilt left something to be desired, if contemporary accounts are to be believed. Emily Crawford speaks of 'the want of whipcord in his thews [which] proclaims that he is no Highlander'.[27] In general, the kilt was not becoming to 'gentlemen of German physique', she maintained. 'It needs the feline cleanness of build and muscularity of the mountain Celt for the bare knees and legs to look well.'

If the Prince Consort was no hero to his tailor, he likewise lacked valour in the eyes of the gillies with whom he stalked, for quite early he sought to introduce Teutonic efficiency into what had hitherto been a casual sport. Among his 'German tricks', as the gillies called them, the Prince caused to be constructed an elaborate system of trenchworks on a favourite feeding-ground of the deer; this was so that His Royal Highness could approach closer to his quarry before aiming. The Marquis of Huntly overheard two gillies condemn this unsporting practice in no uncertain terms. Also, the Prince was fond of hunting with stag-hounds, and these dogs would often tear the deer to shreds while it was still alive.* Donald Stewart, the Queen's forester, undoubtedly voiced the disgust of the other gillies when he declared, 'I would rather give a man a week's shooting in the forest than to let loose a hound on a single occasion.'[84]

To make matters worse, Prince Albert was anything but a skilled performer with a gun. He himself was candid enough about his shortcomings. On his very first visit to Balmoral we find him writing to his step-mother, the Dowager Duchess of Coburg, on September 11, 1848, 'I, naughty man, have been creeping stealthily after the harmless stags, and today I shot two red deer—at least, I hope so, for they are not yet found.'[95] On another occasion he confided to his step-mother that, having spotted three deer, he 'shot like the Lord of Freudenfeuer at the Dragon, and missed.'

It is on these early deer-stalking expeditions that we get our first glimpses of the gillies who were to become such

---

* The Prince later discontinued this practice; however, it was fairly widespread judging by the prominence which Landseer gives to deer-hounds in his early Highland sketches.

great favourites of Victoria and Albert—'tall and hand-some' Macdonald, the Prince's *Jäger*, who looked so natty in his hunting jacket and kilt; dour-faced John Grant, whose pawkish humour and quaint way of talking won the Prince's heart. 'He has an ill fashion o' sheeting by them', Grant would say of a sportsman who was a notoriously bad shot. Of the stags, who were ever alert and watchful of their hinds, he would caution the Prince, 'Ye maun tak' care, they're jaylous the day.' Grant became the Queen's Head Keeper, a position he held for nearly thirty years.

The first mention of John Brown in Queen Victoria's journals occurs in an entry dated September 11, 1849, when he is noted as one of the gillies who accompanied the Royal couple when they set out from Altnaguithsach to climb the hills behind Glen Muich. On this occasion the Queen had difficulty with her pony, who took fright at the bogs, but when she exchanged it for Colonel Gordon's mount she discovered that this latter was 'broken-winded, and struggled very much in the soft ground', which she found even more alarming. There were other unnerving incidents involving the Queen's carriage manoeuvring on narrow mountain roads, and as a result Prince Albert decided that an undergroom should be appointed to ride on the box. John Brown was the likeliest candidate, as he was the youngest and sturdiest of the gillies. Accordingly, in 1849 he was selected to go with the Queen's carriage, and two years later he was taken on permanently to lead the Queen's pony on all Highland excursions. As one contemporary newspaper explained it, 'The Prince Consort [was] struck by his magnificent physique, his transparent honesty, and straight-forward, independent character.*

If anyone was struck by that magnificent physique, it most probably was Queen Victoria, who was peculiarly susceptible to masculine good looks. A photograph of Brown, taken in 1851 when he was twenty-five years old, shows him wearing a kilt of grey Balmoral tartan and a

* The *Aberdeen Herald and Weekly Free Press*, March 31, 1883.

peaked cap, and looking big, raw-boned and uncomfortable, like a hired hand on his day off. This unsmiling gillie, one feels, would be more at home striding up a mountain path with his long, springy gait than in a photographer's studio, where his presence seems a threat to the ornamental furniture and bric-à-brac.

Yet the young Brown, judging from this picture, was undeniably handsome. There is nothing here of the arrogance or dourness which characterize many of his later photographs. The upper lip is clean-shaven, and the sparse side-whiskers make no attempt to conceal the fact that he has a chin. This, in itself, would have impressed Queen Victoria, who was terribly conscious of the lack of chin on the part of her two sons, particularly Albert Edward, the Prince of Wales. ('Handsome I cannot think him, with that painfully small and narrow head, those immense features and total want of chin', she confided to the Princess Royal.)[151] Nor, judging from this early photograph, was the whipcord lacking in John Brown's thews, as was so noticeably the case with Prince Albert, according to Emily Crawford. Sassenachs were inclined to run to flesh, Mrs Crawford opined, whereas the sparsely-fed Highlander made only muscle.

Appointing John Brown to lead the Queen's pony turned out to be an ideal arrangement from Albert's point of view, for, with the Queen thus taken care of, he himself could slip away more often to pursue the deer. At first Her Majesty tried to keep up with him. ('The Queen seems quite as keen as the Prince about deer-stalking and often goes out with him', Eleanor Stanley wrote to her mother in September, 1854, adding, 'It is shrewdly suspected he wishes she would let [it] alone.')[130] But the Prince's wish seems to have communicated itself to his wife, for in the end she let him go off alone. 'Albert is away all day long', Queen Victoria wrote in a letter to the Empress Augusta. The company of her children was no compensation, she added. 'I only feel properly à mon aise and quite happy when Albert is with me.'[150]

Not only was the Prince away all day, but he took to spending the night under canvas in Glen Gelder in order to get an early start after the stags. Later he had his own bothy built at Feithort, where he could absent himself from his family for even longer periods.

Left on her own, the Queen filled her time at Balmoral as best she could, organizing sketching expeditions for herself and her ladies with the handsome, young John Brown to guide them. But it was not to be expected that she would leave dearest Albert undisturbed for long. In fact, she pursued him right to the door of the Feithort bothy ('Albert's little encampment', as she called it), getting John Brown to lead her pony up the steep, winding path. 'Albert was still absent, having gone out at six o'clock', she wrote in her journal, 'but Lohlein* and some of the gillies were there.' The bothy itself, with its little stove and shelves for keeping a few provisions, she found 'not at all uncomfortable'. When Albert returned, the two of them had lunch at the open door of the 'little housie'. 'There was a second hut for the people', she noted.

Looking back on those early sojourns at Balmoral, one is puzzled by Albert's evident neglect of his wife, then still in her early thirties. The Prince seemed to find time for everything but the company of his wife and children, plunging into work as though he were in headlong flight from reality. When not stalking deer, he was designing a model dairy on the latest sanitary principles, or supervising the planting of silver fir trees. He seemed to find in intense activity an anodyne to some inner stress. Again, a certain effeteness of character, an attenuation of the Royal strain, seems to have been operative in drawing the Queen and the Prince Consort to the Highlands. Were they not, unconsciously no doubt, seeking by means of contact with a more

* The German valet whom Prince Albert brought with him from Coburg, and whom Queen Victoria retained in her service after Albert's death.

vigorous and primitive people to renew their own strength? Shades of Marie Antoinette again, who insisted upon living at the Petit Trianon as a private person in an effort to escape the cloying atmosphere of Louis XVI's Court. 'Examining all the manufactories of the hamlet, seeing the cows milked, and fishing in the lake, delighted the Queen', according to her companion, Madame Campan, 'and every year she showed increased aversion to the pompous excursions to Marly.'

Playing at being 'simple folk' has long been a favourite pastime of Royalty, but it does not entirely explain the alacrity with which Victoria and Albert embraced some of the more primitive Highland customs. It is difficult to explain their patronage of the barbarous 'deer dances' that were held after a good day's stalking. The deer themselves, of course, did not dance, but lay cold and stiff on the lawn in front of Balmoral castle while drunken gillies with lighted torches danced around them. 'Much whisky and inspection of raw meat', was the way Sir Henry Ponsonby described these 'larders', and he avoided them whenever possible. Not so Queen Victoria, who always came out after dinner to join in the festivities.

Sometimes the process worked in reverse, as witness the Braemar Gathering. This annual event originated in the eleventh century when King Malcolm Canmore called the clans to the Braes of Mar to select, by trials of strength, 'his hardiest soldiers and his fleetest messengers'. Until the advent of Queen Victoria on Deeside, the Gathering had served as an excuse to pipe and dance and to toss the caber and had been innocent enough; but the Queen by her presence unwittingly transformed it into a cruel trial of physical endurance, for in competing for the privilege of receiving a silver snuff-box or a cairngorm brooch as prize from Her Majesty's hands, the athletes often pushed their exertions beyond the limits of prudence.* In her journal

* Her Majesty's presence also had the unexpected result of diverting attention from the competitors. All eyes were upon the Queen.

entry for September 12, 1850, Victoria herself described one such feat of endurance, the so-called 'long race', which was won that year by one of her own gillies, Charles Duncan. 'It looked very pretty to see them run off in the different coloured kilts', the Queen thought, but as they rose to the summit of Craig Cheunnich they were no longer running but crawling on all fours. Duncan, whom the Queen described as 'an active, good-looking, young man', ended by coughing up blood, and 'has never been so strong since'.[145] Presumably as a result of this mishap, the race was discontinued the following year.

Following the Gathering Albert was initiated into the art of 'leistering', or salmon-spearing, and the spectacle of the Prince floundering about in the Dee among the gillies, including Duncan, who seemed none the worse for loss of blood, had 'a very pretty effect', the Queen noted. When Captain Forbes of Strathdon and his clansmen, on their way home from the Gathering, came to the banks of the Dee, nothing would do but that the Balmoral tenantry should carry them piggy-back to the other side, a bit of horseplay which Queen Victoria found 'very courteous and worthy of chivalrous times'. A spirit stronger than chivalry may have animated the company, for, arrived safe and dry on the south bank of the Dee, Captain Forbes pulled off his boot, filled it with whisky and toasted the Queen. 'Our people in the Highlands are altogether primitive, true-hearted and without guile', was Prince Albert's comment in relating this episode to his step-mother, the Dowager Duchess of Coburg.[95]

'A little before seven the joyous cry of welcome was heard, and they drove up smothered in turbans and blue

---

Visitors, in particular, felt cheated by the plainness of the Queen's dress, which 'they would not have considered ... good enough for a Queen's scullery-maid', according to *Tait's Edinburgh Magazine*. This same periodical quotes one matron as exclaiming indignantly, 'Hoo can she be Queen, wha's nae sae braw's the lady o'Innercaul?'

veils.'[131] Thus did Lady Augusta Stanley, one of the Ladies-in-Waiting, describe the Royal couple's arrival at Balmoral on September 7, 1855, to take possession of their new castle. In their absence during the winter the old castle had been almost totally demolished and, in its place, had risen a baronial structure of almost opalescent hue, so white was the feldspar of the granite. Built to Prince Albert's designs, the new castle was a hotch-potch of styles, its notched gables being distinctly Flemish, while its projecting windows were early French renaissance, the whole being redeemed by a high, square clock-tower with turrets in corbel, evocative of Albert's beloved Rosenau.

But Queen Victoria scarcely paused to admire the castle's façade so eager was she to inspect the interior arrangements. As she swept inside, an old shoe came sailing through the door as a token of good luck. Soon the building echoed with 'ohs' and 'ahs', as the Queen and her ladies, still swathed in their blue travelling veils, pronounced 'the house charming, the rooms delightful; the furniture, papers, everything perfection'.[145] She elaborated on this verdict later, exulting, 'All has become my dearest Albert's creation. His great taste, and the impress of his dear hand, have been stamped everywhere.'

While the impress of that dear hand is to be found everywhere at Balmoral today (when the original flock wallpaper with its 'VR' monogram becomes faded the castle's present owner simply has it renewed), many have come to question its taste. Even in Victoria's lifetime that perfection of which she speaks was severely challenged. Tactfully Lady Augusta Stanley found that there was 'a certain absence of harmony' in the interior appointments, while Lord Rosebery, many years later, put the matter more succinctly: 'I thought the drawing-room at Osborne the world's ugliest until I saw the one at Balmoral.'[113] His Lordship, no doubt, had the use of the thistle motif in mind —Lord Clarendon maintained that there were enough thistles in the drawing-room alone to choke a donkey—

Above: Queen Victoria and Prince Albert in the Highlands—a
luncheon at Cairn Lochan, 1861
Below: An afternoon drive in the rain at Balmoral

Above: The Queen
at Osborne, 1866.
Engraving after
the painting by
Sir Edwin Land-
seer

Right: Queen Victoria
and John Brown

or perhaps he was referring to the 'tartanitis' rampant.

The carpets were of red Royal Stuart and green Hunting Stuart, while the chairs and sofas were covered with the same pattern whose angularity Tsar Nicholas II was to find so jarring many years later that he fled the place in horror.[27] Until Queen Victoria appeared in one, no lady south of the Tweed would have been seen in a plaid dress. After Landseer painted Her Majesty wearing Royal Stuart, this most garish of all tartans became the rage. Today Queen Victoria's influence on the Highlands can be discerned in the tartan trimmings that decorate the tea-caddies and shortbread tins in the souvenir shops along Edinburgh's Princes Street. In their debased way they serve to keep alive the memory of once proud Scottish kings.

3

INFATUATION

ASIDE from the mentions in Queen Victoria's journals, one of the earliest glimpses of John Brown we catch is through the thoughtful, grey eyes of the Honourable Eleanor Stanley, one of the Queen's Maids of Honour. Miss Stanley, an attractive, fair-haired girl, came into waiting at Balmoral for the first time in the autumn of 1854, being plunged into the wilds of Scotland directly from the gaiety of the London Season, where she had been the belle of many a ball. To add to her chagrin, many of the guardsmen who had partnered her in the quadrilles were either on their way to the Crimea or were actually engaged in the fighting there, and such news of them as filtered through to Balmoral was ominous indeed. 'The Coldstream' Miss Stanley wrote home, 'has been awfully unlucky . . . there was not one Captain or Lieut-Colonel in the Coldstream fit for duty.' She was referring to an outbreak of cholera.

But the memory of the young is mercifully short; it was not long before Miss Stanley was writing home about 'the most fascinating and good-looking young Highlander, Johnny Brown', who was on the box whenever the Queen went out for a ride. A few days later, in a letter to her grandmother, she referred again to 'a good-looking Highland ghillie sitting on a little sort of perch behind the carriage'. Still later we find her consoling herself for the absence of her Coldstream partners by dancing with 'Johnny' Brown and the other gillies at their annual ball. By this time the Hon. Miss Stanley thought the kilt and goat-hair sporran every bit as attractive as the red tunic and brass buttons of the Guards. 'I don't know whether that becoming dress may have something to do with it,' she wrote home, 'but really the men looked just as gentleman-like, and less awed and embarrassed at being shown off before the Queen, than most of our gentlemen do on similar occasions.' It is an exceptional gillie who can charm both a Queen and the gentlewoman serving her, and it is time now that we had a closer look at John Brown.

As with all else concerning him, John Brown's family background is a matter of considerable controversy. His denigrators maintain that he came from poor, ignorant, peasant stock, he himself being 'as rough as one of the stots he tended before he went to Court', in the words of that weekly gossip sheet, *The World*. At the other extreme, certain well-wishers have tried to connect Brown with the aristocracy, no doubt from a desire to make him appear worthy of the interest the Queen took in him. Thus he was said to be descended from Sir John Brown of Fordel, in Fifeshire, who joined the Covenanters in the reign of Charles II, and whose estates and title were consequently forfeit. Unfortunately I have been unable to find any evidence to substantiate this claim.* Queen Victoria herself tried her hand at the genealogy game, or rather she prevailed upon her factor, Dr Andrew Robertson, to draw up Brown's family tree. Not surprisingly, the results linked the gillie with some of the great Highland clans.

All that is known with any degree of certainty is that Donald Brown, the grandfather of John, had emigrated from Kirriemuir, in Angus County, to Aberdeenshire in 1770. He had crossed the Grampian range on foot via the Keppel Pass† from the top of which he could see the sails of the fishing boats in the North Sea, then descended into the green valley of the Dee. It may well have been that Donald left Kirriemuir under something of a cloud; for

* In 1861 Brown was the third most common surname in Scotland. There were 33,820 persons answering to it.

† The pass is so called because this was the route taken by General Keppel in 1745 in advancing through the Highlands on the right flank on the Duke of Cumberland's main army.

the Browns had come out in 1745 and, after the Battle of Culloden, had been hunted and persecuted like all others suspected of Jacobite leanings. On Deeside he was able to acquire a small holding on the Monaltrie estate of the Farquharsons. Here he married Janet Shaw and sired six sons, one of whom was named John and was to be the father of the Queen's Highland attendant.

There was nothing of the ignorant peasant about John Brown the elder. He taught in a school until he married Margaret Leys, daughter of the Aberarder blacksmith; indeed, he was the author of a *Deeside Guide*, if local legend is to be believed. After marrying he settled down to become a successful tenant farmer at Crathienaird, where the farmhouse is still standing opposite Balmoral on the north side of the Dee. It was there on December 8, 1826, that John Brown, the Queen's gillie, was born, the second of eleven children.

'Well-to-do' is the way the Marquis of Huntly describes John Brown's parents, adding that they belonged to the 'retainer class' of farmers who were proud of their 'almost hereditary association' with the neighbouring lairds.[67] Certainly the Browns were well off in comparison with the average crofter in Crathie parish, whose sole wealth would consist of two or three half-starved cows, a Highland pony, and a few score sheep, all turned loose to shift for themselves on the hills. Bush Farm, to which his family moved when John Brown was five, was several cuts above the average crofter's cottage, judging from its appearance today.* The latter, with its walls of unhewn stone and roof thatched

---

* Bush Farm, which is virtually unchanged, now belongs to a Mrs Sheriff, a widow, who lets the land as pasture and takes in a few holidaymakers for 'Bed and Breakfast' in summer. The farmhouse is the familiar 'but and ben,' except that proper windows have been put in since John Brown's day. What now serves Mrs Sheriff as kitchen, dining-room and living-room was once the 'ben' end of the cottage, as is evident from a comparison with old photographs. The farmhouse still has no electricity, but its gas-mantle lamps are an improvement on the 'cruises', or boat-shaped oil lamps, of John Brown's day.

with heather or broom, was usually indistinguishable from the surrounding countryside.

Mrs Hilda Harris, Brown's great-niece, has a photograph of John Brown's mother which shows her wearing the plaid shawl and white muslim 'mutch' of the typical Highland woman, and holding her knitting in her hand. Her hair is rather severely parted in the middle, her face is round and kindly, its strong features not unlike those of her famous son. The great tragedy of her life came in the winter of 1849 when a typhoid epidemic swept Crathie, carrying off two of her sons and a daughter within a month. They are buried with their parents in the old part of Crathie cemetery, their common grave being marked by a handsome, granite head-stone which John Brown later erected to their 'loving memory'. As for the father, we catch a glimpse of him in the twilight of life in the entry in Queen Victoria's journal for November 13, 1871, which describes him, then aged eighty-one, as he sat in Crathie kirk, wearing a large plaid and looking 'very much bent'. When old Brown died five years later he was given the Highland equivalent of a State funeral. Not only did the Queen attend, but she commanded the greater part of her household to do likewise.

But to return to John Brown, his upbringing was not unlike that of other Highland lads. He learned to use fishing rod and gun almost as soon as he had learned to walk, for trout and game birds were an important part of the diet in a village like Crathie, where a butcher shop was unknown. (A baker from Ballater visited Crathie only once a week in those days.) As a child he also helped with the farm chores; he and his brothers learned the art of 'fogging the walls', stuffing bits of moss into every crack and cranny of the farmhouse in order to keep out the bitter wind, and of 'cocking', which consists in fencing with thorns the kail-yards in order to keep out the sheep.

As for formal education, for a few 'raiths' or terms, Brown attended the parish school, where Gaelic was the dominant language. (It is still spoken by Crathie school-

boys as I discovered after listening to a busload of
youngsters chattering on their way home from school in
Ballater.)

Most of his education, however, John Brown received
from his father, who had lost none of his ability as a schoolmaster. Such an education, though narrow and limited, can
be thorough, as we know from the experience of Robert
Burns with his tutor Murdoch, who came to live for a while
with the Burns family on their farm. The spelling book and
the Bible were the staples of Burns' intellectual fare as a boy,
but Murdoch also introduced his pupil to Fisher's *English
Grammar* and to Masson's *Collection of Prose and Verse,*
which included extracts from Shakespeare and other great
English writers. Burns, in turn, was expected to instruct
his younger brothers and sisters, as was undoubtedly the
case with John Brown, as the second eldest of a large brood.
'Brown was shrewd, a great reader, and was capable of
giving a considered opinion on most matters,' declared the
Marquis of Huntly, who, as Lord-in-Waiting to the Queen,
had ample opportunity to observe the Highlander.[67] There
is no reason for doubting this verdict.

With so many brothers and sisters to be fed, John Brown
could not be spared for long at home. He found work first as
an ostler's helper at the coaching inn at Pannanich Wells, a
mineral springs near Ballater,* then as a pony herd at
thirteen shillings a week on the Balmoral estate, which was
leased by Sir Robert Gordon. How Brown, together with
the other gillies, was taken over by Queen Victoria when she
leased the estate after Gordon's death has already been
related. Mention has also been made of his rise in Royal
favour, how he was appointed first as an under-groom to go
with the Queen's carriage, then to lead her pony on moun-

* It was to Pannanich Wells that Lord Byron was brought as a boy
of eight to recover from an attack of scarlet fever. The 'steep, frown-
ing glories' of Lochnagar so impressed him that he later put them into
a poem, which in turn was set to music and is sung in Scotland today.
As for the coaching inn at Pannanich, much restored, it is still standing by the side of what has now become the A973 road.

tain treks, and thus 'advanced step by step by his good conduct and intelligence', as Victoria described it in her journal. It was not until 1858, however, that the Queen, through a combination of circumstances, became acutely aware of 'Johnny Brown', as she now referred to him, and began to pay him marked attention.

It was at Balmoral on September 29, 1855, that the Princess Royal, aged fourteen, was betrothed to Prince Frederick William of Prussia, eight years her senior, an event which occasioned some heart-searching on the part of her parents. ('She is still half a child,' the Queen fretted in a letter to Princess Augusta of Saxe-Weimar.) The proposal, in the best romantic tradition, was made while the two young people were on an outing to Craig-na-Ban, the Prince carefully plucking a bit of white heather for good luck before asking Vicky to be his wife. But Queen Victoria was uneasy in her mind because of the disparity in their ages, and on the eve of the wedding at St James's Palace two years later she still complained to Prince Albert, 'It is like taking a poor lamb to be sacrificed.' When the time came to pose with the Prince Consort and her daughter for a wedding picture the Queen trembled so violently that her features registered as a blur on the daguerreotype.

The year following Vicky's betrothal Miss Florence Nightingale was a visitor at Balmoral. The Royal couple had expected to find a formidable, perhaps an unfeminine, personality; instead, Miss Nightingale was extremely lady-like and modest. She quite charmed Prince Albert with her facts and figures. ('She put before us all the defects of our present military hospital system, and the reforms that are needed,' he wrote in his diary.)[95] The Queen showed Miss Nightingale a photograph album she had had made up of soldiers wounded in the Crimean war, including an armless veteran who was Her Majesty's particular despair 'because his friends help him to the brandy bottle . . . and the results are so sad'.[131] Miss Nightingale commiserated, but thought that the Queen's influence would 'generally keep these poor men straight'. Finally, she completely won Queen Victoria's heart by telling her that of all the British soldiers who had fought in the Crimea the Scots had borne pain the best.

Another visitor to Balmoral that autumn of 1856 was Lord Clarendon, the Foreign Secretary, who complained of frostbite. Not only was there no fire in the dining-room, but in the drawing-room there were only 'two little sticks which hissed at the man who attempted to light them', as he wrote to his wife. 'The Queen, thinking, I suppose, that they meant to burn, had a large screen placed between the royal nose and the unignited wood.'[23] A few days later, after standing in the cold for two hours at the Braemar Gathering, his Lordship claimed that his fingers were too cold to hold a pen. But Clarendon's greatest scorn was reserved for the Crathie kirk service, which he felt obliged to attend with the Royal family. 'I don't like the service at all', he wrote to his wife. 'There is a good deal of singing (very bad) . . . The congregation appeared to be devout and attentive, but there is no kneeling, and they never say the Lord's Prayer. The whole thing gave me more the impression of some saintly meeting at Exeter Hall.'

This, of course, was in the days before Victoria's presence had transformed the Sunday service into a kind of circus sideshow, with sightseers parking their gigs a half mile each side of the ugly, white-washed kirk in the hope of catching a glimpse of their Queen (the more enterprising brought Dolland's binoculars the better to observe her at worship). In those early days the Queen and Prince Albert sat in the gallery in what were known as the 'manse pews', occupied by the lairds of Invercauld, Mar Lodge, Monaltrie and Abergeldie; and when the dilapidated ladle that served as collection plate was passed around by one of the elders, the Royal couple put their offerings in along with the rest.

In those days the resident minister was a Dr Anderson, who was noted chiefly for his habit of taking his collie Towser (which Clarendon erroneously described as a 'large,

rough greyhound') into the pulpit with him.* When Queen
Victoria first came to Balmoral, the Reverend Dr Anderson
was afraid that she might object to this, so one Sunday he
kept Towser locked up in the manse. The following day Her
Majesty sent an Equerry to enquire after Towser's health.
Thus it was that by Royal command the collie was restored
to his former privileged position. Actually, the dog served a
useful purpose, for if the sermon were a few minutes longer
than usual he would get up, stretch himself and yawn.[75]

On April 14, 1857, Queen Victoria gave birth to her ninth
child, Princess Beatrice, whom she was to call 'the flower of
the flock' and 'my Benjamin', and who, in truth, was to be
her mother's chief prop in old age. 'The christening of little
Beatrice is just over—and was very brilliant and nice', the
Queen wrote to her Uncle Leopold from Buckingham Palace
on June 16.

Queen Victoria was severely criticized for leaving for
Balmoral early that autumn while Parliament was still in
session and the Indian Mutiny was at its height. At Balmoral
the Queen seems to have realized the seriousness of the
situation, for in September she wrote to Leopold, 'Troops
cannot be raised fast or largely enough. And the horrors
committed on the poor ladies . . . make one's blood run
cold.' Characteristically, not a word concerning the Indian
Mutiny is allowed to disturb the serenity of the Queen's
published Highland journals. Instead, there is an account
of a distribution of clothing to the old women on the
estate. ('I gave her a warm petticoat, and the tears rolled
down her old cheeks', she wrote of the local distiller's
mother, aged eighty-eight.) However, Prince Albert broke

* This practice was not unique to Crathie kirk. Donald Macleod
claims that after the clearances in Kildonan, Sutherland County, the
congregation of the parish church was reduced to eight shepherds and
their dogs, numbering between twenty and thirty. During a service
when the 120th Psalm was sung 'the four-footed hearers became
excited, got up on their seats, and raised a most infernal chorus of
howling'.

into an account of a deer-stalk in Glen Gelder to inform his brother Ernest, 'We have an army of 80,000 armed men against us, and the few Europeans are totally cut off . . . It is impossible to speak of the horrors which happen there.'[2]

When Palmerston, the Prime Minister, suggested that October 7 should be proclaimed as a day of 'solemn fast, humiliation and prayer', Victoria objected strenuously. A day of 'prayer and intercession for our suffering countrymen' would be more appropriate in the opinion of the Queen, who did not know the meaning of the word 'humiliation'. In the event, the effect of the proclamation was rather spoiled, for on the evening she signed it she gave a ball to the tenants of the Balmoral and Abergeldie estates.[56]

In reading Queen Victoria's letters and extracts from her journal it is evident that her attitude towards John Brown underwent a change during the autumn of 1858. As we know, Prince Albert often preferred deer-stalking to the Queen's company at Balmoral, a preference that became more marked as time went on. But in 1858 another circumstance arose to alter the balance in the Queen's relationship with Brown. John Macdonald, the tall, handsome *Jäger* whom Prince Albert had specially trained, developed tuberculosis and could no longer accompany their Highland expeditions.* Brown, with his cheerful ways and his elastic stride, was promoted to take Macdonald's place, which meant that he was brought into much more intimate contact with the Royal couple. For there was no room for ceremony on these excursions, where all were equals as the party struggled to brew tea over a fire of damp kindling, or attempted to dry out their clothes, or applied embrocations to each other's mosquito bites. In addition, Brown was expected to keep the Queen company and to amuse her, while Albert crept off into the bushes after the stags. The Highlander could make himself extremely complaisant when the spirit moved him. Thus he was quick to supply the Ralegh touch

---

* Macdonald died of consumption at Windsor, in May, 1860.

when the Queen came to a marshy place on one of these outings, joining arms with Duncan to form a cradle upon which she was urged to seat herself. 'I sat safely enough, with an arm on each man's shoulder, and was carried successfully over.'*[145]

He also knew how to return a compliment neatly. Referring to Prince Albert's good nature when he shot at a stag and missed, Brown told the Queen, 'Everyone on the estate says there never was so kind a master.' He could not, however, forbear to add in an ingratiating manner, 'Our only wish is to give satisfaction.' The Queen's comment was: 'I said they certainly did.'[145]

But it was not just a question of propinquity. From reading Queen Victoria's letters to the Princess Royal during this period it is evident that she was experiencing something akin to the 'crystallization' which Stendahl described as the first stage in falling in love, and which he defined as 'a certain fever of the imagination which translates a normally commonplace object into something unrecognizable'.[133]

When, in announcing Brown's promotion, Queen Victoria wrote to her daughter in October, 1858, that there couldn't be 'a nicer, better, or handier' servant, was she not already beginning to crystallize? The gruff, uncultivated Highlander was already becoming unrecognizable under the layer of diamonds with which the Queen had encrusted him. 'Brown has had everything to do for me,' she went on; 'indeed had charge of me and all, on all those expeditions, and therefore I settled that he should be specially appointed to attend on me (without any title) and have a full dress suit ... He was so pleased,' she added, 'when I told him you had asked for him.'[151] To her daughter all of this must have

---

* The following year, when Jane Churchill caught her heel in her dress and fell, the incorrigible Brown remarked in picking her up, 'Your Ladyship is not so heavy as Her Majesty.' 'Am I grown heavier, do you think?' the Queen enquired. 'Well, I think you are,' was Brown's plain-spoken reply.

sounded like the artless prattle of a schoolgirl with a 'crush'.

In the same letter we learn that 'Johnny Brown' had now been made privy to such family secrets as the fact that the Princess Royal was expecting a baby,* and that he had nearly given this secret away to her twelve-year-old sister Princess Helena, or Lenchen, as she was called. ('I could not tell such a child as Lenchen about you,' the Queen wrote. 'Those things are not proper to be told to children, as it initiates them into things which they ought not to know of till they are older. Affie [Prince Alfred] knows nothing either.') Alfred, be it noted, was then fourteen years old and getting ready to join the naval cadets.†

In the year 1858 Queen Victoria experienced not only a new awareness of John Brown, but an almost neurotic dread when the time came for her to leave Balmoral ('this blessed place . . . this enchanting life of liberty—these dear people', as she wrote to the Princess Royal), and to return to 'tame, dull, formal England and the prison life of Windsor'. On the last day of her stay, she awoke to find snow on the ground and immediately expressed the childish wish that the party should be snowbound ('How happy I should have been could it be so,' she confided to her journal). Even after she had returned to Windsor she continued to pine for the Highlands. 'Oh! I think I never felt going away from Balmoral more painful than this time, I know not why,' she wrote to her eldest daughter. 'I feel the regret more vividly than I did last year.'

What had happened to cause this heart-sickness? Granted that she hated Windsor Castle, which she once likened to a 'living grave', this would hardly account for the violence of her reaction. Why did she regret leaving Balmoral 'more

* A son, the future Kaiser Wilhelm II, was born on January 27, 1859.
† Lady Longford throws another interesting sidelight on the sex education which Queen Victoria's children received. Prince Arthur, then aged fifteen, complained at lunch that he had never seen such an ugly crinoline as that worn by his aunt, Princess Leiningen. 'She is expecting an addition,' a Lady-in-Waiting whispered. 'What for?' he demanded.[77]

vividly than I did last year'? When this admission is seen in context one cannot help but wonder if it did not have something to do with the man whom she had just appointed to be her special servant, who had had 'everything to do for me', and whom she would not be seeing for another year. When she interrupts her letter to her daughter to quote a snatch from 'My Heart's in the Highlands', the impression is confirmed. 'My heart's in the Highlands . . . Yes, that is my feeling', she wrote, 'and *I must fight and struggle against it!*' (My italics.) What is the meaning of these enigmatic words? What must she 'fight and struggle' against? Her infatuation for Brown? The implication is there, and it becomes clearer when she expresses her resentment that Albert does not love the Highlands as much as she does. 'Unfortunately', she wrote to her daughter, 'Papa . . . is annoyed at my living in recollections of the past! But this I can't help.'

In looking back over Queen Victoria's sojourn at Balmoral that autumn of 1858 it is difficult not to conclude that she experienced some sort of emotional crisis, born perhaps of Prince Albert's neglect, but certainly similar to Stendahl's crystallization. Undoubtedly the real nature of that crisis remained hidden from the Queen; indeed, it would not be revealed to her with full force until many years after the Prince Consort's death. As Stendahl observes, just because a man leaves Bologna on his way to Rome does not mean that he has already arrived at the gates of Rome—there are still the Appennines to be crossed.[133] But the crystallization process had begun, as was evident when the following autumn Prince Arthur wanted to borrow Brown for an expedition of his own. 'Impossible!' the Queen objected. 'Why, what should I do without him? He is my particular gillie!'[83] By 1861, the year of Prince Albert's death, John Brown had become so crystallized in Queen Victoria's imagination that she could write to her Uncle Leopold, 'It is quite a sorrow for me to leave him behind. (Brown) takes the most wonderful care of me', she added, 'combining the offices of groom, footman, page, and maid, I might almost say, as he is so handy about cloaks and shawls.'[147]

The autumn of 1860 saw the first of those 'Great Expeditions', as Victoria called them, which were the Royal equivalent to 'roughing it', and which were to become a unique feature of Balmoral life; for the Queen loved nothing so much as to travel incognito in Scotland, putting up at country inns unrecognized and sharing in the lives of her humblest subjects. Not for a moment were the canny country people taken in by their Sovereign's disguise, but they were shrewd enough to pretend that they were and to keep their mouths shut.

The first Great Expedition was to Glen Fishie, in Landseer country, in September, 1860, the Royal couple taking with them Grant, who acted as Prince Albert's valet, and Brown, who served the Queen in a similar capacity (to clean her boots and brush the mud from her skirts were among his duties). The group travelled as 'Lord and Lady Churchill and party' (Jane Lady Churchill, the Queen's Lady of the Bedchamber, accompanied them as 'Miss Spencer'), and there was great amusement when Brown forgetfully addressed the Queen as 'Your Majesty' when she was getting into the carriage, and Grant, on the box, saluted Prince Albert as 'Your Royal Highness'.

Having put up at the coaching inn in Grantown and decided to take dinner in their room, the Royal couple encountered an unexpected difficulty. 'Grant and Brown', the Queen wrote in her journal, 'were to have waited on us, but were "bashful" and did not.' In Scotland the word 'bashful' is a euphemism for intoxicated. (Ivor Brown recalls hearing this adjective used when he was a boy in Banffshire to describe the condition of a gamekeeper who was famed for his sword-dancing but who was too far gone in drink to perform after supper.) Possibly Brown and Grant had fortified themselves with whisky as a protest against their new roles as male serving-maids. The two gillies were 'very merry' in the hotel's commercial room later that night, according to the Queen's journal, whereas she 'had not slept very soundly'. Brown did not escape without a wigging. ('I spoke to him and to Grant . . . about not having waited on us, as they ought to have done . . . and Brown answered, he was afraid he should not do it rightly. I replied we did not wish to have a stranger in the room, and they must do so another time'.) This is one of the few references to Brown's intemperance that appear in the journals, and perhaps the only instance where a Royal reprimand to the faithful attendant is recorded.

The Queen gives an amusing cameo of the 'ringletted woman' who waited at table in place of the gillies, viewing her with the cool detachment with which one woman assesses another. Leaving early next morning, the Queen looked up from her carriage and espied the ringletted maid, this time with her hair in curl-papers, frantically waving a Union Jack from an upper window. So much for the credibility of the Queen's 'Lady Churchill' disguise.

Queen Victoria was to look back upon these carefree days as among the happiest in her life. On this first, and 'never to be forgotten expedition' she was full of praise for everyone from General Grey, her secretary ('he seemed entirely to enjoy it'), to Brown ('one of my best servants anywhere'), to Fyvie, her Highland pony ('dear Fyvie is perfection'). But most of all the credit belonged to 'my dear Albert', whose idea it was. Apparently he had made similar expeditions in his student days, travelling incognito with his tutor, and had found them delightful. For poor Albert, the Glen Fishie expedition was a valediction of sorts; there were not many such adventures in store for him.

In her enthusiasm for Highlanders, Queen Victoria invented a whole mystique to account for their peculiar qualities. Thus to live amid magnificent mountain scenery was in itself ennobling. Balmoral, she wrote to Uncle Leopold, was free 'of all contact with the mere miserable frivolities and worldliness of this wicked world! The mountains seem fresh from God's hand . . . and the primitive people to have kept that chivalrous loyalty and devotion—seen hardly, indeed, now nowhere else!'[148] Albert agreed that Highlanders were Nature's noblemen, 'marked by that honesty and sympathy which always distinguish the inhabitants of mountain countries'.[95]

As time went on the Queen imputed other qualities to the Scots. Not only were they better at bearing pain, as Florence Nightingale had informed her, but they were possessed of unique healing powers, as she knew from her own experience.* When John Brown in later years rescued her from a mad Irish youth who threatened her with a pistol, she attached great significance to the fact that it was a Highlander who had saved her. Finally, unlike the English peasant, the ordinary Scot was full of poetry, the Queen assured the Princess Royal, adding, 'One does require that to lift one up above the heavy clay which clogs our souls.' With her the romantic stylization of the Highlander begun by Sir Walter Scott reached its apotheosis. The wild, cattle-reeving clansman who rose to follow Bonnie Prince Charles in 1745 is unrecognisable as the noble, chivalrous, poetic child of nature, the typical Highlander as seen through the Queen's eyes.

But even Scott was alive to the wrongs which the Highlands had suffered during the clearances, when the crofters were 'dispossessed by an unrelenting avarice'. One would search Queen Victoria's letters and journals in vain for any such word of condemnation.†

* Two of Queen Victoria's physicians-in-ordinary, Sir James Clark and Sir James Reid, were trained at Scottish universities, as were her accoucheurs, Sir Charles Locock and Dr Ferguson. Thanks to Scottish doctors, the Queen's last two confinements were eased by the use of chloroform.

† When, much later in her reign, crofters on the island of Skye rose and demanded that the idle land be restored to the people, the Queen blamed 'Irish agitators' for the trouble. It would never do, she told the Home Secretary, Sir William Harcourt, to encourage the crofters in 'their wild and impossible demands, the result to a great extent of Irish agitators' persistent preaching of sedition'.[47]

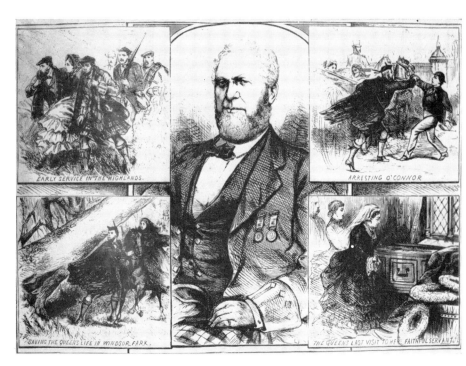

Above: A cartoon tribute to John Brown which appeared posthumously in *The Penny Illustrated Paper*, showing incidents fancied and real from his life
Below: Balmoral Castle, the south front

Victoria did not come to the throne until after the great Sutherland clearances, when 10,000 crofters were driven from their homes; but she could hardly have escaped knowledge of them, for the memory of those brutal evictions lingered for generations. When the Queen and Prince Consort planned to visit the Sutherland estate in 1849 a reporter from the *Inverness Advertiser* advised her to try her hand at sketching 'the blackened ruins of burnt-down cottages'.

Moreover, the Highland clearances lasted well into Queen Victoria's reign. The truncheons which the police used on the women of Strathcarron in 1854 in the so-called 'Massacre of the Rosses' bore the Royal cypher 'VR' burned into their wood causing people to believe 'that Her Majesty sanctions, nay, encourages and authorizes, these evictions', as a reporter from the *Northern Ensign* wrote. All this must have been known to the Queen, but the fact remains that she never once raised her voice in defence of her dispossessed Highland subjects, either to stop the evictions or to ameliorate the sufferings which they brought about. Viewed in this light her pose of being *ceanncinnidh*, or clan chieftain seems a mockery.

Queen Victoria returned to Windsor from the Glen Fishie expedition refreshed in mind and body and little reckoning on the cruel ordeal that lay ahead of her. The first blow fell early in March, 1861, when her mother, the Duchess of Kent, died at the age of seventy-four after a brief illness. ('She is gone! That precious, dearly beloved tender mother . . .' she wrote to her Uncle Leopold.) Curiously, in view of the morbid fascination which death was later to hold for her, Victoria seems to have been totally unprepared for the possibility of losing anyone from her own family circle. As a result she was stupefied by her mother's death, and collapsed in a nervous breakdown. She cried all day long, finding tears 'soothing to the bruised heart and soul', as she wrote to the Princess Royal.[151] Her head was 'fearfully sensitive' to the least noise, particularly to the sound of Bertie, the Prince of Wales, talking. ('His voice made me so nervous I could hardly bear it'.) As late as a month after her mother's death, she was still taking her dinner alone in her room. In fact, her grief, in which a great deal of guilt appears to have been mixed, completely blinded her to the condition of her husband, whose health was rapidly failing.

That even Albert's physical appearance had altered is evident from the last photographs taken of him. Although he was then only forty-two, the Prince Consort looks at least ten years older. The white hairs sprout plentifully among his side-whiskers, while the hair on top is nearly gone. There is a puffiness beneath the eyes, which have that same ineffably sad expression that the Queen's Ladies-in-Waiting were so quick to remark. It is as though his gaze is already fixed on death.

The Highland expeditions organized in the autumn of 1861, to Fettercairn and to Loch Avon, were not the gay, carefree affairs of the previous year. Then 'dearest Mother' had been alive; now Victoria interrupts her journal to observe that 'in the midst of cheerfulness I feel so sad!' This time the Royal couple were accompanied by Princess Alice and Prince Louis of Hesse-Darmstadt, who had become engaged the previous December,* and, perhaps it was due to the presence of these charming young lovers that the Queen gradually became her old self. On one of the last outings Prince Albert stopped behind with his head keeper Grant to look over some land in Glen Muich which he intended to plant as deer forest for the Prince of Wales. Half jocularly he broke off giving directions to Grant to observe, 'But you and I may be dead and gone long before that.'[145] His words were prophetic as far as he himself was concerned, for in less than three months he had died of typhoid fever, apparently without a struggle. 'The Prince always had a fixed idea,' Major Elphinstone noted in his diary, 'that he would die of the first fever he got. It proved true . . . he never even tried

* They were married on July 1, 1862, at Osborne.

to rally from the moment the illness commenced.'[83] Almost
to the end Queen Victoria refused to believe in the seriousness of her husband's condition, but the Prince knew that
he was dying, and asked Princess Alice to summon the
Prince of Wales, who hastened from Cambridge to be at his
father's bedside. Albert died because 'his purity was too
great . . . for this poor, miserable world', Victoria told her
Uncle Leopold.[147] But later she was to deliver a harsher,
almost a contemptuous, verdict. 'He died,' she told Lord
Derby, 'from want of what they call pluck.'[78]

4

BROWN COMES SOUTH

'ONE cold, sunny morning, with the frost glistening on the sweeping lawns of Osborne, Victoria sat listlessly at the window. She saw John Brown walking through the grounds leading "dear little Loch-na-gar", harnessed to her own carriage . . . for the first time since the death of the Prince Consort, Victoria smiled.'[139] So E. E. P. Tisdall describes John Brown's arrival at Osborne with the pony-cart to serve the widowed Queen. 'Victoria's face lit up,' Tisdall tells us, while 'into her heart flooded something of the happy spirit of those days at Balmoral, unclouded by stabbing grief . . .' As for Brown, 'he was almost given to believe that he had saved his mistress from madness if not from death', according to Tisdall. 'In those first few weeks at Osborne John Brown,' his biographer continues, 'did what the doctors could not do. By his simple attentions and kindly care, by talking to her as an affectionate brother to a sister who was emerging from a great sorrow, he gave the Queen of Great Britain a new grip on life.'

This picture of Brown's arrival, with the frost glistening on the lawns, is a pretty one, but inaccurate in several respects. For one, Brown came south in December, 1864, and not in March, 1862, as Tisdall contends. For another, far from it being a surprise to Queen Victoria, as Tisdall pretends, Brown's advent at Osborne had been carefully planned. It was Princess Alice (by then married to Prince Louis of Hesse-Darmstadt) who instigated the move, for since her father's death Princess Alice had been the Queen's chief comfort, and by October, 1864, she was beginning to find her responsibility irksome. When Dr Jenner suggested more exercise in the open air for the Queen as an antidote to her moping Princess Alice remembered the pony rides at Balmoral that her mother had so enjoyed. It was natural, too, that she should think of John Brown in this connection, for the Queen had developed an aversion to seeing new faces about her. And so Brown had been sent for.

Tisdall's suggestion that the Queen may have been saved from madness and her grip on life restored by the simple expedient of sending for Brown is also exaggerated but contains a germ of truth.

Queen Victoria's strange behaviour following the Prince Consort's death can be understood only in the light of her fear that she was losing her mind, a fear that had haunted her intermittently all her life. That the Queen had inherited a tendency towards insanity from her grandfather, George III, was a proposition that was tacitly accepted not only by the Household, including her physicians, and by her Ministers, but by the Queen herself and her family. Everyone watched for tell-tale signs. (The Queen's high colour after meals, or when she became over-animated in talking was interpreted as one such sign.) Emotional crises of any kind were to be avoided, as they might trigger off the incipient madness. Pregnancies were a particularly anxious time, for then the Queen was at her lowest ebb. ('I think much more of our being like a cow or a dog at such moments', she confided to the Princess Royal; 'our poor nature becomes so very animal and unecstatic.')[151] Sir James Clark, the Queen's physician, had gone so far as to warn Prince Albert in 1856 that another child might prove fatal to the Queen's sanity. 'Unless she is kept quiet and still amused, the time will come when she will be in danger.'[78]

Thanks to recent medical research, we now know that all all of these fears were groundless. Far from being insane, George III, according to the latest medical evidence, suffered from an obscure, but hereditary, disease known as porphyria, which is a metabolic disorder affecting the liver, and which is still incurable.[19] Nor was George III the only sufferer from porphyria, which takes its name from the purplish colour of the urine its victims pass. By a remarkable piece of medical detection, Dr Ida Macalpine and her son Dr Richard Hunter have been able to trace this disease from Mary Queen of Scots through thirteen generations spanning a period of more than 400 years. Porphyria may well account for George III's irrational behaviour over the American colonies, as well as George IV's habit of taking laudanum. It may also explain such mysterious deaths as that of James I, thought to have been poisoned.

But by no stretch of the imagination could it account for Queen Victoria's high colour, nor for her own irrational actions upon occasion. For, by some fluke, the dreaded disease skipped the Queen entirely, though her father, Edward, the Duke of Kent, apparently suffered from it.* 'Victoria's long and healthy life gives no indication of the disease and her descendants may therefore also be presumed free of it', the medical research team concluded.[19] Had these medical findings been available a century ago Queen Victoria might have been spared much anguish. Not only that, but Her Majesty's advisers might not have been blackmailed into giving in to the Queen so easily, under threat of provoking an emotional upset.

But as things stood, so much was the Hanoverian taint of insanity taken for granted that when the Queen's mother died in March, 1861, the Earl of Clarendon hoped that Queen Victoria might not become prey to that 'morbid melancholy to which her mind has often tended, and which is a constant cause of anxiety to Prince Albert.'[22] When, nine months later, the Prince Consort himself lay on his deathbed, Clarendon warned, 'A national calamity may be close at hand—the loss of her reason would be nothing else.'[23] Nor were Clarendon's fears calmed when he visited

* The Duke of Kent was thought to have died of pneumonia brought on by not changing out of wet stockings. But Doctors Macalpine and Hunter claim that from his early twenties he suffered from 'rheumatism' and 'colic', which probably were symptoms of porphyria.

the widowed Queen at Windsor Castle in June, 1862. All
went well until Clarendon began to talk politics, mention-
ing the possibility of a change of Ministry, whereupon the
Queen's manner underwent a violent change. Her face
became flushed, her eye feverish. 'My reason, my reason!'
she cried, tapping her forehead.

'She sees the trees budding, the days lengthen, the
primroses coming out, but she thinks herself still in the
month of December . . .' Thus Victoria, in a letter to Lord
Derby, compared the vernal changes at Osborne, that
Spring of 1862, with the gloomy state of her own mind. In a
sense, time stopped for the Queen—for the rest of her life the
hands of the clock would be pointing at 10.50 p.m., December 14, 1861, the hour when her beloved had passed away.
The rest of her days would, in fact, be dedicated to preserv-
ing things exactly as they were at the moment that this
most precious life was snuffed out. At the Queen's express
desire, the longest mourning period in modern times was
decreed for the Prince Consort. Members of the Royal
Household remained in black for a full year, at the end of
which time the ladies were allowed to vary their raven
garments with grey, violet and even lilac. Before being
sealed, the Blue Room at Windsor where Prince Albert had
died was carefully photographed to guard against it being
changed in any way, and to its door was affixed a plaque
stating, 'Every article in this room my late lamented
husband selected for me in the twenty-fourth year of my
reign.' On the right side of every bed the Queen slept in
hereafter, above the empty pillow, hung a photograph of
Prince Albert taken on his deathbed. Within easy reach was
a plaster cast of his hand.

To return to the Spring of 1862, the Queen made the
mistake of visiting Balmoral while her grief was still fresh.
Was not this, more than any other Royal residence, linked
with her beloved? Had she not, herself, written of the new
castle that 'all has become my dearest Albert's creation'?

Now, in hideous fashion, this Highland bower was to be transformed into a Gethsemane, where every tree and every stone spoke to her of Albert. Even the heavens wept when Queen Victoria, accompanied by two of her now fatherless children, arrived at Balmoral on May 2, for in a letter to the Princess Royal she speaks of the rain, and of there being no one out to greet her, only Dr Robertson at the door, with Grant, the headkeeper, lurking in the hall. 'Oh! darling child,' she wrote, 'the agonizing sobs as I crawled up with Alice and Affie! The stag heads—the rooms—blessed, darling Papa's room—then his coats—his caps—kilts—all, all convulsed my poor shattered frame!'[152] Queen Victoria told Clarendon later that on three separate occasions at Balmoral she thought that she was going mad. Twenty-seven years were to pass before she spoke of this period again, and then she wrote to her daughter, the Princess Royal, who had just lost her husband, 'I too wanted once to put an end to my life here, but a Voice told me for His sake —no, "Still Endure." ' Making all due allowance for her tendency to over-dramatize, there is still the implication that the Queen, perhaps fearing madness, as she had confided to Clarendon, had actually contemplated taking her own life while at Balmoral that Spring.

Certainly it is in anticipation of an early demise that we find her back at Windsor making out her last will and testament, and otherwise putting her affairs in order. 'Feeling ill and weakly and longing, as the poor wretched Queen does, to join her dearly beloved and adored husband, her mind is naturally much occupied with leaving this world,' she explained to Earl Russell. To Leopold she wrote, 'I think my life will end more rapidly than any of you think.'[148] Ironically, the very process of writing out final instructions seemed to take the Queen's mind off her troubles. She became absorbed in her task, and thereafter sounded more cheerful in her letters.

In September, 1862, Queen Victoria made a pilgrimage to

Coburg, Prince Albert's birthplace, 'this beloved place, where the very air seems to breathe of her precious one', as she wrote to Major Elphinstone. One of the highlights of her stay was when a group of German choral societies, with a logic that was truly Zen, telegraphed a 'unanimous solemn cheer'.

The Queen returned to Windsor to prepare for the first anniversary of the Prince Consort's death ('this dreadful, dreadful day'), and for the transfer of his remains from St George's Chapel to the Royal Mausoleum at Frogmore, then under construction. Although it is not generally known, Prince Albert himself had had a hand in the planning of this, his final resting place, which cost more than a quarter of a million pounds, and took nine years to complete. Cruciform in shape, and vaguely Italianate, the lower part of the building was faced with pink granite, the rest Portland stone, the whole being surmounted by a copper roof which quickly turned a brilliant shade of green. A yellowish light seeped through the stained glass beneath the dome and onto the recumbent figure of Prince Albert, sculpted in white marble by Baron Carlo Marochetti, who made the companion effigy of Victoria placed alongside the Consort thirty-nine years later. As the years passed the mausoleum was gradually filled with paintings after the manner of Raphael, and with statues, including a group by William Theed entitled 'Allured to brighter worlds and led away', which shows Albert, one arm encircling his wife's waist, the other pointing to Heaven.

The Queen looked upon the Frogmore mausoleum as a place of refuge, going there whenever she felt the need to be alone and to meditate. The keys to the tomb she kept on her person and would let herself in, undoing the bolts of the imposing bronze gates and unlocking the door of the sanctuary itself. Far from having a depressing effect upon her, these visits seemed to comfort her. It was all part of the strange cult of the dead which the Queen fostered, and which caused her to advert to the dead Prince's opinions as though he were in the next room. 'Indeed, it was difficult not to think that he was', observed Clarendon, after an audience with the Queen at Windsor.* 'Everything was set out on his (Albert's) table', Clarendon added, 'the blotting book open with a pen upon it, his watch going, fresh flowers in a glass.'[92]

But at the Frogmore mausoleum the Prince Consort's presence was felt especially strongly, which was why the Queen, on the eve of the Prince of Wales's wedding, took her son and his bride-to-be there. 'I opened the shrine and took them in', she wrote in her journal; 'Alix (Princess Alexandra) was much moved and so was I. I said, 'He gives you his blessing!' and joined Alix's and Bertie's hands, taking them both in my arms. It was a very touching moment and we all felt it.'[90]

The wedding itself, in St George's Chapel, Windsor, proved to be a painful ordeal for the Queen in the absence of that 'principal figure of all, the guardian angel of the family'. At one moment she felt as though she were going to faint ('Only by a violent effort could I succeed in mastering my emotion'). She remained seated in the Royal Closet overlooking the chapel, feeling 'strange and bewildered'. The Rev. Norman Macleod took away with him two vivid impressions of the wedding. One was the sight of the Royal princesses weeping into their bouquets as their brother, the Prince of Wales, stood alone, nervously waiting for his bride. The other was the expression on Queen Victoria's face as, with eyes raised to heaven, she listened to Prince Albert's *Chorale* being sung by the massed choirs. 'She seemed to be with him alone before the throne of God', was the Rev. Macleod's awe-struck comment.[88]

Of a more profane nature were the observations of Benjamin Disraeli, who, not having seen the Queen since her

* According to *Le Mémorial Diplomatique*, Queen Victoria, at about this time, settled the thorny Schleswig-Holstein question by withdrawing from a Privy Council to consult Prince Albert's shade. After retiring to her closet, she returned to announce that 'the Prince was hostile to any act of war by England.'

tragedy, now took advantage of his opportunity. Being
near-sighted, Disraeli raised his eye-glass in order to get a
better view of the sable figure in her Gothic cabinet. 'I saw
H.M. well, but unfortunately caught her glance', Disraeli
wrote. 'I did not venture to use my glass again.'[22]

In bereavement the normal human reaction is to avoid
those persons or things that serve as reminders of the loved
one. But the opposite was true of Queen Victoria. She told
Gladstone that she found it an effort to see anyone who had
not known Prince Albert, and she instanced the pain it had
cost her to receive the Emperor of Austria, simply because
the Prince had not known His Imperial Highness.[98] Nowhere was this resistance to change, this effort to preserve life in aspic, more evident than at Balmoral, where
the Queen clung stubbornly to old ways. When the Deeside
railway was extended from Aboyne to Ballater in 1866 she
refused to use it at first. Instead, she insisted upon driving
the extra ten miles to Balmoral in a barouche hired from the
Huntly Arms, because 'this was the way it was done in
Albert's time'.

The burden of the past weighed heavily on all those who
shared the Queen's life at Balmoral. Sir Henry Campbell-
Bannerman thought the castle was like a convent ('We meet
at meals and when we are finished each is off to his cell').
But in what other convent did the head abbess remain invisible most of the time, and communicate with the other
inmates by note only? The Queen kept the footmen busy
delivering her messages to various members of her Household, including her secretary, who, likely as not, would be
sitting in the next room. These edicts covered every aspect
of Balmoral life, from regulating the arrivals and departures
of her children and guests, to deciding who was entitled to
use the Smoking Room and when. Invisible she might be,
like the Great Lama, but nothing escaped the Queen's
eye.

Discipline was very strict. No one was allowed to leave the

Castle until the Queen herself had gone out (Gladstone once broke this rule and was pulled up short). Nor could the Queen's ladies go off on picnics of their own without proper chaperonage—the Queen personally vetted the list of those who proposed to go on such outings. Her own daughters were not encouraged to go junketing with members of the Household, and this applied equally to her granddaughters, who were told, 'Remember, your dear Grandpapa did not approve.'[93] On her own drives the Queen continued to visit the same beauty spots year after year for no other reason than that dearest Albert had enjoyed the view.

The climax of the Autumn season at Balmoral occurred each year on August 26, Prince Albert's birthday, when the gillies and tenants on the estate put on top hats and black coats and assembled at the Obelisk to toast the departed Prince. The Queen drove there in her carriage with two grey horses and an outrider, but Her Majesty left shortly after the prayer in memory of her husband, possibly in order to avoid the pagan rites that followed, when whisky was freely dispensed from a trestle table at the back of the wood. Soon the assembly was three parts intoxicated. It was not uncommon for visitors who went for a stroll in the afternoon to come across a man in top hat and frock coat curled up fast asleep in the woods. Still, it was how dearest Albert, who had thought only of the happiness of others, would have wanted it, or so reasoned his widow, turning a blind eye to the bacchanalia.

It was while obeying what she took to be the ordinands of her dead spouse that Queen Victoria met with a carriage accident in October, 1863. The Queen was returning home on a mountain road at about 7 p.m. when the sociable in which she was riding overturned. Her Majesty was shot out of the carriage, and suffered facial contusions and a sprained thumb. Providentially, the Queen's two daughters, who were accompanying her, the Princesses Alice and Helena, escaped unhurt. From the entry in her journal concerning it, the Queen leaves no doubt as to the cause of the mishap: Smith, the coachman, was drunk, or 'confused', as Her Majesty preferred to describe it.*

It was quite dark when the Queen and her daughters started for home after a day's outing at Loch Muick. John Brown was on the box next to Smith, and, to add an exotic touch to the excursion, Princess Alice's blackamoor serving-boy whom she had brought with her from Darmstadt, was up behind. 'From the first,' the Queen wrote, 'Smith seemed to be quite confused . . . and got off the road several times, once in a dangerous place, when Alice called out and Brown got off the box to show him the way. After that, however though going very slowly, we seemed to be all right, but Alice was not at all reassured, and thought Brown's holding up the lantern all the time on the box indicated Smith could not see where he was going . . .'[146] Suddenly the sociable began to tip up on its side. The Queen had time to reflect whether she would be killed or not ('there were still things I had not settled and wanted to do') before the carriage overturned with a crash, throwing Her Majesty clear ('I came down very hard, with my face upon the ground'). Brown, who had hurt his knee in jumping clear of the carriage, came hobbling over, crying, 'The Lord Almighty have mercy on us! Who did ever see the like of this before! I thought you were all killed!'

It was nearly ten o'clock when the party, on borrowed ponies, arrived back at Balmoral, by which time the Queen's face had swelled, and her right thumb was giving her pain (she thought at first that she had broken it). Dr Jenner bandaged her head and wanted to put her to bed at once, but she would not go ('people were foolishly alarmed . . . and made a great deal of fuss').

Oddly, the Queen's first thought after the accident was not of herself, nor of her narrow escape from death, but of

---

* The coachman was pensioned the following year. 'We all agreed that Smith was quite unfit to drive me again in the dark' the Queen noted laconically in her journal.

Prince Albert—how 'terrible not to be able to tell it to my dearest Albert', she confided to her daughter Alice, to which Alice replied, 'But he knows it all, and I am sure he watched over us.'[146] Next she examined her conscience: Had the accident resulted from any carelessness on her part? Had she departed from Albert's instructions by so much as a jot or a tittle? She could find no fault. 'I am thankful,' she wrote, 'that it was by no imprudence of mine, or the slightest deviation from what my beloved one and I had always been in the habit of doing, and what he sanctioned and approved.' When Gladstone, who was at Balmoral as Minister in attendance at the time, lectured her about the folly of driving around the countryside after dark, the Queen told him coolly that 'all her habits were formed on the Prince's wishes and directions, and she could not alter them'.[98] Moreover, she was furious with Gladstone for having informed Lord Palmerston, her Prime Minister, of the accident. 'That, dear Mr Gladstone, was quite wrong.'

Undoubtedly the accident had much to do with the Queen's decision to bring John Brown south with her the following year to become her permanent attendant. For Brown, who 'had hurt his knee a good deal in jumping off the carriage', had exhibited that presence of mind for which he was so remarkable. He had, in fact, been 'indefatigable in his attention and care', and when leading the Queen's and Princess Alice's ponies home 'would not let go for fear of another accident'.

'Have now appointed that excellent Highland servant of mine to attend me always', Queen Victoria wrote to Leopold from Windsor in February, 1865. 'It is a real comfort', she added, 'for he is so devoted to me—so simple, so intelligent, so unlike an ordinary servant, and so cheerful and attentive . . .'[146] To signalize his new appointment Queen Victoria conferred upon Brown the title, 'The Queen's Highland Servant', and fixed his salary at £120 per annum, an amount which was to be more than doubled over the next four years.

His new duties were set out in a memorandum dated February 4, 1865.[78] He was to attend the Queen both indoors and outdoors, whether riding or driving or on foot, and to take orders from none but herself. 'He is to continue as before cleaning her boots, skirts and cloaks unless this proves too much', the memo continued. (This soon proved to be the case. In fact, Brown ended up with a batman of his own to polish his boots.) Provision was also made for holidays. Brown was to be allowed to stay on at Balmoral a few days after the Queen's departure, if he so desired (in practice he never did). The Queen also renewed her promise to build her attendant a cottage at Balmoral if he should marry.

The empire which John Brown built for himself and his kinsfolk extended 'even unto the ultimate far-stretching margin of Scotch cousinhood', according to *The World*. Like most gossip repeated about Brown this was an exaggeration, but the Highlander did manage, through his influence at Court, to keep his five brothers in employment, and to take care of quite a few cousins besides.* In leaner times two of his brothers had decided to seek their fortunes overseas. James Brown, the eldest, emigrated to Australia, while Hugh opted for New Zealand, where he married a Christchurch girl and settled down to the life of a sheep farmer. However, hearing of brother John's good fortune these would-be emigrants lost no time in returning home, James to become a shepherd at Balmoral, and Hugh to take on the duties of Keeper of Her Majesty's Kennels at Windsor. A third brother, Donald, was Keeper of the Queen's Lodge, Osborne. Archie Brown, the youngest, did even better for himself. First he became a valet to Prince Leopold, then Page of the Royal Presence ('an excellent, trustworthy young man', is the way Queen Victoria

* The office of 'The Queen's Highland Attendant' became the exclusive property of the Browns for two generations. When John Brown died his brother Hugh stepped into his shoes as Extra Highland Attendant, sharing his duties with nephew Francis Clark. When Clark died, William Brown's son took over.

described him). Alone of the five brothers, William Brown remained on the land, as their father and grandfather had done before them. But, in time, even he benefited from Royal favour, when Queen Victoria gave him the farm known as Tomidhu ('Black Hillock') on the north bank of the Dee, where he died in 1906. John Brown's nepotism, as already pointed out, was not confined to his brothers, but included a host of Clarks and Leys, all distant kinsmen of his.

If Sir Henry Ponsonby is to be believed, John Brown owed his spectacular rise to the fact that the British Monarchy was a Constitutional one. For Constitutional Monarchs, frustrated in their attempts to impose their will on stubborn Ministers (Palmerston and Gladstone, in Queen Victoria's case) were apt to exercise a despotic rule over their servants. 'Thus', Ponsonby concluded, 'they come gradually to govern personally those things which the servants can rule over, and everything connected with their servants' lives and actions becomes of surpassing interest.'[110] In Queen Victoria's case, the peculiar 'Kitchen Court' which she held at Balmoral four months in the year actually enabled her to share power with Brown in a way that would have been unthinkable in any other part of her realm. This explains her preoccupation with the minutiae of Balmoral life, in which she was abetted by Brown in the role of ungazetted Lord Chamberlain.

The stables, for example, were Queen Victoria's special preserve, Her Majesty taking the same interest in her 'dear little Highland ponies' that the present Sovereign takes in her race horses, although she lacked the expertise which Queen Elizabeth II brings to a Newmarket sale of yearlings. To protect her dear ponies from being overridden, the Queen and John Brown put their heads together and devised a complicated merit system whereby the eighteen ponies were divided into five categories and assigned to the Household and guests on the basis of their ability to ride.

The Queen kept the same tight control over stag-hunting. Not a rifle left the Castle's gun-room without the permission of Her Majesty, who studied the 'Stag Book', in which each day's sport was written up, with the same absorption that the present Queen is said to study Ruff's *Guide to the Turf*. Whenever a particularly well-antlered head was brought home, Queen Victoria herself made a pen-and-ink sketch of it in the margin of the 'Stag Book'. When the first snows fell in the Highlands, the Queen, who was usually then at Windsor, would telegraph her Head Forester to remind him to lay out food for the deer.

As the years passed Balmoral life parodied Court life more and more. The presentation of flannel petticoats to the old cottar women, for example, became the Balmoral equivalent of a Buckingham Palace levee, while the dubbing of John Brown as 'The Queen's Highland Servant' was accompanied by all the solemnity of an investiture. Similarly, a quarrel between Brown and John Grant over the fishing rights to a particular stretch of the Dee was apt to assume the proportions of a Cabinet crisis, with the Queen taking a more lively interest in it than she might in a dispute between Mr Gladstone and his Secretary of State for Ireland over the Home Rule question. The trouble was that while Brown and Grant were apt to shake hands and to go off fishing together the next day, a Cabinet split on Home Rule could bring down the government.

Queen Victoria's inordinate interest in her servants also had the effect of involving her Household and her children, notably the Prince of Wales, in a series of kitchen feuds. It all ended in true Montague-Capulet fashion with the servants, themselves, cocking snooks, while their masters walked stiff-legged and bit their thumbs at one another.

The title, 'The Queen's Highland Servant' is misleading in that it gives no real idea of Brown's importance. He took his orders from Queen Victoria, and from no one else. His main responsibility, in turn, was to keep the other Highland servants in line, transmitting the Queen's orders to them direct, for the Equerries could not be entrusted to give orders to the Queen's kilted servitors for fear of hurting their delicate sensibilities. As the Queen reminded Major Elphinstone, 'It will never do to speak harshly and dictatorially to Highlanders; their independence and self-respect and proper spirit . . . make them resent that far more than an ordinary . . . English servant.'[83]

Brown reported to Queen Victoria twice a day. 'He comes to my room—after breakfast and luncheon to get his orders —and everything is always right,' the Queen wrote to the Princess Royal in April, 1865. 'It is an excellent arrangement, and I feel I have here always in the House a good, devoted Soul . . . whose only object and interest is my service, and God knows how much I want to be taken care of.'[78] (One can read into this last phrase the Queen's almost pathetic desire to submit, to be fussed over and spoiled.)

Had Brown's sphere of influence been confined to the Highlanders, all might have run smoothly, but unfortunately, at those bedside briefings, Her Majesty also was in the habit of giving him orders to transmit to members of her Household. Brown, of course, was not noted for his tact, and in time the words 'Her Mad-jesty says' became a hated sound. Lord John Manners was startled by Brown's method of selecting those Household members who were to grace the Queen's dinner-table. Lord John was sitting in the billiard room one day when Brown thrust his head inside the door, scanned the assembled company, and bawled out, 'All what's here dines with the Queen.'[7] If any dispute arose concerning Brown's interpretation of Her Majesty's orders, Queen Victoria invariably took Brown's side. The Queen's writ extended to his brothers as well.

Mention has already been made of Archie Brown, the youngest of those brothers. Shortly after being promoted to the position of Prince Leopold's valet in April, 1866, Archie became involved in a furious row with Lieutenant (later Colonel Sir) Walter Stirling, a young cavalry officer, who had joined the Household as Prince Leopold's governor. Stirling was a hearty, extrovert type (his *Who's Who* listing describes him as a 'lover of fox-hunting, shooting, and all sports and outdoor games'), and accustomed to Army discipline. Apparently no one bothered to take the lieutenant aside when he arrived to explain the hieratic system at Balmoral, therefore he began to order Archie Brown around as though he were an orderly, unaware of the special deference that was due to John Brown's kith and kin. Archie went running to brother John, who, in turn, went running to the Queen. Result: Stirling was summarily dismissed.

Major Elphinstone, who was Prince Arthur's governor, intervened on the young cavalry officer's behalf, suggesting that he be transferred to Prince Arthur's Household, but the Queen would have none of it. Stirling lacked 'enlarged views', she wrote to Major Elphinstone. The cavalryman was also devoid of that 'softness and kindliness of manner' which was requisite to the education of her sons. The Prince of Wales's personality, she went on to note, had suffered as a result of 'so-called "manliness" (falsely called) being forced into him', and she was determined that there should be no repetition of this in the case of her other sons. [83]

Thanks to incidents such as this, the anti-Brown cabal had grown considerably by 1866, and included the Queen's secretary, General Sir Charles Grey. Grey's daughter, Louisa, Countess of Antrim, claimed that the enmity between the two men sprang from the General's military ideas of discipline. 'Brown came into his office one day with a verbal order from the Queen which he delivered in an off-hand manner,' the Countess recalled. 'My father refused to accept the message in this form.' [7] Thereafter Brown bore the 'Gineral' a grudge, which Grey returned in kind, according to his daughter.

Queen Victoria, of course, was not put off by opposition of this sort to Brown. Contention brought out the best fighting qualities in her. And now, like a good general, the Queen prepared for the counter-attack.

5

A PEDIGREE TO ORDER

IF Queen Victoria could make an Archbishop of a butcher's son, as was her frequent boast,* what was to prevent her, by a wave of her wand, from giving John Brown a family background that would connect him to some of the great Highland clans? The Queen's reasoning, of course, was never this crude. Indeed, it is doubtful whether ratiocination played a great part in the process whereby Brown was transformed in the Queen's mind. Rather, she acted upon a genuine belief that anyone so noble as Brown, so worthy of confidence and respect, must, of necessity, be of high birth. It was a question, therefore, of restoring this male Cinderella to his rightful heritage. Of more immediate concern, such a restoration would give Brown standing in the eyes of the Royal Household, and pave the way for his acceptance as a trusted cup-bearer by the Queen's own family. Accordingly, Her Majesty commanded Dr Andrew Robertson, the Balmoral factor, to draw up Brown's family tree.

Dr Robertson, a dapper little man who came originally from Tarland, was uniquely qualified for this task. For one thing, he had brought John Brown into the world, as well as every other baby in Crathie parish up to the time of his retirement to become the Queen's factor in 1848. (As the only doctor within a fifty-mile radius, Dr Robertson in those early days had spent much of his time in the saddle making his country calls. He thought nothing of riding to the borders of Banffshire or Inverness-shire before breakfast, according to his daughter.)[75] For another, he and Brown

---

* Dr William Thompson, the Archbishop of York, was the son of a linen draper, and not of a butcher, as Her Majesty had fondly supposed.

were distantly related, having a common ancestor in Laird
Shaw of Badenoch.* The factor also had the makings of a
courtier. When Victoria asked him to trace Brown's
ancestry he knew exactly how to season the dish to suit the
Queen's taste. His memorandum, dated June 2, 1865, and
written in beautiful copperplate script, did two things: by
implication, it linked Brown with the great clans, notably
the Farquharsons of Inverey;† and it implied that Brown
was of good Jacobite stock, thus flattering the Queen's
Stuart pretensions.

The good doctor hurried over the Browns of Kirriemuir,
Angus, in order to dwell lovingly upon the Shaw side of
Brown's paternal ancestry. (John Brown's grandfather
Donald, it will be recalled, married Janet Shaw, the
daughter of one 'Captain' James Shaw, of Badenoch; the
couple had six sons, of whom one was the father of Queen
Victoria's attendant.) From Dr Robertson's memorandum
we learn that Brown was 'every inch a Shaw'. 'It is from
this blood that John has derived those qualities which have
recommended him to your Majesty', the factor assured the
Queen. Dr Robertson claimed that when very young he had
seen 'Captain' Shaw, John's great-grandfather, and that he
still retained 'a vivid recollection of his fine aristocratic
appearance'. Moreover, by a startling coincidence, John
Brown was the very image of this 'remarkably handsome
man', who was of 'a warm generous disposition, possessing
all the high and chivalrous feelings of the Highland gentleman'. (At this point the memorandum sounds almost as

---

* That the two men grew to detest one another to the point where
Dr Robertson threatened to resign after a row with Brown only adds
comedy to the situation.

† The Farquharson connection, in reality, was nothing much to
boast of. The Farquharsons were cateran in origin and had arrived
late on Deeside, where they tricked the Gordons out of some of their
best land, including the Balmoral estate. The 11th Marquis of Huntly
referred to Col James Farquharson contemptuously as 'Piccadilly
Jim'. Whenever he dined at Balmoral Huntly, who was a Gordon,
never failed to remind his hearers that the Farquharsons were up-
starts who had been on Deeside a mere 200 years.

though it had been dictated by Queen Victoria, herself, so neatly does it coincide with Her Majesty's own views concerning Highlanders in general.) The factor concluded his litany by citing 'Captain' Shaw's 'shrewdness, high intelligence, and knowledge of the world.'

When he came to discuss 'Captain' Shaw's military career however, Dr Robertson got completely muddled. He claimed that the captain had fought with a Highland regiment in the American War of Independence, been taken prisoner, escaped and, 'after many hardships and adventures', made his way back to England, where he married a Miss McDonald soon after. But 'Captain' Shaw would already have been a grandfather when the American colonies rebelled, according to my time reckoning (his daughter Janet was born in 1751, married in the early 1770s), and so most likely would have been rejected as too old for service overseas. The Balmoral factor may have confused 'Captain' Shaw with his eldest son, Lt Alexander Shaw, who was killed in a pistol duel in 1808 near Cromarty.

Queen Victoria caused Dr Robertson's memorandum to be circulated widely among members of the Household and her own family. But her efforts to refurbish Brown's family tree went further. In 1866 the Queen put up money for the publication of a book entitled *Highlanders of Scotland*, by one Kenneth Macleay, Esq., Royal Scottish Academy. In this unique work portraits of a select few of the Royal retainers are shown cheek-by-jowl with those of representatives of the great Highland clans; thus Brown finds himself unexpectedly in a distinguished company of Macdonalds, Gordons, Frasers and Forbes. But it is a Brown who is totally unrecognizable: the granite-like features have been softened, the chin sanded down, the mouth given an almost feminine expression. He is shown wearing a grey hunting kilt and a modern turn-down collar and Royal blue cravat such as no gillie on Deeside would be seen wearing even in his coffin. A massive gold watch-chain is looped high in his waistcoat, a grey plaid neatly folded and pendant from his arm. His dagger is visible above the right stocking top. This son of a crofter who started life as a stable hand is made to look like the foppish fashion-plate of some Edinburgh kilt-maker.

It is easy to ridicule Queen Victoria's efforts to make John Brown shine in the eyes of the world, but she was actuated only by kindness. A parallel can be found in the frantic efforts she made in later years on behalf of Brown's successor, Abdul Karim, otherwise known as the Munshi. The Munshi's father was an apothecary at the local prison at Agra, but the Queen insisted against all evidence that he was a retired Surgeon-General of the Indian Army, and that he had accompanied General Roberts in 1880 on his celebrated march, at the head of 10,000 troops, from Kabul to Kandahar to rout the Afghans there. (Evidently she had heard these stories from the Munshi himself.) When Frederick Ponsonby, lately in India as Aide-de-Camp to the Viceroy, told the Queen of his interview with the Munshi's father at the Agra jail, she said she was sure that he had talked to the wrong man, but young Ponsonby was banished from her dinner table for a year.[113] Having pestered three Prime Ministers, two Viceroys and most of her Household about 'Munshi business', as Sir Henry Ponsonby called it, over the years, Queen Victoria got her final revenge on all doubters by awarding Abdul Karim the Order of the Indian Empire in 1895. As Emily Crawford observed, 'Who can blame an old lady who had been breathing the atmosphere of flattery the greater part of her life, if the pungent Oriental incense pleased her more?'[27]

In time, the Highlander's influence extended even to Queen Victoria's travels abroad, the Queen arranging her itineraries so as to avoid those countries where her personal attendant was not well received. This, of course, was not the only consideration governing her travels, but it was an important one. Thus, after Leopold's death, the Queen usually journeyed to Germany via Cherbourg and Paris, bypassing Brussels because the Belgian Court had been hostile to Brown, and had persisted in treating him as a mere lackey. In Germany Her Majesty insisted, wherever she went, that a suite of rooms be set aside for Brown, preferably near the suite where the Queen herself slept so that she could rest secure in the knowledge of his protection.

In Paris, where the Queen frequently stopped overnight on her Continental journeys, the various French political personalities, accustomed to dealing with eccentric foreigners, came to understand the Queen and her foibles quite well. Far from looking askance at Brown, Jules Grévy, the French President, used to bow to the Scotsman very politely, and telegrams would go to the various watering-places where the Queen was to stay that Brown was to be treated 'according to the Queen's estimation and with tact'.[27] As a result Queen Victoria quite fell in love with republican France. Brown himself seems to have taken a great liking to William Henry Waddington, the half-English French Premier, who had been educated at Rugby and Oxford. When the Queen stopped in Paris en route to Baveno, Italy, Waddington called on her at the British Embassy and, in coming away, the Premier noticed Brown hanging about outside the door as though to intercept him. 'They shook hands,' Waddington's wife recalled, 'and Brown begged him to come to Scotland, where he would receive a hearty welcome.'[153]

But in 1865 there was no question of Brown being snubbed when Queen Victoria took him with her on a visit to Princess Alice at Darmstadt in August of that year. For whatever Princess Alice may have thought of the gillie privately, she was all surface cordiality at the prospect of welcoming him ('How it will amuse and please me to show the excellent Scotchman our home,' she wrote to her mother). The main purpose of the Queen's visit was to unveil a bronze statue of the Prince Consort on his forty-sixth birthday anniversary. All nine of her children were present at the ceremony. It was the first time the family had been reunited since Albert's death. Trumpets blared, cannon, thundered salutes, and two hundred young ladies in white laid wreaths at the foot of the statue—'It was,' the Queen proclaimed, 'most beautiful, touching and solemn . . .'

But Brown, whose kilted figure had attracted as much attention in Germany as Princess Alice's blackamoor had on Deeside, was restive. Most likely it was as a result of his prodding that Queen Victoria left for Scotland almost immediately following her return home. This time Her Majesty's destination was not Balmoral. Instead, she was the guest of Lord Dalhousie at Invermark, which she had visited in the company of Prince Albert the year of his death. Now, four years later, all seemed different, 'strange, unnatural, and sad', as she recorded. 'For the first time I was alone in a strange house, without either mother or husband . . .' And yet not entirely alone, for John Brown was just down the passage. With typical methodicalness, the Queen noted the location of Brown's room in her journal 'The two maids, Lenchen (Princess Helena) and Lady Churchill, and Brown were all in our passage, away from the rest of the house.' Victoria liked to have Brown near her when she visited a country house whose layout was not too familiar. The Highlander gave her a sense of security; she seemed to sleep better knowing that he was close at hand.

On the other hand the Queen showed a reckless disregard for her own safety by insisting once more upon driving around the countryside after nightfall. In this instance the Queen and her party got lost after dark in a blinding rainstorm while en route to Dunkeld, where Her Majesty was to be the guest of the Duchess of Athole, and this time even the Queen suffered an attack of nerves ('I became much alarmed, though I would say nothing'). Grant took a lamp out of the carriage and walked in front of the horses, while Brown led them ('this reassured me'). Brown's temper seems to have worn thin, for when General Grey asked a direction of the Duchess of Athole, who was riding in the

Queen's carriage, Brown answered for Her Grace: 'The
Duchess don't know at all where we are!' As Queen Victoria
tactfully explained in her journal, 'It was so dark she could
not recognize familiar places.' Safely arrived at the
Duchess's shooting-lodge at Dunkeld, the Queen again
noted down the sleeping arrangements, 'Brown, the only
other servant in the house, below, Grant in the adjoining
buildings to the house. The General and Lady Ely were at
the hotel.'

The adventure in the rain had a painful sequel. In her
journal two days later the Queen wrote, 'Was much dis-
tressed at breakfast to find that poor Brown's legs had been
dreadfully cut by the edge of his wet kilt on Monday, just
at the back of the knee . . . Today one became so inflamed,
and swelled so much, that he could hardly move.' This
mishap, as trivial as the mosquito bite which gives rise to
malaria, may well mark the onset of the streptococcus infection which was to plague Brown for the rest of his life,
and eventually to cause his death. On this occasion Brown
appears to have been suffering from cellulitis, a form of
swelling and induration of the tissues, which can begin from
just such small abrasions, the streptococci entering from
various sources of infection. Brown's illness will be discussed in detail later, but suffice it is to say now that, from
this point onwards, he was to have continual trouble with
his legs. Even then, in the autumn of 1865, the subject
bulked large in Victoria's journal. On October 13, Brown
insisted that he was well enough to accompany Her Majesty
on one of her outings, but the Queen confessed, 'It was
really most distressing to me to see what pain poor Brown
suffered, especially in going up and down the hill. He could
not go fast, and walked lame, but would not give in.
His endurance on this occasion showed a brave heart
indeed.'[146]

In February, 1866, Queen Victoria opened Parliament for
the first time since the Prince Consort's death, consenting

largely because she had a financial interest at stake: Parliament was to be asked to vote a £30,000 dowry for Princess Helena, whose engagement to Prince Christian of Schleswig-Holstein had just been announced. Still she could not bring herself to go to Westminster graciously, but likened the opening to a public execution, to which she 'a poor, broken-hearted widow, nervous and shrinking (was) dragged in deep mourning . . . to be gazed at without delicacy of feeling.'[148]

Queen Victoria might just as well have stayed at home, for not many of her subjects were in a holiday mood. On the Continent Austria and Prussia were poised on the brink of war; at home the Russell government faced a crisis over its Reform Bill. Even had they been holiday-minded, the crowds would have found very little to their liking, for the Queen had decreed that there should be no pageantry, no trumpet fanfares, no gingerbread coaches. Instead, Her Majesty arrived at Westminster Palace in a modest equipage and shunned the Royal Entrance to sneak in at a side door reserved for peers. Emily Crawford, who must have had a front seat in the Distinguished Visitors' Gallery, observed Her Majesty closely as the Lord Chancellor read the Queen's speech. 'Not a nerve in her face moved . . . but her nostrils quivered and widened'. Mrs Crawford reports. 'Tears gathered on the fringe of the drooping eyelids. A few rolled down the cheeks.'[27]

In March Queen Victoria revived another custom when she visited Aldershot and reviewed troops for the first time since the Prince Consort's death. Earlier in her reign the Queen, who delighted in these reviews, had taken the salute while seated on her horse Alma and wearing a scarlet military tunic with brass buttons and gold braid, but this time she remained in her carriage, sharing the limelight with the stolid Highlander on the rumble. 'Gillie Brown', *The Morning Post* noted, 'seems by degrees to have fallen into the position in the household of the Queen such as was occupied by Roustaen, the Mameluke, near the person of

Napoleon the Great.'* This, as far as I have been able to determine, is the first, but by no means the last, mention of John Brown in print.

Queen Victoria refused to postpone her usual Spring trip north for anything so tiresome as a Ministerial crisis ('She could not go on working as she does . . . if she did not get that change of scene and that pure air . . .').[148] Consequently, she was at Balmoral, 600 miles from the capital, when the Russell government resigned in June, after having been defeated on an amendment to its Franchise Bill. The reaction of the Establishment as the Queen continued to delay her return to Windsor was one of profound disgust.

'No respect or loyalty seems left in the way people allow themselves to talk of the Queen,' Lady Amberley, Earl Russell's daughter-in-law, wrote in her diary.[6] She quoted the grumbling remarks of those around her, 'What do we pay her for if she will not work?' and 'She had better abdicate if she is incompetent to do her duty.' More tellingly, the gossipers now began to link Queen Victoria's name with that of John Brown. The reason she did not return to Windsor, they whispered, was that 'John Brown will not let her come.'[6] It was a full week after the government's resignation before the Queen could be prevailed upon to return to Windsor, and to call upon Lord Derby to form a government, which he did with Disraeli as Chancellor of the Exchequer.

But the Queen had personal worries alongside which the Ministerial crisis paled to insignificance in her eyes. The out-

---

* Roustaen's life reads like something out of the *Arabian Nights*. Born in Georgia, he was kidnapped by pirates and sold as a slave to the Bey of Alexandria in whose house he was brought up. Napoleon brought the Mameluke back to France in 1799, and for the next fifteen years he accompanied his master on every battlefield, acting partly as outrider, partly as valet. His devotion, however, did not extend to following Napoleon into exile, for Roustaen made off with a considerable sum of money on the eve of the Emperor's departure for Elba.

break of the Seven Weeks' War between Austria and Prussia found her two eldest daughters, Vicky and Alice, on opposite sides; indeed, all of the Queen's German relatives were threatened with involvement in the conflict on one side or another. To cap it all the Princess Royal's infant son, Sigismund, died as the result of convulsions on June 18.

In her grief Vicky turned to Queen Victoria for solace ('My little darling ... my pride, my joy, my hope, is gone ... God's will be done ... but oh how bitter is this cup'). Owing to the Austro-Prussian hostilities, the Queen could not personally console her daughter, whose place at that moment was with her husband's people in Berlin. Instead, she sent the Princess Royal a volume of suitably mournful poems—had not she derived great comfort after Prince Albert's death from reading Tennyson's *In Memoriam?*—and her advice to her daughter now was that which Tennyson had addressed to the Queen herself: 'Break not, O woman's heart, but still endure ...'

In writing to the Princess Royal a curious thing happened—the Queen left the door to her own heart ajar. In discussing grief the Queen had been thinking not of Prince Albert, nor of Tennyson and his *In Memoriam*, but of John Brown, who represented the quick, as opposed to the dead. It began with the Queen comparing the merits of her various spiritual advisers as comforters in bereavement. Big, jovial Rev. Norman Macleod, who used to read Burns aloud to the Queen, was the best of these spiritual brethren, though the Rev. Gerald Wellesley, who had been her Dean of Windsor for twelve years, could be very tender on occasion, but Dean Stanley was cold '& to me as if he were of no sex'. [78] The best comforter of all, the Queen decided, was Brown. None other had done her more good, she confided to her daughter. But here the Queen was confronted by a dilemma. Was it wrong to seek solace from this man who was not her husband? Was she being unfaithful to Prince Albert's memory? Thoroughly perplexed, the Queen rushed to Dean Wellesley with her problem, which she outlined in general terms. Should she reproach herself that the grief for the Prince Consort was waning? Was it wrong to accept comfort and sympathy from another? The Dean, who probably guessed the true import of her questions, thought not. A 'settled mournful resignation' was better than acute grief, the Dean told her. If God saw fit to put in our way comforters with 'congenial natures' and special healing powers we should not question it.[78] Dean Wellesley's words were undoubtedly balsam.

It had taken the shock of grief, in this case the death of a grandson, to force Queen Victoria's love of Brown and her emotional dependence upon him into her consciousness. The crystallization process was now complete; the love object had been wholly transformed by the imagination; the humble bough by this time had become heavily encrusted by gems, cairngorms, perhaps, if not diamonds of the first fire.

'John Brown will not let her come . . .' As previously remarked, the Establishment did not hesitate to blame John Brown for delaying the Queen at Balmoral during the Ministerial crisis in June. From now on the gillie was to be made the scapegoat for many of the Establishment's discontents. 'John Brown will not let the Queen do this . . . John Brown will not let the Queen do that . . .' The power which the gossips attributed to the Highlander over his Queen was equal to that which the Russian Court later attributed to Rasputin.

Encouraged by these signs of disloyalty on the other side of the Channel, a Swiss newspaper, the *Gazette de Lausanne*, in September, 1866, reported that not only had the Queen and Brown been secretly married, but that she was at that moment with child by him. In making these assertions, the *Gazette's* 'Special Correspondent' took refuge behind the anonymous 'on dit' of the professional gossip columnist.

'They say, that with Brown and by him she consoles herself for Prince Albert, and they go even further.

94

They add that she is in an interesting condition, and that if she was not present for the Volunteers Review, and at the inauguration of the monument to Prince Albert, it was only in order to hide her pregnancy.

I hasten to add that the Queen has been morganatically married to her attendant for a long time, which diminishes the gravity of the thing.'

Although the British Minister at Berne immediately lodged a formal complaint against the Lausanne newspaper with the Swiss government, the Queen's Household was slow in learning the contents of the offending article. 'We do not know what the libel is', Ponsonby, then an Equerry, confessed to his brother. 'I believe that the Queen is as ignorant as any of us', he added, 'but I hope she will not hear of it, as I believe it to be a statement that she has married John Brown, and the idea that it could be said she was marrying one of her servants would make her angry and wretched.'[110] Much later Ponsonby contradicted himself and asserted that Queen Victoria was not only aware of the libel, but that, far from feeling 'angry and wretched', she had actually 'laughed at it and said she was sorry any notice had been taken of it.'[118] (One wonders whether, in recalling the event many years after it happened, Ponsonby's memory may not have been at fault, for the rumour that she was pregnant would hardly have been treated by the Queen as a laughing matter.)

In his letter to his brother Ponsonby went on to explain, 'Brown . . . has lately been raised to be personal attendant —that is, all messages come by him. As he is always dressed as a Highlander he is conspicuous and so is talked of. Besides which he certainly is a favourite. But he is only a servant and nothing more, and what I suppose began as a joke about his constant attendance has been perverted into a libel that the Queen has married him.'[110]

The British Minister at Berne would have done well to allow the libel to die a natural death, for in protesting to the

Swiss government he merely ensured that the slander would gain wider currency. *Reynolds's News*, which was no friend of the British monarchy, quickly got wind of it, reported that the Swiss government had declined to prosecute the offending newspaper despite the British complaint. (The complaint was actually withdrawn as unauthorized by the Foreign Office.) In commenting editorially on the subject, *Reynolds's* made the cryptic observation, 'We do not care to reproduce in our columns the many extraordinary causes that are assigned for the Queen's seclusion in the pages of our foreign contemporaries.'

Another explanation of Brown's hold on the Queen that began to gain ground at this time was that the gillie was endowed with unique psychic powers, and that the Queen used him as her medium to contact Prince Albert in the spirit world. This theory would hardly merit more than a passing reference were it not for the persistence with which it has been urged by its advocates.

All Highlanders, of course, are supposed to be second-sighted, a gift which appears to be confined to the melancholy business of foretelling death. In this connection it is only fair to set down that Brown had some sort of premonition of disaster in the autumn of 1861 during the Prince Consort's last stay at Balmoral. For as that stay drew to a close Brown remarked to the Queen, 'I hope you will all be well through the winter and return here safe. *Above all, I hope you will have no deaths in the family.*'[151] (My italics.) On the last day of the Royal couple's stay, Brown returned to this morbid theme, recalling how he himself had lost two brothers and a sister in the typhoid epidemic which swept Crathie in 1849. 'This struck me as so dreadful that I told it to Papa and several others', the Queen wrote to her eldest daughter in November, after Her Majesty had returned to Windsor. By this time death had already struck twice within one week in her family. Typhoid had carried off the Queen's two cousins, King Pedro V of Portugal and his

Top left: Funereal brooch created by Collingwood, the Royal jeweller, to commemorate John Brown's death. In gold with a chaste Greek border, this particular brooch was apparently given to one of Brown's nieces, for engraved on the back is the legend. 'Uncle John, March 27, 1883, from VRI.'

Top right: John Brown's mother shown wearing the white 'mutch' and plaid shawl of the typical Highland woman

Below: Medals awarded to John Brown. In the centre is the silver medal bearing the head of Ludwig III of Hesse. On either side are the silver Faithful Service Medal, with bar denoting ten additional years of service; and the gold Devoted Service Medal, which bears on the reverse the legend, 'To John Brown, Esq., in recognition of his presence of mind and devotion at Buckingham Palace, February 29, 1872.' These medals fetched £550 when auctioned by Spink and Son in July, 1965

Extract from Queen Victoria's diary, dated Osborne, August 4, 1883, but bearing no salutation. It was found among Mr Hugh Brown's effects when he died

brother, Ferdinand. The Queen immediately recalled Brown's remarks. 'These two coincidences . . . keep returning to my mind', she told the Princess Royal, 'like as if they had been a sort of strange presentiment.'[151] Within one month her own husband was dead of the same fever.

Having stated this much, I should add that Brown gave no further indication of the gift of prophecy during the remainder of his life. Queen Victoria, however, has become a prize exhibit of the spiritualists over the years, taking her place in that small, but select pantheon of notables that includes Arthur Conan Doyle, Sir Oliver Lodge, and Hannen Swaffer, among others. That Queen Victoria was superstitious there can be no doubt—as an example one might cite the number of times the word *unberufen* (meaning 'touch wood') occurs in her letters. Like most of her contemporaries, the Queen took a lively interest in the psychic antics of Daniel Dunglas Home, whose seances were attended by Sir Edward Bulwer and the Brownings, and in the table turnings of the Fox sisters, who enjoyed a vogue in the 1850s. The Queen and Prince Albert even tried their hands at table turning themselves at Osborne in 1854—more as a parlour game, though Her Majesty was 'quite provoked' when General Sir Charles Grey expressed incredulity.[115] But this mild intellectual curiosity has nothing to do with an active interest in spiritualism.

Emily Crawford was largely responsible for encouraging the belief that Queen Victoria dabbled in the occult. According to Mrs Crawford, the Queen, whenever she wanted inspiration to solve some complicated political or domestic problem, would sit and gaze at a bust of the Prince Consort. If this were not convenient 'she held some relic of him . . . and concentrated her thoughts on some of his sayings'.[27]

What would be more natural in these circumstances than that the Queen should allow her gaze to stray now and then from the cold marble features to the homely, but very much alive countenance of Brown, Mrs Crawford reasoned? Had not the Prince himself chosen Brown to be the Queen's guide? But there was another reason why the Prince Consort should reveal his mind to the Queen in Brown's presence. As Mrs Crawford so grandly expressed it: 'Some men were the shadow of the truth, others the reflection of the truth, but Brown, she was satisfied, was the truth itself.'[27]

From this bit of tortured logic it was only a short step to the theory that Brown was Queen Victoria's medium. The spiritualists, however, added another link to the causal chain, and that link was Robert J. Lees, journalist, lecturer, founder of a spiritualist centre at Peckham. From infancy Lees seemed destined to be the catalyst who would reveal John Brown's latent psychic powers, for we are told that 'even in his cradle he could not be left alone at night until he saw a Scottish Highlander sitting beside him'. (*Two Worlds*, October 7, 1951.) At the age of thirteen, Lees succeeded in contacting Prince Albert on the 'Other Side', a feat which was not long in reaching Queen Victoria's ears. Summoned to Windsor Castle, young Lees declined the post of Resident Medium on the advice of his spirit control, Myhanene. 'Instead, he was "told" that the Queen had a servant on her Balmoral estate who could act as her medium.' (Roy Stemman, editor of *Psychic News*, in *The Sunday Telegraph*, August 30, 1964.) Brown's mediumistic gifts thus revealed, the Queen used him to maintain regular contact with her lost Consort, 'the Prince continuing to advise her on many questions of State' (*Two Worlds*, March 7, 1959).

This farrago would not be dealt with at such length had not the same threadbare fabrications been rehearsed again and again in the spiritualist press. (*Psychic News* has a fat file of newspaper cuttings all dealing with Queen Victoria's supposed spiritualist inclinations.) A study of her character will reveal that Queen Victoria, superstitious though she may have been, was much too hard-headed and practical to indulge in hocus-pocus of the sort attributed to her. Besides, such seances could scarcely have escaped the notice of her Household, particularly of her sceptical secretary, Sir Henry Ponsonby, who would certainly have commented on them in his letters to his wife. As for Brown, he was too strong a Calvinist to look upon table turnings and spirit rappings as anything but works of the devil. His comment on all who engaged in such satanic practices would probably have been the same as that which he once used to describe the Catholic clergy: 'Nasty "beggars"!'[78]

6

ALL IS BLACK THAT
IS NOT BROWN

THERE was a thrill of expectancy when the Royal Academy opened the doors of its annual Spring Exhibition to the public on May 6, 1867, for word had leaked out that this show, the Royal Academy's ninety-ninth, was an exceptional one. As *The Times* put it, 'It is long since we have seen an Exhibition of such great and various interest.' The Royal Academy was then housed in what is now the National Gallery (it was not until 1869 that it moved to its present quarters, Burlington House in Piccadilly), and so, as the crowds made their way across Trafalgar Square on opening day, there was a considerable congestion of horse-drawn traffic.

The opening day visitors 'knew what they liked', and what they liked were pictures that told a story. It was the heyday of genre painting, of Academicians like Frith, Ward and Maclise, whose big, tasteless canvasses depicted the humorous, the anecdotic, the sentimental. Characteristically, the one artist among those exhibiting whose work would survive, J. A. McNeill Whistler, was discreetly ignored. His 'Symphony in White, No. 3', an achromatic experiment, was lost among the 872 paintings, drawings and miniatures that were hung, one above the other, like postage stamps in some gigantic album. As *The Times* tactfully observed, 'Mr Whistler, who in his own way is abstract enough, takes a place by himself . . .'

The Times' critic had some testy things to say about Academicians who pre-empted for themselves the most commanding positions on the walls of the various salons. But the critic's strictures were undoubtedly lost on the cluster of

admirers that gathered in front of W. P. Frith's big painting
of 'King Charles II's Last Sunday', which depicted that
unhappy monarch 'all dissoluteness', as the Diarist Evelyn
described him, profaning the Sabbath a week before his
death. His Majesty toys with one of his favourites (the
Duchess of Portsmouth?), while French musicians tootle and
scrape, Courtiers stake their gold at basset, and spaniels of
that breed which bears the King's name lap milk from a
silver dish at his feet.

Thomas Faed's picture of a blind beggar receiving alms
from a fisherman and his children drew an appreciative
audience, as did Poynter's 'Israel in Egypt' depicting Jewish
slaves dragging a red granite Sphinx. Millais had his following, too. This talented painter had long since forsaken his
Pre-Raphaelite friends to become a crowd-pleaser, and now
his canvas 'Asleep' drew audible 'ohs' and 'ahs' from spectators. It was the portrait of a little girl, her 'sweet rosy
face . . . moist with the dew of slumber', in the words of *The
Times*' critic, who singled out for praise the finish which
Millais had given to the quilted satin counterpane at the
foot of the child's crib ('simply consummate . . . finished
almost to the point of illusion').

The magnet which drew the crowds to the Great Room
was not to be found among these canvases, however. The
sensation of the Royal Academy's 99th Exhibition was Sir
Edwin Landseer's equestrian portrait of Queen Victoria
entitled 'Her Majesty at Osborne, 1866'. A big (4′9″ x 6′10″)
canvas, it showed the Queen reading a despatch while
sitting side-saddle on a glossy, well-fed black horse, just as
though she always 'did her boxes' in this equestrian fashion.
The Queen is cocooned in black from head to toe like a nun
from some contemplative order. Strewn at Her Majesty's
feet are her gloves, the empty despatch box, various letters
and envelopes, and dogs, including her favourite terrier,
Prince, who stands on his hind legs as though begging the
Queen to toss him the communiqué which absorbs her
interest. In the background is the square tower of Osborne.

Landseer's eyesight had begun to fail long before he attempted this portrait of Queen Victoria, which accounts for the crudeness of its finish. Also, he had become a prey to what would probably be diagnosed today as acute melancholia. ('Flogging would be mild compared to my sufferings,' he wrote to his sister Jessie. 'No sleep, fearful cramp at night, accompanied by a feeling of distressful feebleness'.) The spectators who flocked in front of Landseer's painting on opening day had, of course, no way of knowing the artist's physical or mental state at the time he did this portrait, but they stared with fascination at his subject matter. And, as they stared, a titter, barely audible at first, ran through the crowd; the titter, in turn, gave way to frank laughter that was punctuated in places by guffaws and ribald comments that scandalized the critic of *The Saturday Review* ('If anyone will stand by this picture for a quarter of an hour and listen to the comments of visitors he will learn how great an imprudence has been committed,' the critic stormed).

The 'imprudence' which provoked all of this rib-digging and risibility was the inclusion in Landseer's canvas of the figure of John Brown. The Queen's Highland Servant is shown holding the horse's bridle, and, possibly in deference to the surrounding gloom, is wearing a black kilt.

This is no cap-in-hand menial whom the artist has placed at the horse's head. Brown appears as bold as brass, watchful, yet very much in command of the situation. Anticipating no doubt the public reaction, *The Saturday Review* felt that it was a mistake even to exhibit the painting. 'We respect the privacy of Her Majesty,' the weekly magazine observed, 'but when Sir Edwin Landseer puts the Queen and her black favourites into what are, during the season, the most public rooms in England, he does more harm to her popularity than he imagines.' *The Illustrated London News* agreed that the painting was an unfortunate one: 'We trust it will be deemed no disloyalty either to the Sovereign or to

the reputation of the painter to say . . . there is not one of
Her Majesty's subjects will see this lugubrious picture without regret.'

Until now Brown had been merely a blurred figure
glimpsed on the box of Queen Victoria's carriage, as far as
the public was concerned; a subliminal image that was
flashed onto the mind to be instantly forgotten until some
concatenation of events served to bring it to the forefront
again, this time in sharp focus. The Landseer painting
served this purpose: by juxtaposing the figures of the Queen
and her gillie, Landseer, unwittingly no doubt, seemed to
make explicit a relationship which until then had been
nebulous. If one could have recorded the comments which
The Saturday Review found so scandalous they would, in all
probability, have run something like this: 'Ah, so this is how
it is! This is how the old girl spends her time in retirement!'
And because their Sovereign was shown suddenly to be
human, and capable of all the folly that the word implies,
the spectators giggled appreciatively, and the giggles became
guffaws.

It should be added that Queen Victoria was pleased with
the painting, so much so that she ordered Sir Edwin
Landseer to make an engraving of it. ('The likeness of herself [rather a portly elderly lady] and her good faithful
attendant and friend are both, she thinks, very good', as she
told Sir Howard Elphinstone.)[83] Poor Sir Edwin, who, at
that time was being driven half-mad by failing eyesight, was
not to be left in peace until he had made certain alterations
suggested by Her Majesty, and filed by him in his correspondence under the heading 'Royal Fusseries'.[72] In this
case, Lady Caroline Gordon acted as go-between in conveying the Queen's suggestions to Landseer at his London
studio in St John's Wood. On July 1, Lady Caroline wrote
enclosing a batch of photographs of John Brown, showing
the Highlander with his beard shorter than Landseer had
portrayed it in the Royal Academy painting. 'She (the
Queen) wishes much to know if this could be introduced

into the engraving and whether you would think it an improvement', Lady Caroline wrote, signing herself 'your everlasting tormentor'. Whether or not Landseer thought it an improvement, Brown's beard was trimmed according to the Queen's wishes, which brought to an end this particular 'fussery'.* Meanwhile, a brash new humour magazine called *Tomahawk* coined a bon mot which quickly made the rounds of the London drawing-rooms. After surveying the unrelieved gloom of the Landseer painting, *Tomahawk* declared, 'All is black that is not Brown.'

The year 1867 itself had begun gloomily when Queen Victoria was booed when she went in State to open Parliament. This personal appearance was intended as a favour on Her Majesty's part to Lord Derby, who had become her Prime Minister the preceding June, and it was to Lord Derby, therefore, that General Sir Charles Grey expressed the Queen's disappointment. 'Her Majesty says there was a good deal of hissing and even groaning at times', her secretary wrote, adding that the Queen had had a presentiment that 'something unpleasant' might happen 'with the existing agitation about Reform, and the numbers of people out of employment.'[33]

The times were, if anything, more apocalyptic than Her Majesty had painted them. For not only had tens of thousands of unemployed gone hungry that winter, but there were cholera outbreaks in East London, colliery disasters elsewhere (340 were killed in a mine explosion near Barnsley, Yorkshire), ending with a meteoric shower on November 14 (1,200 meteors were counted at the Twicken-

---

* Queen Victoria was no less critical of portraits of herself, as witness the following comments written in her own handwriting on the proof of the engraving which eventually was used as the frontispiece to *More Leaves:* 'The face is too short. The bows of the bonnet might be brought below the cheek . . . The distance from the nostril to the eye is rather too short . . . The eyes are too much closed. The upper eyelid should be slightly lessened in thickness.' (See Helmut and Alison Gernsheim: *Queen Victoria.*)

ham Observatory), as though the very heavens were out of joint. Added to these natural and man-made phenomena were the agitations of the Reform League and of the Irish Republican Brotherhood (Fenian), both of which were on the rampage.

As 1867 dawned the one bright spot as far as Victoria was concerned was the emergence of Benjamin Disraeli, who, as Chancellor of the Exchequer in the Derby government, was now for the first time brought into close contact with the Queen. To celebrate the beginning of this new partnership *Tomahawk*, in its issue of June 1, 1867, ran a prophetic cartoon entitled 'Pygmalion and His Statue', showing Disraeli, spit-curl plastered on forehead, goatish tuft of hair sprouting from chin, putting the finishing touches to a statue of the Queen. But Gallatea has come alive, and she is exclaiming, 'Dizzy—Dear Embodiment of all that is good, and grand, and great, how I do love thee.'

Writers on the subject have been hard put to reconcile the wily and sophisticated Disraeli with that other mascu-line influence in the Queen's widowed life, John Brown. How could Victoria accommodate the one's peremptory 'wumman', and the other's fawning 'Faery' at one and the same time? Actually the contradiction was more apparent than real, for each played Pygmalion to the Queen in turn. (They held one another in high regard, incidentally, for Brown sent Disraeli salmon he had fished from the Dee, while Disraeli was always careful to enquire after 'Mr Brown' in his letters to the Queen.) Brown's claim on the Queen was, of course, the stronger: he had renewed her interest in life at a time when that interest was waning, and this through the simple expedient of treating her as a woman. Disraeli not only treated the Queen as a woman, but he made her an Empress, which Brown did not have it within his power to do. Thus, far from being mutually exclusive these two male influences were complementary.

Undoubtedly it was the Byzantine side of Disraeli's character which appealed to Queen Victoria initially, for the

Queen was fascinated by the East, and in her imagination she associated Disraeli with all of its gorgeous panoply, an illusion which he was at no pains to dispel. It was not only the Orient that attracted her, but anything exotic or out of the ordinary. And Disraeli, with his dyed hair, his use of scent, his habit of wearing his rings over his gloves, was nothing if not exotic. Who but Disraeli would think of asserting that nightingales fed on glow-worms? The Queen, who could not pass a gypsy on the road without stopping her carriage to talk, who was attracted even to Italian organ-grinders, clearly found Dizzy irresistible.

As early as 1852, when she had invited Disraeli and his wife to dinner at Windsor, the Queen had described his appearance as 'most singular'. . . . The expression is disagreeable, but I did not find him so to talk to', she wrote in her journal, adding that 'his language is very flowery'.[78] Ten years later Dizzy earned her gratitude when he intervened in a Commons debate to champion the Albert Memorial, and, in appreciation, the Queen sent him a copy of Albert's speeches bound in white morocco and inscribed from 'the beloved Prince's broken-hearted widow'. But it was not until 1867 that Dizzy's spell really began to work.

In his capacity as Chancellor, Disraeli wrote to the Queen in the style of his novels, making the opposition to his Reform Bill sound like romantic intrigue at the Court of Louis XVI. 'It was a *conspiration des salons*', he began a typical letter describing the Parliamentary scene in June, 1867. 'The Ladies' Gallery', he continued, 'was full of fascinating conspirators; all the stormy petrels of politics, all the statesmen out of place, revisited the House of Commons . . .'[148] One has only to compare this racy approach with the dry-as-dust reports which Gladstone sent to the Queen when he was Prime Minister to understand why, under Dizzy's aegis, the Queen began to take an active interest in politics. As Clarendon observed, 'Dizzy writes . . . telling her every scrap of political news dressed up to serve his purpose, and every scrap of social gossip cooked to amuse her. She declares that she had never had such letters in her life . . .'[23]

While her Chancellor held Queen Victoria in thrall, she had less cause to be enchanted with her Prime Minister, who was responsible for embroiling Her Majesty in a needless row with the Reform League. For in banning a Reform League meeting in Hyde Park, called for May 6, 1867, Lord Derby gave as his reason that the meeting would 'interfere with the object for which Her Majesty has been pleased to open the park'; namely, public recreation. Accordingly Edmond Beales and his Reform League followers decided to defy the free speech ban by 'taking an airing' in Hyde Park at 6 p.m. on May 6th for the sake of their 'political health'.

The result was a complete and bloodless victory for the forces of progress, or 'the most disgraceful day . . . in political history' (*The Saturday Review*), depending upon your point of view. At any rate, by 6.30 p.m. the park swarmed with an estimated 100,000 free-speech lovers out for a stroll, and they were harangued by Reform League speakers from no fewer than ten platforms. *The Times*, yielding to hysteria, claimed that Beales & Company were 'the actual government of the country'. The frightened Derby government took refuge from the mob by hiding behind Queen Victoria. Specifically, it brought in a new Parks Prohibition Bill, which would have enabled the authorities to ban meetings in Hyde Park on the grounds that it was Crown property. It was class legislation, pure and simple, designed to protect 'the fastidious and insolent whims of Rotten Row', as Beales expressed it, referring to the swells who rode horseback in that part of Hyde Park. By invoking Her Majesty's name, the Bill, which was later dropped, only served to increase her unpopularity.

Mention has already been made of *Tomahawk*, which was founded in May, 1867, as 'A Saturday Journal of Satire'.

This humour magazine was to provide Queen Victoria with some of her biggest headaches before the year was out. Starting with a cartoon entitled 'Where is Britannia?', showing an empty throne with the British lion dozing behind it, *Tomahawk* now published a series of cartoons, each more anti-Royalist than the other, which raised its circulation, and with it the hackles of those at Court who cared for the Queen's reputation.

The art of impaling Royalty with a political cartoon is lost today, possibly because present-day Royalty lead such exemplary lives that there is nothing visible into which the cartoonist can sink his harpoon.* *Tomahawk*'s merit was that it harked back to an older, more robust tradition when Royalty was considered fair game, when Gillray delighted fashionable London with his caricatures of George III as a pinchpenny frying his own sprats in order to economize, and of his son, the Prince Regent, as an unrepentant voluptuary who divided his time between the banquet table, the gambling hall and Mrs Fitzherbert's boudoir. Although his style in no way resembled Gillray's, Matt Morgan, *Tomahawk*'s chief cartoonist, was a worthy successor to the Prince Regent's scourge, and whatever brilliance *Tomahawk* achieved during its brief career it owed almost entirely to Morgan, who was also a scenic designer at the Covent Garden Opera.

The cartoon which sent *Tomahawk*'s circulation soaring (and with it Queen Victoria's blood pressure) was a double-page drawing which appeared in its issue of August 10, and which was entitled 'A Brown Study'. The scene is the same as in the cartoon cited above, with the throne still empty, only this time a rather sinister-looking John Brown is shown leaning against the throne as he smokes his clay pipe. The British lion that was shown dozing in the previous

---

* More likely it has to do with what Kingsley Martin calls the 'glorified, religious view of royalty' which prevails today. 'The Queen is not allowed to wear a crown,' Martin declares; 'nothing less than a halo will suffice.'[94]

cartoon is fully awake this time, and has assumed a begging posture at Brown's feet, while the grim-visaged Highlander looks down at it thoughtfully as though to say, 'Down!' In the background the Queen's Crown rests underneath a glass bell.

Accused of being scurrilous and vulgar, *Tomahawk* pleaded guilty to three unpardonable vices. 'We are young, successful and speak the truth,' Arthur a'Beckett, its editor, claimed. The humour magazine was certainly successful—that point was beyond dispute, though older heads might question its version of the truth. But had not the older heads on *Punch*, for example, been guilty themselves of baiting the Monarchy? As early as September, 1865, *Punch* had criticized Queen Victoria's retirement from public life by picturing her in a cartoon as the statue of Hermione in Shakespeare's Winter's Tale with whom Britannia, disguised as Paulina, pleads: ' 'Tis time! Descend: be stone no more!' And was not *Punch* the first to attack the Queen's favourite by holding him up to ridicule in a mock 'Court Circular' published in its issue of July 7, 1866? The editors of *Punch* could find nothing more noteworthy of Court news to chronicle than the following:

> 'Balmoral, Tuesday.
> Mr John Brown walked on the slopes.
> He subsequently partook of a haggis.
> In the evening Mr John Brown was pleased to listen to a bagpipe.
> Mr John Brown retired early'

If Mr Punch, that model of respectability, saw fit to ridicule the Queen and her favourite in these terms what was to prevent others less scrupulous and less talented from having a go? Following *Punch*'s example, the gossip columnists made John Brown the scapegoat for their animosity towards Queen Victoria, great play being made of his pre-eminence at Court, his insolence to those around him, and his predilection for hard liquor. Curiously, in view of

Brown's origin, the Scottish provincial press was the greatest offender in this respect. Thus, in August, 1866, the *John-O'-Groat Journal* published a letter from its London correspondent which read in part:

> 'I suppose all my readers have heard of the great court favourite John Brown. His dismissal some weeks ago was generally talked about at the time, and I observe that the fact has now found its way into print, coupled with the suggestion of John Brown's probable restoration to power before long.
>
> The reason assigned for his dismissal is an inordinate indulgence in the national taste for whisky, and the restraining of that appetite is mentioned as a likely condition of his re-admission to favour.
>
> Far be it from me to question Mr Brown's powers of suction. They may rival those of one of Dickens' characters, the elder Weller, I think, who would have made an uncommon good oyster if he'd been born in that sphere of life . . .'

This rumour concerning Brown's alleged dismissal for drunkenness was picked up by other newspapers and given wide currency. It was even repeated on the other side of the Channel.

Brown was the subject of another *Tomahawk* cartoon, this one entitled 'Pictures in the Fire', showing an Indian fakir gazing into the flames where he sees 'The Mystery of the Season'—Brown, again propped up against the empty throne. But this drawing lacks the audacity of 'A Brown Study'. The magazine crowned its impudence by suggesting in May, 1868, that the Prince of Wales be appointed Regent in view of the 'deplorable state of health, both physical and mental, in which our unhappy Queen is'. *Tomahawk* folded early in 1870, and Matt Morgan left soon afterwards for America. Jerrold claims that Morgan received a large bribe 'to exercise his talents on the other side of the Atlantic', but this hardly seems likely, for in 1874 Morgan wrote from

New York to Arthur a'Beckett proposing that *Tomahawk* be revived.*

The *Tomahawk* cartoons and the comments concerning Brown's presence in Landseer's portrait of the Queen must have been terribly wounding to the Highlander, who saw himself hoisted into public notoriety overnight and made the butt of coarse jokes. No doubt he complained loudly to the Queen about those 'nasty beggars', the penny-a-liners of the press who kept the meretricious rumours concerning him alive. He may even, as the Scottish provincial press had suggested, have threatened to resign from the Queen's service. That the Queen and her Highland attendant quarrelled frequently is a fact well attested to by members of her entourage. The quarrels were hastily composed as a rule, the reconciliations being accompanied often by expensive gifts from the Queen to Brown.

In view of the press attacks on Brown, and in view of his explosive temper, unusual interest attaches to an item which appeared in *The Manchester Examiner* at about this time. Headed 'The Queen's Gillie', the item, which appeared on September 3, 1867, stated: 'It is understood that the Queen will shortly lose the personal services of her faithful Highland gillie, John Brown . . . It appears that despite the confidential post assigned to him in the royal household, he is desirous to redeem the troth long ago plighted to a young Scotch woman of his own grade.' The newspaper added that the married couple were to be given a lodge at Balmoral as residence. Although nothing more was heard of these nuptials, it was not the last time that John Brown was rumoured about to marry. In the end he remained wedded to the Queen's service.

The brouhaha concerning Brown, of course, did nothing to improve the Queen's popular standing. Moncure Conway,

* The practice of bribing artists was not uncommon in Georgian times. Receipts in the Royal Archives at Windsor attest to sums paid out by George IV to suppress drawings and caricatures that showed him in an unflattering light. Among the recipients was George Cruikshank.

the rationalist preacher, recalled dining at the Urban Club at St John's Gate at about this time, when a kinsman of Lord Macaulay, a young man named Babington. refused to rise when the Queen's health was proposed. 'There was a noisy discussion,' Conway declared, 'but a goodly number defended Babington's right so to express his opinion.' 'It became plain to me,' he added, 'that the Queen was not popular.'[25]

As though Queen Victoria did not have enough to contend with from disloyal clubmen, satirical cartoons, and jeers concerning her portrait in the Royal Academy Exhibition, her Prime Minister took it into his head that she should invite to England some of the Heads of State who were then attending the Great Exhibition in Paris, notably Tsar Alexander II of Russia, the Sultan of Turkey, and the Egyptian Khedive. Lord Derby saw in the proximity of so many notables an excellent opportunity for England to mend its Eastern fences, and had he been more tactful he might have won the Queen's consent. But the gout-ridden Lord Derby was a country squire of the old school, accustomed to expressing himself bluntly, and completely unschooled in the flattery that characterized his Chancellor, Disraeli. As a result of Lord Derby's blundering approach, Queen Victoria saw in the propinquity of these Eastern potentates a plot to disturb her peace of mind, and she had no intention of giving in without a struggle. From Balmoral she dispatched this message to Lord Derby: ' . . . the Queen is UTTERLY incapable (overwhelmed with work, and the responsibility of her arduous position, in which she is naturally unaided) of entertaining any Royal personage as she would wish to do . . . The Queen feels compelled to take as much care of her health as she can, and quiet is the principal thing she requires . . .'[148]

'Quiet is the principal thing she requires . . .' Queen Victoria hit upon the perfect weapon to use in her never-ending war with thoughtless Ministers and in the employ-

Left: Undated note in Queen Victoria's handwriting reminding Mrs Hugh Brown to place a wreath of flowers on John Brown's bed, presumably on the day of his funeral at Balmoral

Right: Queen Victoria's draft of an inscription for John Brown's tombstone. In the left hand corner the Queen has made a sketch for the tombstone

Left: John Brown's tombstone in Crathie cemetery. Next to it is the gravestone which Brown erected to the memory of his parents, and of the five brothers and sisters who predeceased him. The iron railing which Queen Victoria caused to be placed around the grave was used for scrap iron in World War II and has never been replaced

Right: The bronze statue of John Brown by Sir Edgar Boehm with the inscription suggested by Tennyson carved on its pedestal

ment of this weapon she was ably assisted by her physician in ordinary, Dr (later Sir) William Jenner. Among other things, Dr Jenner was an expert on drains, and as such he could have found enough work at Windsor Castle alone to fill his days. When making alterations to the castle in 1825 Sir Jeffrey Wyatville had warned 'There will be a terrible stink one day,' and as late as January 1862, when Jenner began sniffing around, many of the unventilated cesspools beneath the castle had still not been cleared. As for Buckingham Palace, Dr Jenner was still detecting bad smells there as late as July, 1878, one of the worst portions of the palace being that occupied by the Queen herself during her rare visits there.

Unfortunately, Dr Jenner did not confine himself to smells, but became the Queen's compliant tool as far as medical matters were concerned. To make matters worse, the doctor, who was an ardent Tory, exercised a political influence on the Queen, in particular prejudicing Her Majesty against Gladstone, whom he detested. (Gladstone returned the compliment, referring to Jenner as 'this feeble-minded doctor' upon one occasion.)

Consequently, it was Dr Jenner whom the Queen put up in July, 1867, as her foil to counter Lord Derby's suggestion that she entertain the Sultan of Turkey. The doctor would tell Lord Derby 'the real state of her health and nerves', the Queen assured her Prime Minister. Dr Jenner obliged with a hair-raising account of the Queen's physical and mental state, which Lord Derby, in turn transmitted to his Cabinet ('Dr Jenner told him that any excitement produces the most severe bilious derangement, which induces vomiting to an incredible extent, and his fear is that . . . the mischief could fly to the head,' Lord John Manners declared after the Cabinet meeting which heard the report on the Queen's health).[157] Queen Victoria was not content to let the matter rest there, but insisted that Jenner insert in *Lancet* a paragraph explaining that she could not attend 'public evening festivities' because 'agitation, over-worry, or much talking in the evening is followed by restless nights, most distressing sick headaches and sense of great exhaustion'.

Lancet's announcement would have carried more conviction had the press not reported earlier that Her Majesty had been pleased to attend a Balmoral ball given on the occasion of her birthday and attended by upwards of two hundred tenants and keepers on her estate. As it was, *Lancet*, in its issue of August 3rd, felt obliged to answer the sceptics who had 'impugned the accuracy of the paragraph'. 'Upon a subject of so much delicacy,' the medical journal began, 'we spoke with what we believe to have been a becoming and justifiable reserve. Our report was in no respect sensational or over-stated.' *Lancet* went on to assert that 'even those in immediate attendance upon the Queen are not always in a position to arrive at a correct knowledge of Her Majesty's condition', and that she was in fact subject to 'bodily suffering of a character most difficult to be borne'.

The Queen's pleas of ill-health failed to move Lord Derby, so she fell back on her second line of defence: there was no room at any of the Royal residences to entertain the Eastern notables properly. Her Majesty instructed her secretary to write to Lord Derby that she would be quite willing to do her part 'if the country would build her a Palace for the purpose of lodging foreign Royalties, and make her a handsome allowance for entertaining them.'[33] The Queen's suggestion was only half in jest. Meanwhile, under pressure she reluctantly consented to the Sultan of Turkey being housed at Buckingham Palace, but the Khedive of Egypt, who would arrive in London earlier, would have to go to Claridge's, she decreed. The visitor's suite at Buckingham Palace would not be ready in time for the Khedive's arrival was the lame excuse given. Immediately there was an uproar in the House of Commons. Why could not the Khedive be put up at St James's Palace, an irate Member of Parliament wanted to know. Or better still, why not Clarence House, which at that moment was empty in the absence of

Prince Alfred, the Duke of Edinburgh? *Reynolds's News*
thought it knew the answer to these conundrums. In a leading article entitled, 'The British Monarchy—Is it Practically
Dead?' *Reynolds's* pointed out, 'Almost every one of our
palaces is converted into a . . . royal rabbit-hutch, or else
into an almshouse for decayed and pauperized aristocrats.'
The Sunday Times agreed with its radical rival. 'We might,
as far as the mighty fellowship of the nations is concerned,
as well be dead', *The Sunday Times* declared. 'There is dust
on the curtains and rust on the hinges of the doors.' At the
eleventh hour Lord Dudley saved the day by offering to
place his magnificent mansion in Park Lane at the Khedive's
disposal, a gesture 'gratefully appreciated by all who are
jealous of the national honour', *The Times* declared.

The Queen's objections to playing hostess to His Highness
Abdul Aziz, the Sultan of Turkey, were of a different order.
Her Majesty required assurances that the Sultan would not
be accompanied by a harem. Lord Lyons, the British
Ambassador at Constantinople, wrote hastily to guarantee
that neither women nor slaves would be accompanying the
Sultan, nor would there be anything 'shocking to our notions
or peculiar in the habits of the Sultan or his suite'. The only
eccentricity in Turkish dress would be that of the Sultan's
guards who at no time removed their fezzes, the Ambassador added. As for the Sultan himself, he had at least one
quality which should endear him to Her Majesty: he was a
fresh air addict, and had a horror of over-heated chambers.
As the Ambassador explained, 'The Sultan is subject to
rushes of blood to the head, and may not be able to stand
much of hot rooms . . .'[119]

But before Sultan Abdul Aziz could set foot on English
soil a crisis rose which, in Queen Victoria's mind made his
impending arrival and the inconvenience to her plans which
it entailed pale to insignificance. For this new situation involved John Brown, which meant that it affected the Queen
more nearly than it did the billeting of a hundred Egyptian
Viceroys, or the concubinage of an equal number of Turkish

Sultans. The crisis concerned Brown's presence at a military Review in Hyde Park scheduled for July, and has already been dealt with at length in an earlier chapter. Lord Derby, it will be recalled, had dared to suggest that the Queen leave Brown at home when she went to inspect the troops in the park. The mere sight of Brown on the box of her carriage might touch off a riot on the part of Mr Beales and his Reform League followers, the Prime Minister had hinted.

7

THE FENIAN SERPENT

THE Emperor Maximilian's execution before a Mexican firing squad providentially had given Lord Derby his pretext for cancelling the Hyde Park Review, and thus avoiding a show-down with Queen Victoria. But it had been a near thing. Just how close may be gauged from the fact that viewing stands and decorations costing £2,000 had already been put up in the park, and three regiments of cavalry had been dispatched from Aldershot by the time the cancellation orders came through.

Queen Victoria found the episode most vexing. Not for a moment was she fooled that the prospect of 'a scuffle with Mr Beales and his party' was the real reason why Lord Derby wanted her to drop John Brown from her retinue. All this talk about an 'unpleasant incident' being likely to occur if Brown accompanied her to the Review was 'mere panic', she wrote to Lord Charles Fitzroy, her Equerry, after the Review had been cancelled. Had she not received assurances from Inspector Mays, of the Windsor police, and from Sir Richard Mayne, the Metropolitan Police Commissioner, himself, that the 'state of London', described to her as being so dreadful, had been 'greatly exaggerated'?[148]

No, Lord Derby obviously had been listening to 'ill-natured gossip in the higher classes', and the fact that his informant concerning the planned anti-Brown demonstration had been Lord Portman merely increased the Queen's suspicion. For Lord Portman was a notable purveyor of society tittle-tattle, and he and his wife, Lady Emma Portman, a one-time Lady-of-the-Bedchamber to the Queen, had been involved to the hilt in the Lady Flora

Hastings affair.* The Queen therefore would be sure to discount any reports emanating from this quarter. As for her own popularity, Her Majesty had indirect assurances from the press† that it was as great as ever, and that any talk to the contrary was 'shameless rubbish, not to be listened to for a moment.'[148]

The intended snub to her good faithful Brown would not be easily forgotten. The death of 'poor Max' in Mexico had made it unthinkable that she should fulfil her public engagement, but it would be 'very long before she forgets all the worry and uneasy sensations' caused by the plot against Brown, she assured her Equerry. The entire episode had left 'a painful, bitter feeling in her heart, towards many—not easily to be eradicated'. Fortunately for all concerned, Queen Victoria's mind was soon distracted from thoughts of revenge by the arrival in England of her 'Oriental brother', His Imperial Highness Abdul Aziz, Sultan of Turkey.

The Sultan's visit went off much more smoothly than the Queen had anticipated. Abdul Aziz had truly splendid eyes, 'ate most things', and showed himself to be a democrat by shaking hands with everyone at the Guildhall banquet which the Lord Mayor gave in his honour. After attending a gala at the Covent Garden Opera, His Highness was invited to shoot a stag in Windsor Great Park, the rest of his party being kept 'well out of the way' on the orders of Colonel Francis Seymour, the Groom-in-Waiting, who evidently did not trust the Sultan's marksmanship.

The highlight of the Sultan's visit, however, was the Spithead Naval Review which he attended as Her Majesty's guest. The Sultan in an unguarded moment having ex-

* In 1839 Lady Flora Hastings, a Lady-in-Waiting to the Duchess of Kent, was falsely suspected of being pregnant, and treated shabbily by members of the Royal Household and by the Queen, herself. When Lady Flora died of an enlargement of the liver a few months later the Queen was overcome by remorse.

† Probably through Sir Arthur Helps, Clerk of the Privy Council, who acted as the Queen's go-between to the press on several occasions.

pressed an interest in the Navy, the Foreign Office, anxious to impress him, had assembled all available ironclads in the roadstead off the Isle of Wight. As luck would have it, the weather turned nasty, and the Queen, who herself was a good sailor, was thus obliged to receive the Sultan aboard the Royal yacht *Victoria and Albert* in a howling storm. They must have made a strange pair as they sat outside the deck saloon, the homely little widow of Windsor and the dissipated-looking Oriental, who spoke no known language, according to Ponsonby. As interpreter, Fuad Pasha, the Egyptian Viceroy, sat between the two rulers, his short legs scarcely touching the deck. Queen Victoria's journal entry for this occasion was masterly in its understatement. 'The Sultan feels very uncomfortable at sea', she noted, ' . . . he went below, followed by the rest of his suite, and did not reappear on deck until after we had half passed through the Line.' 'He was continually retiring below and can have seen very little', she added. 'Still, it was a very fine sight.'

Abdul Aziz did, however, remain on deck long enough for Queen Victoria to invest him with the Order of the Garter, 'though I should have preferred the Star of India, which is more suited to those who are not Christians'. There was a horrible moment when it was discovered that the Garter insignia had been left ashore, but a quick whip-round was held among the Royals present, a silver Star being snatched from one, a gold George from another, with Prince Louis of Hesse being divested of his Garter ribbon. (The Sultan later stoutly refused to consider replacements for these bits of heraldic finery, maintaining that they had been given to him by the Queen's own hand.) The Sultan ran up a number of unpaid bills during his visit, including one for twelve quarts of Farma's Eau de Cologne, seven pints of rosewater, and an unspecified quantity of essence of jasmin. He left England on July 23, trailing clouds of scent behind him.

A month later Queen Victoria left for the Scottish border town of Kelso on a private visit to the Duchess of Rox-burghe, taking with her John Brown. Thanks to the cartoons of him that had appeared in *Tomahawk*, the Highlander had now become a national celebrity, and so the press 'covered' him when he travelled with the Queen. The reporter from the *Inverness Advertiser*, for example, noted the alacrity with which Brown alighted from his own railway carriage to open the door of the Queen's carriage on the train's arrival at Kelso. 'But for the intervention of the Duke and Duchess of Roxburghe, the Duke of Buccleuch, and other distinguished company on the platform, the stalwart Highlander would have conducted his Sovereign across the platform and through the triumphal arch to the royal carriage at the outside of the station', according to this self-appointed Boswell. He then went on to describe Brown's entry into Kelso on the box of the Queen's carriage: 'John, who was dressed in full Highland costume, seemed immensely proud of his position; and it was certainly amusing in the extreme to see him now and again, with a broad grin, bowing his acknowledgments for the cheers raised for Her Majesty, some of which he probably thought were intended for himself.'

There was one awkward moment when the Royal party, in rounding a corner, were confronted by banners proclaiming, 'Welcome to the Borders—John Brown!' and 'God Save the Queen—John Brown!' Was this 'an impudent joke perpetrated by some stupid citizen', the *Inverness Advertiser* wondered, or had some crypto-republican 'with more waggishness than sense' sought by this means to call attention to his cause? Apparently, it was neither. The 'John Brown' whose name was so sensationally linked with that of the Queen was, it turned out, a local shopkeeper, who was not above combining a bit of self-publicity with a display of loyalty to the Crown. This explanation received, Sir Thomas Biddulph and others of the Royal Household breathed more easily. But even after the Queen had been installed at Floors, the magnificent 18th century Roxburghe country seat designed by Sir John Vanbrugh, the press continued to pursue Brown. Thus, on a visit to nearby Melrose Abbey, the

Queen was all but ignored, the journalists preferring to dog
the footsteps of Brown, who was reported as 'anxious to
obtain a good view of the abbey's architectural beauties'.

From Kelso Queen Victoria travelled north via Edinburgh to Balmoral, only to find another serpent threatening
to spoil the peace and solitude of her Scottish Eden. This serpent, apparently one of those overlooked by St Patrick,
called itself the Irish Republican Brotherhood, but was more
commonly known as the Fenian Brotherhood (for Fianna,
the 'bare-armed' fighting men of the legendary Len Finn).
The Fenians were reported to be plotting to kidnap Her
Majesty, no less, and to hold her hostage against the release
of several hundred Fenian prisoners then languishing in
British prisons.

In looking back over the various Fenian 'plots' which had
as their object the abduction of Queen Victoria one is
inclined to dismiss them as exercises in 'black propaganda',
designed to harass the enemy and to spread confusion in his
ranks. However, there is nothing in the record to indicate
that the Fenians, who took their orders from a Head Centre
in New York, had either the brains or the ability to put
'black propaganda' into operation. To the contrary, their
record was one of bungling, as witness the abortive 'rising' of
March, 1867, which ended with a few railroad ties being torn
up and a handful of police barracks being captured or
burned to the ground. In reading through the reports from
Dublin Castle, now on file with Home Office papers at the
Public Record Office, one gets the impression that the
various kidnap scares were really the work of impecunious
but thirsty narks, anxious to earn their beer money by passing on fictitious reports to the police.

Was it entirely coincidental, for example, that the 'plot'
to snatch Queen Victoria from the arms of John Brown at
Balmoral should have been hatched in a Manchester pothouse, where the police informer just happened to be drinking with a gang of Fenian desperadoes? In passing the tip

along to Scotland Yard, the Chief Constable of Manchester vouched for the informer's reliability; this particular nark was not only intelligent, but 'perfectly sober when he made his statement' according to the police chief. Sobriety perhaps was his trouble, his imagination having been nudged by a terrible thirst, and by the prospect of slaking it at police expense. At any rate, the informer told police that on Sunday afternoon, October 13 while downing a pint of beer in the grogshop, he over-heard a group of Fenians, led by a sinister character named Nuttall, plotting to kidnap the Queen, and that 'nearly every man had a revolver and there were also several rifles in the room and some cartridges'. The plan was for a group of Fenians under Nuttall's orders to go north the following morning, and to put their plot into operation on Tuesday, October 15. After being kidnapped, the Queen was to be taken to a place called 'Saunder's cottage' and held as a hostage for the Fenian prisoners. In view of the Queen's habit of driving at night, which was the despair of her Cabinet Ministers, there is a certain irony in one observation contained in the Chief Constable's report: 'They (the Fenians) believe that Her Majesty goes about the country with very few attendants and no guard, and that there will be no difficulty in accomplishing their design.'[118]

Even so, this report almost certainly would have found its way into the waste basket, along with all the other tips from crackpots and cranks, had it not been for two circumstances. First of all, the Manchester police were still smarting from the daring daylight rescue of two Fenian prisoners that had been carried out under their noses a month earlier. The prisoners, Col. Thomas J. Kelly and Capt. Timothy Deasy,* were being taken from the police court to a jail out-

* Col. Kelly and Capt. Deasy, both veterans of the American Civil War, were typical of the Irish-Americans who volunteered for dangerous Fenian missions abroad. By a weird chance, the pair were arrested as burglary suspects, and it was not until shortly before they were rescued that the police discovered their true identity. Both were smuggled back to America.

side Manchester when the police van conveying them was ambushed by a band of armed Fenians. The prisoners were freed, but in the mêlée a Police Sergeant Brett was shot and fatally wounded. Three of the rescuers (Allen, O'Brien and Larkin) were tried for Brett's murder; and this trio—'the Manchester Martyrs', as they were known—were under sentence of death and awaiting execution at the time of the Balmoral kidnap scare.

The second circumstance which caused the police to treat the kidnap plot seriously was, of course, that it concerned the Sovereign. Wildly improbable though the plot may have seemed, they could take no chances on it proving to be a false alarm. Accordingly, Scotland Yard dispatched to Deeside on the Monday night mail train a party of fourteen plain-clothes police under Inspector Walker, who frequently doubled as the Prince of Wales's bodyguard and who, on this occasion, had instructions to distribute to his men the cutlasses and revolvers in his custody if needed for 'self-protection'. Meanwhile, the Chief Constables of Aberdeen and Perth were alerted to watch all incoming trains for suspicious-looking strangers.

All things considered, an improbable tip emanating from a Manchester pothouse would hardly seem to justify the atmosphere of hysteria which prevailed at Balmoral once the 'plot' became known. Apparently no one stopped to ponder how the kidnappers could slip into Balmoral and out again with their precious bundle, when the only access to the Castle was by means of a narrow glen. And supposing, for the sake of argument, that her abductors were successful in nabbing the Queen while she was out driving, what exactly did they propose to do with Her Majesty? It was the Queen herself who suggested laughingly that they would find her a handful. Much of the blame for the hysteria must rest with General Sir Charles Grey, the Queen's Private Secretary, who sent to Aberdeen for a detachment of the 93rd Highlanders to guard Balmoral. (In approving this action, Lord Derby observed that 'the absolutely unprotected state of

Her Majesty in her late drives . . . renders necessary such precautions as you have taken'.) Two days after he arrived at Balmoral a bored Inspector Walker wired his superiors at Scotland Yard: 'There are no strangers on Deeside. All quiet.'

But General Grey did not give up so easily. If not by train, what was to prevent a posse of Fenians from arriving by boat? To the General it made no difference that Balmoral was located forty-five miles from the nearest coast-line as the crow flew. 'The craft would probably be sent round to some point on the North Coast between Peterhead and Inverness,' General Grey warned the Home Secretary, adding that 'as from the river Don . . . there is a practicable road for carriages, it seems the direction in which an attempt at the abduction of the Queen would probably be made.'[49]

The climax to the Fenian hysteria came in December, when Viscount Monck, the Governor-General of Canada, reported that eighty Fenians had sailed from the New World in a Danish brigantine with the avowed purpose of kidnapping Queen Victoria from Osborne in the Isle of Wight. The brigantine presumably would anchor in the Solent and then the men would row ashore and snatch the Queen while she was out driving with John Brown. Where Lord Monck got his information is not clear, though most likely it was from a Fenian 'plant', whose aim was to sow confusion. What is clear is that His Lordship was recalled from Canada, his career resting under a cloud, before another twelve months were out.

The tip however was good enough for General Sir Charles Grey, who implored Her Majesty to leave Osborne at once. 'It is difficult to believe,' he wrote to the Queen on December 19 'that danger can lurk about the quiet woods and valleys of this island. But . . . it is precisely in these solitary and peaceful places that real danger exists.' [148] In conclusion Sir Charles begged, 'on his knees', Her Majesty to return to Windsor immediately. The spectacle of the good General, his dundrearies quivering with emotion, kneeling at the risk of splitting his silk knee breeches must have provoked a smile; but if so, Queen Victoria repressed it, observing with some asperity, ' . . . she thinks any panic or show of fear would be most injudicious as well as unnecessary. The Queen . . . must ask not to have this again mentioned.'[148] (This exchange of letters took place, of course, while both the Queen and her Private Secretary were at Osborne separated by a few doors.) Meanwhile, Lord Derby felt it necessary to warn that 'Your Majesty's unattended late drives afford an opportunity for desperate adventures against which no vigilance can effectually provide.'

By this time Queen Victoria had begun to smell a plot every bit as dastardly as any that the Fenians had cooked up—a plot to force her out of her retirement and, if possible, to make her take up residence in London, on the pretext that Balmoral and Osborne were no longer safe. Her attitude hardened accordingly. Replying to Lord Derby, she brought him up short concerning his 'groundless apprehensions . . . to her late and distant drives after dark, which never at any time hardly take place here'. She then went on flatly to declare, 'The Queen does not consider Windsor at all safe. And to London nothing will make her go, till the present state of affairs is altered.'[148] In a letter to Gathorne Hardy she enlarged upon her objections to Windsor, where 'there are always a great many nasty people about,' at the same time complaining that, owing to the precautions taken for her safety at Osborne, she was 'almost a State prisoner'.[149]

A State prisoner she was, in effect, for in addition to extra police, nearly 200 troops, including a contingent of Life Guards, had been moved onto the Isle of Wight to guard the Sovereign, while the waters of the Solent swarmed with naval and Coast Guard vessels on patrol. Only the Queen's swift intervention prevented a detachment of cavalry from being sent to the island, according to Gathorne Hardy.[33] The mind boggles at the spectacle of cavalrymen charging after imaginary Irish invaders on the Osborne estate.

The climax to the Fenian farce occurred on Friday, December 20, when a sentry on duty arrested Mr Page, the Queen's Gamekeeper, and an unnamed 'royal personage' for failing to give the proper counter-sign when challenged, according to *The Portsmouth Times*. *Reynolds's News* further identified the 'royal personage' as 'Count X', but I can find no one of this description at Osborne on December 20, although the Dukes of Marlborough and of Buckingham both arrived on that date to attend a Privy Council.

However, there is no doubt that some such incident occurred, for the Queen herself referred to it. 'That Friday, 20th of December', she reminded her Home Secretary, Gathorne Hardy, in a letter, 'every one lost their heads and seemed to think the whole Island teemed with danger, excepting herself, her children, the Ladies, and one or two other Men!' The Queen also revealed that among the 'dangerous people' arrested at the height of the Fenian scare was her own son, seventeen-year-old Prince Arthur, who had arrived at Osborne to spend Christmas with his mother, 'and the Queen's own female servant living at the Swiss Cottage, who was not allowed to go into her own home!!!'

The absurd precautions taken for her own safety did serve to bring to the Queen's notice a shameful case of public neglect. Accordingly she prompted Sir Thomas Biddulph to write to the Metropolitan Police Commissioner calling attention to 'the unprotected condition of the Royal Mausoleum at Frogmore'. 'It has one constable always on duty', Sir Thomas pointed out. 'Perhaps you may think it right to have a second constable placed there during the night', he concluded, knowing that a hint was as good as a command.

Fortunately for her, Queen Victoria had other matters to take her mind off the Fenians during the closing weeks of 1867, for she was preparing for publication *Leaves from the Journal of Our Life in the Highlands*. These extracts from her Highland journals were originally intended for private circulation; but Arthur Helps, Clerk of the Privy Council, and others to whom she had shown the manuscript persuaded the Queen that the book should reach the larger public, who would be gratified to learn how their Sovereign spent 'her rare moments of leisure'. Dedicated to 'the dear memory of him who made the life of the writer bright and happy', *Leaves*, which covered the Queen's visits to Scotland from 1842 to her widowhood in 1861, was an instant success when it eventually appeared in January, 1868. The press was generous in its praise, although *Punch* could not resist the good-natured dig that 'the trait that seems to be most prominent in Her Majesty's book is the tea-tray.' By January 16, 1868, Queen Victoria could write to Theodore Martin with genuine humility, 'The Queen was moved to tears . . . what has she done to be so loved and liked?'[96]

Not surprisingly, such sour grapes as there were came from the Queen's own family and from members of her Household, who took exception to the footnotes concerning her domestic servants with which the pages of *Leaves* are liberally sprinkled. 'We have a very painful feeling about the domestic notes and histories', Lady Augusta Stanley wrote to her sister. 'They give people the idea of a patriarchal system, quite alien to their conception of royal habits —and convince them that all are on the same footing.'[132]

The footnotes make curious reading indeed, setting out as they do not only the servants' pedigrees, but bizarre details concerning their lives. Thus on page 104 we make the acquaintance of Batterbury, the groom, 'who followed me . . . with thin boots and gaiters, and seemed anything but happy', while on page 132 we learn that Mackay, the Queen's Piper, 'unfortunately went out of his mind in the year 1854'. But the domestic note which sent eyebrows shooting up was the twenty-two line entry devoted to John Brown, who, among other things, 'has all the independence and elevated feelings peculiar to the Highland race, and is singularly straightforward, simple-minded, kind-hearted, and disinterested; always ready to oblige; and of a discretion rarely to be met with.'

'No one, before or since, has written like Queen Victoria', remarked Max Beerbohm, who was fond of parodying her style, and who went so far as to imitate her handwriting in inscribing the flyleaf of his own copy of *More Leaves*, 'For Mr Beerbohm, the never-sufficiently-to-be-studied writer, whom Albert looks down on affectionately, I am sure.'[13] In vain, Arthur Helps, who edited *Leaves*, urged Queen Victoria to put her syntax in order, but then Helps ('Lord Help Us', as Ponsonby called him) was a bit of a fusspot; and besides, the Queen was having none of it. 'How could Mr Helps', she asked reproachfully, 'expect pains to be taken when she wrote late at night, suffering from headache and exhaustion, and in dreadful haste, and not for publication?'[96]

Encouraged by the success of *Leaves* ('Rather amusing the literary line the Queen has taken up,' Lady Ponsonby noted in her diary), the Queen was persuaded to attend one of Lady Augusta Stanley's pink teas, where she met fellow authors Carlyle and Browning. Carlyle, in a letter to his sister, described the Queen as 'a comely little lady . . . still looks young (in spite of one broad wrinkle which shows on each cheek occasionally); is still plump.' She had 'a fine, low voice', he remarked. The Queen, for her part, was not favourably impressed, finding Carlyle 'a strange-looking eccentric old Scotchman, who holds forth . . . upon Scotland and upon the utter degradation of everything'.[148] Quickly turning to Mr Browning, whom she found to be 'a very agreeable man', Her Majesty told him how much she admired his wife's poetry. 'Are you writing anything?' she innocently enquired of the poet, who had just published *The Ring and the Book*, one of the longest poems in the English language.

According to Colonel Ponsonby, it was the fear of making just such howlers that caused Queen Victoria to shun the society of intellectuals. Explaining why the Queen preferred the company of Mrs Grant, the wife of her Head Keeper, to that of Mrs Grote, the wife of the historian, Colonel Ponsonby asserted, 'Mrs Grant speaks of her children and the tea cake and scones. These require no preparation. But Mrs Grote might suddenly ask her whether she approved of female doctors.'[110] Whether or not this sense of inferiority was the real reason for Queen Victoria's anti-intellectual bias, the pink tea experiment at Lady Stanley's was never repeated.

Queen Victoria was not writing to please the professors at Oxford ('that monkish old place which I have a horror of . . .' as she once described it). The Queen knew better than Mr Helps, or Lady Augusta Stanley, the public to whom her book would appeal. It was to a lower middle-class audience, many of whose members had been newly-franchised by Disraeli's Reform Bill, that *Leaves* was aimed. Musing aloud in her journal concerning this self-same Reform Bill, had not the Queen herself written, 'The upper classes and aristocracy must "buckle to", or they will deservedly suffer'? 'The lower orders,' she added shrewdly, 'are becoming so well educated that they will push on.'[148] The Queen knew, too, that the kind of pastoral existence portrayed in the pages of *Leaves*, where the Sovereign was shown to be occupied largely with the distribution of flannel petticoats, was the best antidote to any republicanism that might be stirring in the breasts of these educated 'lower orders'. Sir John Elphinstone was quick to sense this in urging that a cheap edition of *Leaves* be published at once—'the sooner the better', as he wrote to Lady Augusta Stanley. As for Queen Victoria, surely there was recompense for the headaches and exhaustion suffered while writing up her journal late at night in this letter from Mrs M. A. Everett Green to Arthur Helps which mirrors so perfectly the lower middle class attitude towards *Leaves*. 'In families where moral tone is natural and beautiful,' wrote Mrs Green, 'it will be read with deep and sympathetic interest.' Mrs Green went on to express her conviction that 'to the purity at

Court, England is greatly indebted for the growing purity of morals in the higher and middle classes . . . The Queen,' she concluded, 'has condescended to become the friend of her people and they love her for it.' Dearest Albert would indeed have been proud of his pupil.*

---

* In his annotated copy of *More Leaves* the irrepressible Max Beerbohm copied out this press blurb, supposedly from *Spectator:* 'Not a book to leave lying about on the drawing-room table nor one to place indiscriminately in the hands of young men and maidens . . . Will be engrossing to those of mature years.'[13]

8

MISUNDERSTOOD

THE republican movement which swept Britain in 1871 had many elements in common with those gorgeous Christmas pantomimes which thrilled Victorian audiences at the Drury Lane theatre with their trick scenery, their pyrotechnics, their elaborate transformation scenes. Mingled with the crowds singing the *Marseillaise* in Trafalgar Square, and calling for a British Republic, were those stock characters of pantomime sired by Roman antiquity out of the *commedia dell'arte*. Scaramouche appeared with a tricolour sash draped around his enormous girth while the lecherous Pantalone bore the red cap of Liberty aloft on a pole. Pulchinella fresh from the barricades of the Paris Commune, made his descent in Trafalgar Square by balloon.

Everywhere in evidence was that reversal of values which is the lifeblood of all good pantomime. In this case the republicans were really pro-monarchist, as they were careful to explain, while Queen Victoria herself was accused of being a crypto-republican. 'Her Majesty, by doing nothing except receive her Civil List, is teaching the country that it can get on quite well without a monarch,' *The National Reformer* pointed out. Certainly the Queen's activities at the beginning of 1871 were rich in comic possibilities. There was the opening tableau, for example, with the Queen standing outside the Houses of Parliament with her begging bowl and a placard reading, 'Needy widow with 9 children to support.' Then there was that other laugh-provoking scene of Royalties, including the Emperor and Empress of Brazil, queuing for rooms at Claridge's while Buckingham Palace stood vacant. (Why can't they stay home, the Queen told Colonel Ponsonby, in effect.)

But what of the Widow Twankey's eldest son, Albert Edward, the Heir Apparent and Principal Boy? Victorian pantomime knew no transformation more remarkable than that which befell him in 1871. The previous year he had been hissed as the wicked Baron Renfrew, whose appearance as a witness in the Mordaunt divorce case had provoked a public scandal.* Again, in 1871, there was a nasty moment when it became known that he was squandering gold sovereigns (from the pockets of the working class, some said) at the kursaals of Baden-Baden. But before the year was out Prince Guelph was to become the object of public adulation such as Britain had seldom known, an orgy of sentimentality which moved one writer to speak of the 'whiskey-inspired howls of an Irish wake'.[164] His death, which at one moment appeared imminent, would have been nothing short of a national calamity affecting millionaire and cottager alike, according to the leader-writers.

Of all the figures who appeared on the scene in 1871 Charles Bradlaugh was most typical of Britain's comic opera republicanism. For one thing, he bore striking resemblance to John Bull, judging from Sickert's pencil sketch of Bradlaugh, now in the National Portrait Gallery, which shows him with snub nose and long, clean-shaven upper lip over a wide mouth. A one-time trooper in the Army before becoming a solicitor's clerk, Bradlaugh called himself 'the Iconoclast', but his image-smashing was almost entirely confined to organized religion and to its received truths (the Trinity he likened to a monkey with three tails), his political thought having very little depth. A professed republican, he was nevertheless anti-Socialist and upheld private property. An anti-monarchist, yes, but the monarchy must be abolished by legal means through repeal of

* Subpoenaed as a witness in the divorce action which Sir Charles Mordaunt brought against his 21-year-old wife in February, 1870, Prince Albert Edward, who had written eleven letters to Lady Mordaunt, had spent an uncomfortable few minutes in the witness box denying that there had ever been any 'criminal connection' be-between himself and Lady Mordaunt.

132

the Act of Settlement passed in Queen Anne's reign. 'It would be treason to do anything to shorten the reign of the present monarch', he told a meeting of the London Republican Club, of which he was president. As may be inferred ,the militant atheist favoured non-violent agitation. 'If we cannot win by reason I will not try to win by force', Bradlaugh assured the same meeting of London republicans.

A republicanism which abjured the use of force, and which would leave the monarchy intact (Bradlaugh favoured an elective monarchy)—all of this was a far cry from Tom Paine, who stigmatized the monarchy as 'the master-fraud that shelters all others'. It was farther still from John Thelwell, the poet and orator at the time of the French Revolution, who cried as he blew the froth from his beer, 'This is the way I would serve all kings!'

The truth was that the republican movement of 1871 was devoid of any real political content. The American republic rather than the French, was the model to which the British *sans-culottes* looked. They were attracted by the American system which opposed merit to privilege and rank. But aside from vague demands for a meritocracy and a larger slice of the national cake, Bradlaugh and his crowd had no real political objectives, and because they had none their movement sank without a trace. In 1871 an estimated eighty-three republican clubs met in the smoky back parlours of public houses up and down the country; by 1873 all but a handful had disappeared.

But before they evaporated the republicans were to give Queen Victoria many a bad moment. In 1871 the criticism of her for neglecting her duties mounted in volume and bitterness, reaching its height when *Reynolds's News* compared her to a horse leech. To make matters worse, during the autumn, the Queen experienced the most serious illness of her lifetime, and at one point was given no more than twenty-four hours to live. She had just cause to complain of being alone and misunderstood, for during this illness the

nation was kept in total ignorance of her condition. There
were no bulletins issued, as was normally the case when a
Sovereign was gravely ill; nor were any national prayers
offered for her recovery. To appreciate how singular this
silence was one has only to contrast it with the wave of
hysteria that swept the nation a few months later after her
son, the Prince of Wales, had been stricken with typhoid.
Then even the commercial life of the nation appeared to
come to a halt as the watch was kept at the Prince's bedside.

The curious part was that Queen Victoria had done her best
to forestall criticism by indulging in a burst of activity at
the beginning of 1871, all calculated to make the monarchy
'visible and palpable to the people', in Gladstone's phrase.
In February she had opened Parliament in person, going
so far in abating her mourning as to substitute a gown
of deep purple trimmed with ermine for her usual un-
compromising black. This process of alleviation was
continued at the wedding, on March 21, of Princess
Louise to the Marquis of Lorne in St George's Chapel
Windsor, where the Queen wore her rubies as well as her
diamonds.

No doubt it was because the bridegroom was a fellow
Scot that John Brown approved the match more than did
the Queen's family (the Prince of Wales thought that his
sister should have married a Prince of the blood). Not only
did Brown organize a backstairs whip-round to buy
Princess Louise a wedding present, but he himself contributed thirty guineas, which was three times the amount
Colonel Ponsonby gave. And it was Brown who threw a new
broom after the married couple when they drove away from
Windsor. It comes as something of a surprise, therefore, to
learn that Brown's admiration for Princess Louise was less
than reciprocated. In discussing with Colonel Ponsonby the
servants she wished to engage, the Princess made it plain
'I won't have an absurd man in a kilt following me about
everywhere.'[110]

In general the marriage of the Queen's daughter to a British subject, rather than to a German princeling, met with popular approval; that is, until Parliament was asked to provide a £30,000 dowry, plus an annuity, for Princess Louise, whereat the columns of *Reynolds's News* blossomed with advice as to how the Marquis of Lorne might earn his living. Boot-riveting was the suggestion of a correspondent from Northampton, who added, 'perhaps his wife could do a little on the machine'. When in August the Queen asked Parliament to provide for Prince Arthur, who had just attained his twenty-first birthday, as many as fifty-one Members voted to reduce the proposed annuity from £15,000 to £10,000, while eleven M.P.s were against providing any annuity at all.

The Queen continued to make herself visible and palpable by holding two Drawing rooms, opening the Albert Hall and reviewing the Household Troops in Bushy Park, but far from giving her credit for these efforts, the national press criticized Her Majesty for her inhospitality to visiting Crown Heads. (Among the summer visitors to London were the Emperor and Empress of Brazil, the Grand Duke Vladimir of Russia, Prince Oscar of Sweden, the Princess Royal and Crown Prince Frederick of Prussia, all of whom put up at hotels or legations, while Buckingham Palace stood empty.) *The Times* dubbed Queen Victoria 'The Great Absentee', while *The Pall Mall Gazette* was even more scathing in its comments concerning 'the invisible Monarch'. 'It is only when startled by the appearance of some Royal visitor at Claridge's that they (the people) remember that the Queen is still living', the *Gazette* maintained, further predicting that 'England might virtually be left without a Sovereign for half a century' in the event of the Queen attaining a ripe age.

The Queen's lack of hospitality lent colour to allegations that she was hoarding at the public expense. These were contained in a remarkable pamphlet titled 'What Does She Do With It?' and written by one 'Solomon Temple, builder', which was published early in 1871.* Specifically, the pamphlet accused the Queen of putting aside nearly a third of her annual £385,000 Civil List by skimping on Royal Household expenses, and of having built up a tidy personal fortune as a result.† The Queen was entitled to none of this fortune, according to 'Solomon Temple', who contended that Civil List unexpended balances should revert to the Treasury at the end of the year as they were intended by Parliament for no other purpose than to 'support the honour and dignity of the Crown'.

The anonymous pamphlet enjoyed a wide circulation. Spotting an advertisement for it plastered on the walls of the Birkenhead railway station, Gladstone, who was en route to Balmoral in late September, groaned, 'Things go from bad to worse.'[53]

If he had been at all sensitive to the feelings of his Sovereign, Gladstone would have stayed away from Balmoral, for his presence there was no tonic to Queen Victoria in her low physical state. What she needed above all else from her First Minister (and what Disraeli, for example, would have given her in full measure) was sympathy and understanding. But these were the very qualities in which Gladstone was deficient. If Disraeli could congratulate himself on having a female as a Sovereign, Gladstone could with equal justice have pronounced it a curse. With a King, now, all would have been straight-forward. There would have been no need of flattery and cajolery, the

---

* Lady Longford attributes this pamphlet to George Otto Trevelyan, the Liberal M.P., but I am inclined to believe that 'Solomon Temple' was Sir Isaac Butt, the distinguished Irish barrister. In his biography of Butt, Terence de Vere White writes: 'His most intimate friend, Barnett . . . with whom he was staying in 1871 at Blackheath . . . stated after Butt's death that it was he who wrote the pamphlet, and that he had asked Barnett to make arrangements for its printing.'

† No doubt Queen Victoria died a very wealthy woman. Lytton Strachey estimates her fortune at nearly £2 million, based on Civil List savings of £20,000 a year, and including revenues of £60,000 a year from the Duchy of Lancaster.

People's William relying upon sweet reason to carry the day. But in the presence of the Queen, whom he held in awe, all of Gladstone's warmth and humanity seemed to dry up. Perhaps he lacked chivalry, as the Queen herself suggested. One sometimes gets the impression that beneath that pious, frock-coated exterior lurked a bully, who, simply because the Sovereign was a woman, was tempted to use badgering tactics which he would never have dared employ with a man. Queen Victoria believed this to be the case, and it explains why, when Gladstone tried logic and reason on her in the autumn of 1871, she gave him the full benefit of her 'repellent power', as he described it. It is from this period that her almost pathological hatred of Gladstone dates.

It all arose from a trivial misunderstanding, when Gladstone asked the Queen to postpone her departure for Balmoral by a few days so that a Privy Council could be held at Windsor directly after Parliament was prorogued. This would have spared the few who were required to attend the Privy Council a 600-mile journey to Balmoral in the summer heat. But the Queen, who felt that she had made enough concessions to Gladstone, refused to delay her departure. Her energy had been severely taxed by her recent public engagements, and now she was exhausted and on the point of a breakdown. This explains the hysterical tone of her letter to the Lord Chancellor refusing the Cabinet's request that she stay for the Prorogation: 'What killed her beloved husband? Overwork and worry—What killed Lord Clarendon? The same. What has broken down Mr Bright and Mr Childers and made them retire, but the same; & the Queen, a woman, no longer young, is supposed to be proof against all and to be driven & abused till her nerves & health will give way . . .'[57]

The failure in communication between Queen Victoria and her Prime Minister cut much deeper. The Queen suspected Gladstone of trying to detain her near London during the Prorogation crisis in order to derive the maximum political advantage from her presence, that it might seem to prop up his detested Liberal government. When Gladstone learned of Her Majesty's suspicions he, for once, lost his Olympian calm, called it his 'most sickening experience' in nearly forty years of public life. 'Worse things may be imagined,' he confided to Colonel Ponsonby, 'but smaller and meaner cause for the decay of Thrones cannot be conceived. It is like the worm which bores the bark of a noble oak tree and so breaks the channel of its life,' he concluded with pardonable exaggeration.[57]

This then was the situation when Queen Victoria left Osborne for Balmoral on August 15. On the whole she emerges from the Prorogation crisis in a better light than her Ministers and her advisers at Court. That she felt utterly alone at a time of great physical and mental distress excites sympathy, for she had no one to whom she could turn for comfort. Her children were next to useless as far as comforting the Queen was concerned, her Ministers were inclined to badger, and even warm-hearted Colonel Ponsonby seemed to withold his usual sympathy, though he did remark to his wife that the Queen, when she left the train at Ballater, 'looked quite knocked-up'. In fact, she had to lean heavily on Princess Beatrice's arm. The following day the Queen noted briefly in her journal that she had been sleeping during the daytime ('very unusual') and reading a book whose title, quite appropriately, was *Misunderstood*.

'Never since a girl, when I had typhoid fever at Ramsgate in '35, have I felt so ill,' Queen Victoria wrote in her journal on August 22, 1871. In 1835 her illness had run its predictable course, though the attack of typhoid had been a severe one, and had left the sixteen-year-old Princess Victoria looking thin and peaked and nearly bald (her thick hair had come out in handfuls). Her 1871 indisposition, however, was an altogether different matter, and frankly baffled her physician, Sir William Jenner. It seemed to fall into three distinct phases, the first of which, a swelling in her throat, was undoubtedly the most dangerous, for it interfered with the act of swallowing, and even with speech. The crisis came on Sunday, August 20, when the Queen suffered tortures until 'something seemed to give way in the throat and the choking sensation with violent spasms ceased'. Before that Sir William thought that she might have no more than 24 hours to live, as he told Ponsonby later.

The second phase, a swelling which quickly became an abscess under the Queen's right arm, equally baffled Jenner. ('He don't clearly know what it is,' Colonel Ponsonby wrote to his wife.) Nor was the Queen's physician alone in his bewilderment. Referring to the abscess, *Lancet* explained, 'If not to the public, at least to medical minds, (it was) not a little disquieting, inasmuch as it signified, under the circumstances, that serious disturbance of the general health had taken place . . .' The arm was still not responding to treatment as late as August 29, at which time it was decided to call in Professor Lister of Edinburgh, then at the height of his fame as the father of antiseptic surgery. Lister, who arrived at Balmoral on September 4, thought it best to lance the abscess, which was then about six inches in diameter. 'I felt dreadfully nervous as I bear pain so badly,' Queen Victoria later wrote in her journal. She need not have feared, however, as Lister carefully 'froze' with ether the affected area before lancing the abscess.* While Lister operated, Jenner worked by means of a foot-pedal bellows the germ-killing 'carbolic spray' which the Edinburgh surgeon had invented. In doing so, he inadvertently allowed some of the vapour to get into the Queen's eyes, much to Her Majesty's annoyance.

Flying gout succeeded to the Queen's other ills, the rheumatic pains settling first in her left ankle, then her shoulder, then her right hand. This time even Gladstone was moved to compassion, writing to Queen Victoria that he

---

* Lister, who was knighted by the Queen in 1883, later boasted that he was 'the only person who ever exercised upon her sacred body the divine art of surgery', which was true. The Queen, for her part, was duly grateful, complimenting Lister on 'a most disagreeable duty most agreeably performed.'

was 'extremely concerned' to learn of Her Majesty's 'suffering state'. The press, too, modified its tone, notably the newspapers north of the border. In fact, the editorial comment about the Queen's illness that appeared in the Scottish press at this time showed a remarkable degree of uniformity, the leader writers taking as their thesis that criticism of the Queen emanating from the 'frivolous classes' of society had brought on her illness, a theme dear to Her Majesty's heart. Thus Queen Victoria's sole delinquency in the eyes of *The Aberdeen Free Press* was 'that she does not lead a fast life, that she does not give balls in the London palaces, parade the London streets . . .' This was also the line taken by *The Dundee Advertiser*, which pointed out: 'They (the grumblers) place inestimable value upon the roll and rumble of royal carriages along the streets—splashing with mud a grateful people . . .' The Dundee paper maintained that the Queen was entitled to retirement, the same as soldiers, sailors and policemen. She was not 'national property, existing for the primary purpose of being made a national show.'

Ponsonby suspected that Sir William Jenner was the orchestrator behind these editorials which appeared in the Scottish press, and that he was responsible for an anonymous paragraph in *Lancet* to the effect that 'Her Majesty is not physically capable of bearing the effects of crowded or overheated rooms or of prolonged residence in London.' When Ponsonby taxed Jenner with authorship of the latter paragraph, the physician denied it vigorously, his denial leading to the following passage at arms:

PONSONBY: I suppose it (the paragraph in *Lancet*) was written at the Queen's desire.

Jenner shook his head and looked out of the window.

PONSONBY: If not, I may say I think it most unfortunate, as it will enable the abdicationists to say at once, 'Why should we wait any longer—she promises not to do more, but positively to do less.'

JENNER: It is far better that the truth should be

known. As to there being any feeling on the subject, I don't believe it. There is no feeling against the Queen.

PONSONBY: All well and good, but if that is the truth . . . many people will see some reason for insisting upon what Gladstone mildly calls an 'alteration in our form of government.'[110]

The argument was renewed a few days later and this time Jenner, in a violent outburst, blamed her Ministers for the breakdown in the Queen's health by their insistence that she remain near London for the Prorogation of Parliament. 'By heavens if she had died I would have borne testimony that they had killed her!' he cried, adding that if she had been a man they would never dared have treated her in so 'outrageous' a fashion.

PONSONBY: No, they would simply have turned her off the throne.

JENNER: Colonel Ponsonby! You must know that there is not a woman in the kingdom who does so much work as the Queen. All the time I am with her she is signing papers, or writing dispatches.

PONSONBY: Well, you will see bye and bye when she asks for money for her next son that there will be considerable difficulty. The middle and lower classes believe she is hoarding, and will vote no more.

JENNER: Nonsense! I know hundreds of middle class people who have the highest respect for her. That there will be difficulty about money I have no doubt. But that is the advancing democracy of the age, and it is absurd to think that it will be checked by her driving about London and giving balls for the frivolous classes of Society.[110]

At the moment when Queen Victoria appeared to hover between life and death Lady Churchill wanted to know why her children had not been sent for. 'Good heavens,' cried Sir Thomas Biddulph, 'that would have killed her at once.'[110]

Colonel Ponsonby agreed that this was the case. 'Other
people have relations, but these relations seem to be the very
people the Queen is least inclined to send for,' Ponsonby
opined. In these circumstances, when the mere sight of her
children was enough to impede her recovery, John Brown's
importance to Queen Victoria once more becomes self
evident. Unlike her children, who were wrapped up in their
own egos, and full of their own family concerns, Brown was
utterly selfless in his devotion to his mistress in her present
distress. Nor did he attempt to lecture her in the fashion of
Gladstone. Instead, he tried to cheer her up and to comfort
her in his own homely way. Aside from her maids and her
physician Brown was, in fact, the Queen's principal contact
with the outside world during the six weeks when she was
most ill.

Astonishingly enough, it was not until nearly a month
after her arrival at Balmoral that Her Majesty would con
sent to see her Private Secretary, though ordinarily she
consulted with Colonel Ponsonby daily. ('Yesterday
Ponsonby wrote to his wife on September 14, 'I saw the
Queen for the first time . . . she looked rather pulled down
thinner and paler . . .') Meanwhile, Brown doubled a
messenger and nursemaid, being equally handy in trans
mitting the Queen's orders to the far corners of the Bal
moral estate, or in the vexatious task of turning Her
Majesty in bed. Brown's easy access to the Queen was bitter
ly resented by her children, banished from her presence. In
another letter to his wife, Ponsonby reported a conversation
with Princess Alice in which she threw out 'anxious hints as
to the influence of one who, though an honest and really
faithful servant, was quite unfit for more than menial
work . . . Yet,' the Princess pursued, 'he alone talks to her
on all things while we, her children, are restricted to speak
on only those matters which may not excite her or which
she chooses to talk about.'[110]

The caution against discussing excitable topics with the
Queen becomes understandable when the tactlessness of

Vicky, the Princess Royal, is taken into account. For Vicky had chosen just this moment when her mother's spirits were at their lowest to get up a round-robin letter for her brothers and sisters to sign warning the Queen of the dangers ensuing from her continued seclusion. ('Your peace and quiet, your authority and popularity seem to us to be at stake.') Chances are that the Queen would have developed an abscess under her left arm had she been shown this letter, but fortunately wiser counsels prevailed.

Although the round-robin was never sent, there was much muttering and shaking of heads among the Queen's children as they gathered outside her sick room. Princess Alice, in particular, was filled with gloomy forebodings concerning the future of the Monarchy. She maintained that the Queen had become a reckless exponent of *aprés-moi-le-déluge*. 'She thinks he (the Prince of Wales) has become so unpopular that it is useless to expect he will come to the throne', Princess Alice confided to Colonel Ponsonby. 'She thinks the Monarchy will last her time and that it is no use thinking of what will come after . . . so she lets the torrent come on.'[110]

As if to lend weight to this view *Reynolds's News*, under the heading 'Panic in High Places', reported that the Prince of Wales had recently been the centre of attraction at a Bad Homburg casino, where spectators had stood six deep to watch him squander his gold—'gold which he obtains from the toil and sweat of the English working men without himself producing the value of a half penny'. The one-time Chartist weekly also seized the occasion to dredge up the Prince of Wales's role in the Mordaunt divorce scandal, concluding: 'When, therefore, the people of England read one year, in the journals, of their future King appearing prominently in the Divorce Court, and in another of his being the centre of attention at a German gaming-table, or public hell, it is not at all surprising that rumours concerning the Queen's health have occasioned in many quarters much anxiety and apprehension.' Gladstone had summed up the situation as far back as December when, in a letter to Lord Granville marked 'Secret', he wrote: 'The Queen is invisible and the Prince of Wales is not respected.'

All was not carbolic sprays and Cassandra-like prophecies at Balmoral while the Queen lay stricken. Life went on as usual within the castle walls, which meant that petty quarrels proliferated. In true pantomime fashion, these tiffs reversed the normal order of things, with masters championing the disputes of their servants.

The origin of these quarrels was usually so labyrinthine as to be impossible to trace. Take, for example, the row which broke out between Prince Alfred and John Brown when the former arrived at Balmoral in September and, in a marked manner, refused to shake hands with Brown. Ostensibly this rebuff had its genesis in the gillies' ball of May, 1870, which had been a particularly noisy and drunken affair. Prince Alfred had ordered the music to be stopped when the ball showed signs of getting completely out of hand and, in doing so, had trodden heavily on Brown's brogues. 'I'll not take this from you or from any other man', he is supposed to have told Prince Alfred. (Brown denied making this insulting remark. His version was that he had told the fiddler, 'Oh, if the Prince ordered you to stop, you were quite right.')

In the wavy mirror world of Balmoral things were never quite as they seemed. In reality, the Prince Alfred–Brown row was rooted in a long-standing feud between Brown and John Grant, who served as Prince Alfred's head gillie, and who refused to take orders from Brown. (There was intense jealousy between these two servants who had entered the Royal service at the same time.) Queen Victoria suspected that Grant had been poisoning Prince Alfred's mind against her good, faithful Brown, but when she voiced these suspicions to Jane Churchill, her Lady of the Bedchamber, the latter replied with heavy sarcasm, 'Oh, no, Mum, I am sure that no one would listen to stories from their servant against anyone.'[110] When Prince Alfred refused to shake hands with Brown the Queen's worst suspicions seemed to be confirmed, and she insisted that the quarrel be patched up immediately. Acting on the Queen's orders, Colonel Ponsonby saw Prince Alfred that same evening to arrange for a meeting between the two protagonists.

PRINCE ALFRED: Very well, if the Queen wishes it, I will see him— I am always ready to obey her desires. Only you must be present.

COL PONSONBY: As a witness, Sir?

PRINCE ALFRED: To a certain extent, yes. If I see a man on board my ship on any subject it is always in the presence of an officer. You have, I believe, the same rule in the Army. Let it be so now.

COL PONSONBY: I ask this, Sir, because the Queen is ill, and the whole of this question annoys her. I am sure Your Royal Highness doesn't wish to make her worse.

PRINCE ALFRED: Of course I don't. But who is it who has irritated her with this question? Not me—for I never raised it—but Brown. He spoke and complained to her.[110]

When Queen Victoria heard of her son's demand that his interview with Brown be witnessed in accordance with naval custom, she was furious. 'This is not a ship, and I won't have naval discipline introduced here,' she stormed. The Queen knew only too well that Prince Alfred was inclined to be overbearing with those whom he regarded as his inferiors, a tendency that had become more marked since, as captain, he had assumed command of the cruiser *HMS Galatea.* He had returned only recently from an Australian cruise with a deep tan and the manners of a martinet. His offhand treatment of Brown the Queen regarded as all the more unacceptable in that, in earlier years, Prince Alfred had been glad enough to accept Brown's services as gillie on deer-stalking expeditions, and to share Brown's pipe tobacco on those occasions.

The actual confrontation between the two was something of an anti-climax, though it was not without its comic aspects as described by Ponsonby in a letter to his wife:

BROWN: Am I right, Sir, in thinking that you are annoyed with something I have done in the past? If so, please tell me, for it is most painful that any of Her Majesty's children should be angry with me.

PRINCE ALFRED: It's nothing that you have done in the past. But I must confess that I was surprised at the extraordinary language you used at the gillies' ball last May.

BROWN: Her Majesty put the whole arrangements for the ball into my hands ... At first I did not know that it was Your Royal Highness who had stopped the music, and I was very angry and lost my temper. I cannot think it possible that I used any nasty words, but if Your Royal Highness says so then it must have been so, and I must humbly ask your forgiveness.[110]

Colonel Ponsonby thought that Brown acquitted himself well until it came to the moment of parting, when Prince Alfred expressed himself as satisfied with the meeting. 'I'm quite satisfied, too', blurted the incorrigible Brown. 'My private opinion', Ponsonby added for the benefit of his wife, 'is that neither is satisfied.'*

If the Prince Alfred–Brown episode settled nothing it at least took the Queen's mind from her own troubles, and it was noticeable that from the moment she felt herself well enough to take a hand in this quarrel her recovery was

* Even Queen Victoria's grandchildren were rude to Brown apparently, for Ponsonby relates an incident involving Princess Charlotte, the Princess Royal's tiny daughter, who was with the Queen when Brown entered the room. 'Say how de do to Brown, m'dear,' her grandmother prompted. 'How de do,' repeated the child. 'Now go and shake hands with Brown,' the Queen continued. 'No, that I won't do,' her granddaughter replied. 'Mama says I ought not to be too familiar with servants.'

accelerated. Soon she was well enough to sit propped up by many cushions in her garden tent, though Ponsonby reported that she looked peaked. Small wonder—she had lost fourteen pounds in the two months she had been ill.

No Drury Lane pantomime could be considered complete without a villain, and the 1871 republican extravaganza had one *par excellence* in the person of Sir Charles Wentworth Dilke, Bart., who was every inch a Demon King, or perhaps one should say a Demon President. Dilke's father had been a friend of the Prince Consort, and encountering the eight-year-old Dilke strolling with his father in Hyde Park one day Queen Victoria had stroked the boy's hair. 'I suppose I stroked it the wrong way', she was to remark much later.

In November, 1871, when Dilke began his attacks against the Monarchy, he was twenty-eight years old, tall, bearded, handsome, with nothing of the demonic in his appearance; indeed the contemporary portrait of Dilke by G. F. Watts which hangs in the National Portrait Gallery shows him with a dreamy expression about the eyes. Elected to Parliament for Chelsea, as a Liberal, in 1868, Dilke proved to be such a promising backbencher that he was singled out to second the Loyal Address to the Crown at the opening of Parliament in February, 1870. The defection of this wealthy young aristocrat less than a year later to the republican cause created, therefore, a major scandal in Establishment circles. More than that, it lent the republican cause an air of respectability, lifting it out of the smoky back parlour of the public house to set it down in the chintz and Chippendale atmosphere of a Chelsea drawing-room.

9

AN EPIDEMIC OF LOYALTY

THERE was no hint of trouble on November 6, 1871, however, when the tall, slim, dignified-looking Dilke rose to address a working-class audience at Newcastle-on-Tyne. His topic, 'Representation and Royalty', sounded innocuous enough, but the speech, as it turned out, was devoted almost exclusively to the rear half of this tandem, Royalty, which he claimed was costing the British taxpayer close to one million pounds sterling a year, and which was 'a centre of waste, corruption and inefficiency in national life'. As examples of waste, he cited such sinecures as the Lord High Almoner, the Master of the Buckhounds, the Exons in Waiting, and the thirty-two physicians, surgeons and apothecaries in ordinary and extraordinary who were retained to look after the Royal family's health. As for the Hereditary Grand Falconer, the Duke of St Albans, he should be made to earn his £1,500 a year stipend by being designated Hereditary Grand Pigeon Shooter, Dilke suggested. It was all good knockabout fun, but shrewdly calculated to appeal to a wide spectrum of opinion.

Sir Charles did not stop there, however, but went on to accuse Queen Victoria of hoarding at the public expense, and of failing to pay income tax on the private fortune she had thus accumulated. He reminded his audience that Sir Robert Peel, in introducing the Income Tax Bill of 1842, had spoken of the Queen's 'determination that her income should be subjected to a similar burden'. 'I have reason to believe that this promise has never been fulfilled,' Dilke remarked drily amid general laughter. Then, having accused the Queen of malversation, he hurried to his peroration, which consisted of a rather damp endorsement of the republican principle. 'If you can show me a fair chance that a Republic here will be free from the political corruption that hangs about the Monarchy, I say . . . let it come!' he cried.

Curiously, in view of the uproar which the speech later created, the press was slow in rising to Dilke's bait. *The Times*, for example, did not bother to report the speech the following day, but three days later, as if caught napping, "The Thunderer" suddenly devoted one and a half columns to a news report of the Newcastle meeting, and in a leading article rounded on Dilke, whom it accused of 'recklessness bordering on criminality'. Gladstone thought so little of the Newcastle speech that at the Lord Mayor's banquet on November 9 he made only a glancing reference to it, without naming Dilke. The Prime Minister did, however, uphold the right of the individual 'to discuss without any limit at all . . . questions relating to the institutions under which we live.'

If Gladstone's impulse was to ignore Dilke, an altogether different view of the matter was held at Balmoral, where Queen Victoria was slowly recovering from her illness. Here Dilke's attack on the Monarchy was regarded as little short of high treason, a crime which would have merited banishment to the Tower of London in former times. If her Premier was hesitant, Her Majesty had no doubts at all as to the proper course of action. 'Gross misstatements and fabrications, injurious to the credit of the Queen, and injurious to the Monarchy remain unnoticed and uncontradicted,' she complained to Gladstone. The country looked to him and to his colleagues 'for some very decided expression of their condemnation,' she added.[57]

The Prince of Wales, who, as Heir to the Throne, might have been expected to react strongly to attacks on the Monarchy, had just returned from a pheasant shoot at Scarborough when the Dilke storm broke. The two seemingly unrelated events—the pheasant shoot and Dilke's Newcastle speech—were to be connected in a subtle way. For it was while staying at Scarborough as a guest of the Earl of

Londesborough that the Prince of Wales contracted typhoid fever, and it was as a consequence of this illness, or rather of the sympathy it engendered, that the pendulum of opinion swung hard towards the Royalists, and away from Citizen Dilke and his republican cause.

Scarborough (pop. 24,081) boasted of itself as 'Queen of the English watering places', but it hardly seems to have been the salubrious spa that its travel brochures gave out. It was in fact 'the worst drained town in England', according to the *British Medical Journal*, which added, 'It is simply not drained at all . . . a mass of middens, and ash-holes, and stinks.' The Prince of Wales and his fellow guests might have hesitated before accepting Lord Londesborough's invitation had they known how high the death rate from zymotic diseases was in this Yorkshire spa. As it was, two of the party, the Earl of Chesterfield, and the Prince's own groom, Charles Blegge, were to succumb within seventeen days of one another to typhoid fever, contracted while imbibing Scarborough's 'health-giving' waters. The Prince was luckier, but even his strong constitution nearly met its match in Scarborough's tough bacteria.

Their host, Lord Londesborough, had inherited an immense fortune at the age of twenty-six, and had then proceded to throw most of it away in backing horses and theatrical flops. There was still enough left, however, to entertain the Prince of Wales in a fitting manner, and on this occasion his Lordship had invited such members of the 'fast' Marlborough set as the Marquis of Hartington ('Harty-Tarty') and his mistress, the lovely Duchess of Manchester, whose complaisant husband tagged along. The guests also included Christopher Sykes, a fearful snob, who slipped readily into the role of Court fool. (Prince Albert Edward's idea of fun was to empty magnums of champagne over the unprotesting Sykes's head.) The company was good, the pheasant plentiful, the Prince seemed set for a pleasant week. In the event, everything went wrong.

Londesborough Lodge, situated on a cliff-top overlooking Scarborough Bay, was no doubt a delightful spot for seaside villeggiatura. Lord Londesborough's grandson, Osbert Sitwell, who as a child knew the house, describes its wind-contorted trees as 'a grove of Daphnes frozen in permanent flight from the cool waves below.'[129] However pleasant its situation, the interior of the lodge, with its numerous small, box-like rooms, left much to be desired. If one wall had been removed while the week-long shooting party was in progress, the cutaway section would have revealed twenty-seven persons, including the servants, crammed into these boxes.*

The over-crowding was not the worst thing, however. There were the smells. The Lodge's drains were primitive, even by nineteenth century standards, and were subject to the vagaries of the sea, the sewage backing up when the tide rose. All thirteen of the house's water-closets and sinks emptied into two huge cesspools, one of which ('the one most likely to be the source of evil', according to the *British Medical Journal*) was located in the basement directly beneath the Prince of Wales's bedroom. It had not been opened in six years. Londesborough Lodge was, in fact, a veritable pest-house.

At first the Prince and his companions banged away merrily at the pheasants but gave it up in a few days as, one by one, the distinguished company fell ill, suffering from diarrhoea. Dr George P. Dale, Lord Londesborough's physician, admitted that the diarrhoea could have been due to 'offensive effluvia escaping from the house', though he maintained in *The Times* that the Lodge's drains were 'in perfect condition'. As for the Lodge's water supply, the Prince of Wales had drunk nothing but hot springs water bottled at Clifton, Bristol, the physician averred. Whatever the cause of the alimentary disorders, the host, himself, was

---

* Concerning the servants, *Lancet* affords an interesting peek into their quarters. The Prince's valet, for example, slept in a cubbyhole only 6 ft. high, while three maid-servants shared another tiny room without windows or ventilation of any kind. A fourth slept in the linen closet.

a victim. Lord Londesborough was, in fact, too ill to see his guests off at the railway station.

The Prince of Wales returned to Sandringham where, on November 9, he celebrated his thirtieth birthday by giving a ball for some of Norfolk's old County families. His Royal Highness was about to resume his social rounds with a visit to the Maharajah Dhuleep Singh when he had a sudden chill followed by a febrile attack.

Meanwhile, as he continued to stump the country, Sir Charles Dilke began to play down the Monarchy question and to play up his plea for a redistribution of Parliamentary seats. At Leeds, before an audience of 4,000, Sir Charles denied any intentional rudeness towards Queen Victoria ('I care nothing for the ridiculous cry of "treason", but I do care a great deal for a charge of having used discourteous words towards the Queen'). This disclaimer did not discourage hecklers from delaying the meeting for twenty minutes with their catcalls and groans. Elsewhere, his reception was similar. At Dilke's Bristol meeting there were fist fights and the platform was stormed; at Derby cayenne pepper and rotten eggs were thrown. The climax came at Bolton, on November 30, when iron nuts and bolts were hurled through the windows of the meeting-house where Dilke was speaking, killing one of his followers. The rowdyism was carefully orchestrated. Bolton, for example, was liberally placarded with posters inciting the populace to wreck the Dilke meeting, while elsewhere the police deliberately held off giving him protection. At Derby there is evidence that hooligans were plied with free ale before being turned loose on the Dilke meeting, held, ironically, in the Temperance Hall.

Dilke's crime in the eyes of the Establishment was not that he attacked the Monarchy in espousing the republican cause, but that he 'attempted to excite a working-class audience against their existing government', in the words of *The Times*. Had his criticisms of the Monarchy been confined within the walls of his club, or even of the House of Commons, they would undoubtedly have been ignored as the temporary aberration of an eccentric young aristocrat. But 'no party of gentlemen' will tolerate 'calumnies such as he was permitted to utter with impunity before the 'roughs' of Newcastle', *The Standard* warned. Lord Chelsea (afterwards Lord Cadogan) was so incensed that, in a speech at Bath, he challenged Dilke to a duel.

Still, Establishment wrath over this *trahison des clercs* does not entirely explain the mounting violence that accompanied Dilke as he continued to address the 'roughs' up and down the country. For a fuller explanation one must turn to the Court Circulars that appeared in the daily press. Alongside the reports of Dilke's hostile reception at Leeds, for example, there appeared on Thursday, November 24, among other items of Court news, the following bulletin, issued over the signature of Sir William Jenner and three other physicians: 'Sandringham—His Royal Highness the Prince of Wales is suffering from an attack of typhoid fever. There are no unfavourable symptoms.' The press accounts of Dilke dodging a hail of iron nuts and bolts at Bolton appeared cheek by jowl with the news that Queen Victoria had hastened to Sandringham to be with the Prince of Wales, who was delirious with fever.

Looking back, it is difficult to account for the exaggerated emotion which the Prince of Wales's illness aroused in the public breast. 'With the exception, perhaps, of certain periods of the Crimean War and of the Indian Mutiny, public feeling had never been so deeply touched in the present generation,' declared Joseph Irving, the chronicler, who went on to describe the public frenzy: 'Bulletins ... were posted up in all places of resort; newspapers were eagerly bought up, edition after edition, as they were hourly brought out; and whenever two or three friends met, the condition of the Prince was not only the first but the single topic of discussion ... Throughout India, in the colonies, and even in the United States, the daily progress of the disease was recorded and watched . . .'[68]

Unfortunately the Royal family appeared to lose its head along with the rest of the nation, the inability to maintain a dignified mien in the face of tragedy being a family failing. The Queen's children had given ample proof of this lack of judgment during their mother's recent illness, when the Princess Royal had chosen just that moment to lecture her mother, while Prince Alfred had picked a quarrel with John Brown. They were to surpass themselves in foolishness now as they clustered about the stricken Prince's bed.

The cramped quarters at Sandringham had much to do with the undignified scenes that took place there during the Prince's illness. Sandringham, which was located in a flat, bleak Norfolk landscape, was little more than a shooting-box when Prince Albert Edward bought it; and although he had made extensive improvements, the old Elizabethan house was hardly designed to accommodate both the Prince's Household and that of his mother the Queen, plus the Cambridges (Uncle George, the Duke of Cambridge, had hurried to Sandringham as soon as Bertie's condition became serious). The result was that everyone got under everyone else's feet, and on everyone else's nerves, and sickroom gossip was freely bandied about in the drawing-room.

Sometimes the Prince of Wales in his feverish ravings imagined that he was already King, and talked of restoring order: to begin with, the 4th Earl of Onslow would be made to appear at Court wearing tights, the light-headed Prince decreed. This was mild enough, but other reforms which the delirious Prince had in mind for the Royal Household 'set all their hair straight on end', according to Ponsonby.[110] Not all members of the Royal family were on good terms with one another, but they were united in their awe of Queen Victoria. Ponsonby tells of strolling in the garden at Sandringham with one of the Equerries 'when we were suddenly nearly carried away by a stampede of royalties, headed by the Duke of Cambridge and brought up by Prince Leopold, going as fast as they could', he wrote to his wife. 'We thought it was a mad bull,' he added, 'but they cried out, "The Queen, the Queen", and we all dashed into the house again and waited behind the door until the road was clear.'[110]

As the Prince's temperature rose to 104 and his breathing became more rapid, the anxious watchers split into two camps, which Ponsonby labelled as 'improvementors' and 'depressors'. Naturally, Ponsonby himself belonged to the 'improvementors' while Stephy, the Duchess of Roxburghe, was the acknowledged leader of the hand-wringing opposition ('Fools!' cried the Duchess, referring to Ponsonby and his followers, 'they talk as if the Prince were fit to go out shooting tomorrow.'). The Prince may have been less than fit for shooting, but this did not deter his brothers, Prince Alfred and Prince Arthur, from going ice-skating at Sandringham while Bertie supposedly lay at death's door.

Meanwhile, their Uncle George, the Duke of Cambridge, thought he detected a typhoid-bearing smell, and went charging around the house in pursuit of it. Princess Louise's room from which the smell seemed to emanate was declared out of bounds, but when Francis Knollys, the Prince of Wales's secretary, located a smell in the library, the red-faced Duke jumped up, crying, 'By George, I won't sit here another minute.' The smells turned out to be a gas leak, which a plumber quickly put right. Fortunately, the public was spared these scenes, else its sympathy for members of the Royal family in their hour of despair might not have been quite so heartfelt.

As it was, the approach of December 14, tenth anniversary of Prince Albert's death, saw the nation in the grips of what *Reynolds's News* described as 'an epidemic of typhoid loyalty'. 'All England may be said to have gathered at the little Norfolk cottage', gushed *The Daily Telegraph*, thereby setting the tone for much of the editorial comment which appeared on the eve of the awesome anniversary. The *Telegraph* went on to sermonize about 'those angels of God, Sadness and Love', and ended by asserting that 'in a thousand nameless households . . . hearts close together, and hands linked with hands . . . against the dreaded approach of death.' *The Times*, which earlier, as if panic-stricken, had dropped all leaders from its editorial pages except those relating to the Prince, now made its contribution to the solemnity of the occasion by appearing on December 13 with its pages framed by a heavy black border. More ominously, on page 15, it carried two advertisements for Jays, the London General Mourning Warehouse, at 247 Regent Street, announcing that they were prepared to send milliners and dressmakers anywhere in the United Kingdom 'in the event of immediate mourning being required.'*

Thursday, December 14, dawned without any appreciable worsening in Prince Edward's condition. Indeed, there was cheering news that 'dear Bertie' had slept quietly at intervals, and that his respiration was much easier. He had even taken food. After breakfast his mother approached the sick bed. 'He kissed my hand, smiling in his usual way, and said, "So kind of you to come; it is the kindest thing you could do." . . . How deeply grateful we are for God's mercy', the Queen added.[148] By the following day, Queen Victoria, who had regulated the comings and goings at the 'little Norfolk cottage' with the authority of a station-master, had already begun to clear Sandringham of its surplus royalty. Among the first whom she sent packing were her two youngest children, Leopold and Beatrice, and the two princes, Alfred and Arthur, who had annoyed her by ice-skating when their brother was in danger.

The Prince of Wales's illness dealt republicanism a blow

* The only discordant note was sounded by the Irish press. *The Flag of Ireland*, for example, after recalling how Queen Victoria had refused to reprieve the Manchester Martyrs, asked, 'Why then should we sorrow, because the son of this royal lady lies at the gate of eternity?'

from which it never recovered. It was swept aside in the sea of gushing sentimentality emanating from newspapers like *The Daily Telegraph* which, on the December 14 anniversary, had invoked the 'Angelic help' of the Prince Consort, that 'loving father, today in Paradise'. It was drowned in the chorus of 'God Bless the Prince of Wales', which, on Boxing Night, December 26, gallery-goers at the Drury Lane theatre caught up three times running, and which brought even the stalls to their feet to cheer their future King. ('Even Citizen Dilke, himself, if he chanced to be among the audience at Drury Lane, could scarce forebear to cheer,' declared *The Annual Register*.) Well might a radical historian like J. R. Green try to put the best face on defeat by recalling that 'all France went mad with anxiety when Lewis the Well-Beloved fell sick, and yet somehow or other '89 came never the later'; the fact remained that overnight all hostility towards the Monarchy had dissolved in a salt solution of tears. The spectre of republicanism had been exorcised by the cliché of the widowed Queen kneeling at the bedside of her son.

To those who had worked hard to found Jacobin clubs the blow was a bitter one. So much so that some, like E. Morrison Davidson, suspected that the Prince of Wales's condition had been 'purposefully exaggerated', while *Reynolds's News* bluntly labelled it 'a sham panic got up for the occasion to serve a political end'. On the other hand, the Duke of Cambridge saw in his nephew's illness Divine Intervention operating to save England from Red Republicanism. 'Heaven has sent this dispensation to save us', the Duke wrote to his mother. Lord Henry Lennox put it more succinctly. 'What a sell for Dilke this illness has been', he remarked to Disraeli.

What a sell, indeed. As already pointed out, the republicanism of 1871 was purely a negative movement, lacking in anything that could be defined as Socialist content. The great majority of the British working class remained loyal, though inclined to criticize the Monarchy as a wasteful extravagance, and to feel that the Queen was not giving good value for money. But such cheese-paring economies as might be effected by the change were hardly justification for switching from one form of government to another, and once the republican leaders allowed themselves to be side-tracked by the pecuniary argument they gave the game away to the monarchist party. As *The Daily Telegraph* pointed out, 'When we put the Throne of England away in the British Museum, we will, please God, have a nobler reason than that it costs us a million sterling; that is to say, sevenpence three farthings apiece.'

Thomas Wright, a journeyman engineer, and an acute observer of the times, admitted that the republican cause was a negative one. 'Republicanism as it now exists in England', he wrote in June, 1871, 'is founded less on pure admiration of its own professed principles than upon hatred and contempt for royalty and its concomitants.' Wright, who himself was a moderate, went on to say, ' "Take away the baubles" is a cry that sums up the political aspirations of the working classes.'[164] A movement that could inscribe its banners with no slogan more stirring than 'Take away the baubles', that could offer the masses nothing more inspiring than a vague, American-style meritocracy to take the place of hereditary privilege, did not, perhaps, deserve to live.

With republicanism dead, the stage was all set for the big Christmas panto transformation scene: the apotheosis of His Royal Highness Prince Guelph, the Heir Apparent and Principal Boy. Already the gauzes were beginning to lift, one by one, to disclose the dome of St Paul's in the distance. Soon the portly figure of Prince Guelph, disguised as a pilgrim, would be seen making its way towards the cathedral, while Scaramouche and Pantalone, their tricolour sashes and republican mob caps discarded, cheered from the side-lines, and Joey the Clown, with sausages dangling from his pockets, pushed the helmet of a policeman over the un-suspecting bobby's face.

The Thanksgiving service at St Paul's was, in reality, a triumph for William Ewart Gladstone, who showed himself to be the possessor of a talent for showmanship not unworthy of Augustus Harris, the impresario at the Drury Lane theatre. Gladstone's original conception of what such a ceremonial should be like did not differ greatly from the Jubilees of Queen Victoria's latter reign, which also had St Paul's cathedral as their focal point. Nor, for that matter, did it differ fundamentally from the Coronation of the television era, when an Earl Marshal would refer to Queen Victoria's great-great-granddaughter jocularly as 'my leading lady'. In Gladstone's case, however, the leading lady objected strongly to turning a solemn religious occasion into one of 'pomp and show', and so the People's William was forced to curb the public hoopla somewhat.

Others, notably *The Times,* had fewer scruples about the show element. In the columns where mourning clothes specialists had but lately announced their willingness to go anywhere in an emergency, the furnishers of Court suits and diplomatic uniforms now vied for attention with the suppliers of pyrotechnics ('Five guinea cases of selected fireworks, carriage free') and of 'Dolland's celebrated Guinea Opera Glasses of great power'. Elsewhere in *The Times*' classified section there were offers of viewing space along the procession route at prices ranging from ten shillings for a rooftop perch to forty guineas for a 'spacious drawing-room on first-floor, with two windows and balcony, and use of piano', the whole overlooking Fleet Street. One householder on Ludgate Hill had calculated his viewing space with the nicety of a theatrical lessee plotting a house chart, thus—'Second floor, three windows, £40; third floor, three windows, £30; Single seats, ground floor, £3; Top of house, front row, 10s.' Even the Medical Club, that all-male preserve, used *The Times* to announce that on this special occasion it was relaxing its rules to the extent that 'Windows of the club will be made available for ladies—no member to invite more than one.'

This speculative bubble came very near to being pricked. On February 13, the Prince of Wales was 'like new-born, pleased at every tree and flower', according to his mother's description; but a week later his left leg had swollen with gout. By February 22, the Queen doubted very much whether her son could 'undergo the fatigue of the very long Drive etc.—not to speak of the excitement', as she wrote to Gladstone.[57] More to the point, the Queen herself declared that she was looking forward to the ceremony of the 27th 'with much alarm'. On the Sunday preceding the service the Prince was pronounced fit to attend, but when he walked it was with a pronounced limp.

'A Royal Raree-Show . . . fit only to amuse children and nursemaids', was the verdict pronounced upon the Thanksgiving celebration of February 27 by *Reynolds's News*. Not that there was anything particularly colourful about the procession itself. It consisted of a few Horse Guards, a Mace-bearer on horseback, who had difficulty in managing his ponderous weapon, a brass band, a contingent of Lancers and nine State carriages, in the last of which, an open landau drawn by six cream-coloured horses, sat the Queen and her son. The Queen's black silk dress trimmed in miniver 'would have been in no way remarkable upon any other middle-aged lady in the Strand', as *The Echo* noted. As for the Prince of Wales, his uniform, that of a General Officer with the Orders of the Garter and Bath, was at least in keeping with the occasion, though its flamboyance was belied by the Prince, himself, 'pale as yet, and fever-worn', in Tennyson's words. Far from being 'showy', there was very little here on which the imaginations of nursemaids and their charges could feed. Sanger's Circus, which followed through the same streets a few hours later, was brilliant by comparison, for the circus could boast a real lion, gilt cars, and a bare-back rider who rode two piebald horses at the same time.

The 'Royal Raree-show' element lay with the crowds

themselves—the million and a quarter people who lined the seven-mile route along which the procession passed in its journey from Buckingham Palace to St Paul's and back. They were cheerful, in a holiday mood, for the most part. They laughed at the simian antics of the boys who climbed trees in Green Park for a better view.* They cheered the postman who made his rounds down the Strand ahead of the procession, taking bows as he went. Some of those who occupied two guinea window seats overlooking Fleet Street amused themselves by heating pennies and flinging them down to street urchins, finding the howls of pain as the boys burned their fingers irresistibly funny. As the Royal carriage approached there were deafening cheers, which the Prince of Wales acknowledged by repeatedly doffing his hat. 'I saw the tears in Bertie's eyes and took and pressed his hand', the Queen later noted in her journal. 'It was a most affecting day . . .'

Queen Victoria might have been even more affected had she known that among those cheering thousands in Fleet Street was Arthur O'Connor, an undersized, scrofulous, eighteen-year-old, who was armed with a flintlock pistol and a petition for the Queen to sign, and who was awaiting only an opportune time to present both to Her Majesty. However, there were no untoward incidents as the procession mounted Ludgate Hill to St Paul's. As he climbed the cathedral steps the Prince of Wales's lameness evoked sympathetic 'Ahs' from the bystanders.

After the colour and tumult of the street, the hushed atmosphere of St Paul's ('so dull, cold, dreary, and dingy', the Queen thought the interior) was bound to seem an anticlimax to Her Majesty. Nor did she have a good word to say for the service itself. 'Too long,' was her verdict, and one

* Tree-climbers were among the 227 persons hospitalized as a result of celebrating the Prince of Wales's recovery. The injuries sustained by these casualties included two fractures of the thigh, one compound dislocation of the ankle, and eleven simple fractures of the legs, according to *Lancet*, which added, 'not a few of those who met with accidents had, in the excess of their loyalty, drunk deeply'.

fancies that had she been in the little kirk at Crathie she might have held up her fan as a signal to the Archbishop of Canterbury that His Grace was being windy. As her eyes roamed the glittering array of guests assembled for a *Te Deum* under that great dome, they may have been glad-dened by the sight of one repentant sinner, for listed in *The Times* as among those present at the Thanksgiving service was Sir Charles Dilke.

Two days after the Thanksgiving service at St Paul's there occurred the sixth and penultimate of the outrages aimed at Queen Victoria's person during her lifetime.* Owing to its unexpectedness, this outrage frightened the Queen more than all the rest, though the pistol that was thrust to within inches of her face was, as it turned out, unloaded. It happened as Her Majesty was returning to Buckingham Palace after a drive through Regent's Park, an outing which she had undertaken by way of reciprocity for the public affection shown to her at St Pauls.' Arthur O'Connor had seen the Queen leave the palace at 4.30 in her open landau with Lady Jane Churchill beside her, and her two sons, Arthur and Leopold, opposite. John Brown, as usual, was on the box, and two Equerries, General Sir Arthur Hardinge and Lord Charles Fitzroy, rode on either side of the carriage, looking incongruous in their tall hats and frock coats. A pair of outriders in front, and of grooms in the rear, completed this smartly turned-out equipage.

By the time the Queen's carriage returned at 5.30 a large crowd, summoned by that mysterious jungle telegraph which operates on such occasions, had gathered at the palace gates, and Sergeant Jackson, the lone policeman on duty, had his hands full in keeping their enthusiasm within bounds. The newspapers later claimed that the O'Connor

---

* These outrages had many features in common. With one exception, none of the Queen's assailants was of mature years. All showed signs of mental derangement, a condition which the juries, in most of the cases, took into account, in finding the miscreants insane.

boy slipped through the palace gates while the policeman's back was turned but the truth was even more astounding. Having first removed his jacket and placed it on top, the lad managed to scale the ten-foot high railing, apparently unobserved. As he raced across the courtyard to intercept the Queen's carriage which came to a halt at the garden entrance of the palace, O'Connor's luck still held, for he was mistaken for one of the under-gardeners. The Queen's journal takes up the story from there.

'Brown had just got down to let down the steps, and Jane C. was just getting out,' she wrote, 'when suddenly someone appeared at my side, whom I at first imagined was a footman, going to lift off the wrapper. Then I perceived that it was someone unknown, peering above the carriage door . . . Involuntarily, in a terrible fright, I threw myself over Jane C., calling out, "Save me," and heard a scuffle and voices! I soon recovered myself sufficiently to stand up and turn round, when I saw Brown holding a young man tightly . . . Brown kept hold of him till several of the police came in. All turned and asked if I was hurt, and I said, "Not at all." '148

Curiously, although O'Connor had shoved his flintlock pistol over the side of the carriage, the Queen apparently was not aware of it until a few minutes later when the weapon was found on the ground. Then the full horror of the outrage dawned ('All were as white as sheets, Jane C. almost crying, and Leopold looked as if he were going to faint'). In addition to the pistol, police found on O'Connor's person a petition for the Queen to sign ordering the immediate release of all Fenians then being held in Her Majesty's prisons. It had been the boy's original intention to present this petition to the Queen at the point of his pistol as she knelt in prayer at St Paul's. But when he had tried to hide himself in the cathedral on the eve of the

Thanksgiving service, he had been ejected by the verger, who, because O'Connor was small for his age, had mistaken him for a schoolboy larking about on the eve of a public holiday.

That Arthur O'Connor's great-uncle was red-headed Feargus O'Connor, the Chartist leader, who ended his days in a lunatic asylum, explains much about the boy and about the rashness of his deed. It tells us that there was insanity in the family (in addition to espousing the People's Charter, Feargus O'Connor worked for the restoration of the Irish monarchy, with himself as King), and thus explains how the O'Connor boy came to confuse Chartism with the Fenian cause; for the boy clearly worshipped the memory of the fiery Feargus. He told Dr Bond, one of the alienists who examined him, that he would 'feel insulted if anyone spoke disrespectfully of his great-uncle'. Arthur's mother said that she had spoken to him often about the greatness of the O'Connor family, and that Arthur had expressed a desire 'to go to Ireland and see the places where the O'Connors were all-powerful'.

Although living in reduced circumstances, his parents, who were Irish Protestant, had managed to send Arthur to the church school of St Dunstan's-in-the-East, Fleet Street, and afterwards the boy had been apprenticed to a law stationer, until the boy's ill-health had forced his employer to cancel the indenture. From the age of six, Arthur seems to have been plagued by illnesses of one sort or another. He was tubercular; he had scrofula, a condition which had necessitated the amputation of a big toe; and at fourteen he had been knocked down by a cab in Chancery Lane, and had sustained severe head injuries.

Just prior to the outrage against the Queen, O'Connor had shown 'symptoms of mental derangement', according to a family friend writing to *The Times*. At home he had become irritable, complained of sleeplessness and violent pains in the head. The day before the Thanksgiving service at St Paul's,

O'Connor had paid four shillings for the flintlock pistol at a pawnshop in Southwark. The pistol was utterly useless, its flintlock broken, indeed, showing no signs of ever having been fired. In lieu of ammunition, the boy had stuffed the pistol with wads of paper and bits of old leather.

10

THE GREATER ORDER OF BROWN

IF John Brown had done nothing else to earn his keep
during the thirty-odd years he was with Queen Victoria,
his presence of mind on the occasion of the O'Connor outrage would seem to have justified the confidence the Queen
placed in him, and to have repaid all the gossip and ridicule
that she had had to endure on his account. It made no
difference that the Queen was menaced by 'such feeble
instruments as a moon-struck youth and a flintlock pistol',
in the words of the *Daily News*, or that the flint was broken
and the pistol stuffed with wads of paper and leather. What
mattered was that Brown was there to protect his Royal
Mistress, to strike down the arm that had intended to harm
her.

This, at any rate, was the way Queen Victoria reasoned.
'It is to good Brown and to his wonderful presence of mind
that I greatly owe my safety,' she wrote in her journal, 'for
he alone saw the boy rush round and followed him!' 'The
pistol was not loaded,' she added, 'but it might easily have
been.' Later, at Balmoral, the Queen amplified on Brown's
courage, when giving a first-hand account of the episode to
her favourite preacher, Rev. Norman Macleod. After filling
in the clergyman with all the details of the outrage, the
Queen said she 'was sure he would rejoice to think that it
was a Highlander who had seized O'Connor'. The Rev.
Macleod replied that he was 'deeply thankful' to hear it.[146]

Brown seemed to enjoy the rôle of public hero in which he
was now cast, for when he appeared at Bow Street court as
chief witness against O'Connor he beamed upon everyone
from the chief magistrate, Sir Thomas Henry, to the
prisoner at the bar. It was a rare opportunity for the public

to see the Court favourite at close range, for usually he was glimpsed fleetingly on the box as the Queen's carriage sped past. What the public noted was that Brown had put on weight, and that he had aged in Her Majesty's service. His hair had turned almost white. 'A trusty, respectable yeoman,' was the way he was described in *The Echo*.

There was nothing about O'Connor to inspire trust or respect, however, judging from the press comment. *The Times* described Arthur O'Connor as being of 'very mean aspect', while the *News of the World* noted 'a wild expression of eye, a feverish flush in his thin cheeks'. He was wearing a threadbare coat from which his long red hands and wrists protruded, according to this latter newspaper, and a red check neckcloth was loosely folded round his throat with the ends tucked in to conceal his shirt front.

The *News of the World* hurried over these details in order to dwell upon Brown's speech, which it described as 'genuine "Aberdeen-awa" Scotch of the most undiluted character'. 'I gied him a bit shove back,' Brown was quoted as saying of the prisoner O'Connor, and when the boy ran round to the other side of the Queen's carriage, 'I took hold o' him with one o' my hauns, and I grippit him with the other by the scruff o' the neck . . .' till half a dizzen had a grip o' him—grooms, equerries, I kenna how many there was—so then I tocht it time to gie up.' It was a pity that no other newspaper saw fit to render Brown's testimony in dialect, for a complete transcript would have made fascinating reading.

On April 9 Prince Leopold and John Brown were the only witnesses called before a grand jury, which brought in a true bill against O'Connor charging him with 'presenting a pistol at the Queen with intent to alarm her'. Neither of these two witnesses had a chance to repeat his performance when the case came on for trial at the Central Criminal Court, however, for O'Connor suddenly pleaded guilty, against the advice of his counsel. Before passing sentence, the judge, Sir Anthony Cleasby, heard evidence concerning the boy's fitness to plead from four doctors, including Dr Harrington Tuke, at whose lunatic asylum at Chiswick the boy's great-uncle, Feargus O'Connor, had been a patient. Dr Tuke testified to hereditary insanity in the O'Connor family, called the court's attention to the boy's 'irregularly shaped' head (it measured 19″ instead of 20″ one way, and 22″ instead of 23″ the other, the alienist claimed) and to the 'glistening appearance' of his eyes. Despite this evidence, the jury found O'Connor 'perfectly sane' and hence fit to plead, and Judge Cleasby sentenced him to one year's imprisonment at hard labour, during which he was to receive twenty strokes from a birch rod.

Queen Victoria fumed at the 'extreme leniency' of O'Connor's sentence. Her first reaction had been that 'this poor wretch did not mean to kill (but) to frighten', but her attitude had hardened later when she read in *Lancet* that O'Connor was sane. 'To let this deluded youth out again in a year . . . is most dangerous', she complained to Gladstone.* 'The Queen is more unprotected in some ways than any of her subjects as she is a mark to shoot at, and attack from her position', she reminded him.[57] From the tone of her letter, one might have thought that Gladstone, himself, had pointed the pistol at the Queen.

Her confidence in John Brown triumphantly vindicated, Queen Victoria now turned her attention to finding a suitable reward for her faithful attendant. As far back as October, when she had been slowly recovering from her illness, the Queen had considered the creation of a Faithful Service Medal to show her appreciation to Brown and to one or two other servants who had cared for her devotedly during her illness. But when it came to discussing the

---

* Queen Victoria was right as concerns O'Connor. After serving his sentence, he was persuaded to go to Australia; but he returned to England shortly afterwards. On May 5, 1874, he was arrested while loitering outside Buckingham Palace, where one of the Queen's Drawing-rooms was in progress. This time O'Connor was committed by court order to Hanwell Lunatic Asylum.

matter in writing with Gladstone, Her Majesty had sounded strangely flustered.

Arctic explorers were decorated, the Queen argued defensively; so were those who saved lives at sea—yet unrecognized were the Queen's own personal servants, whose services, in many cases, were just as meritorious. ('What can be more important in fact than the faithfulness and discretion and independent unselfishness of those personal servants . . .?' the Queen asked)[57] Her Majesty cited the examples of Prussia and of Grand-ducal Hesse, both of which awarded medals to servants with twenty-five years of service. The Queen proposed to shorten this period to twenty-one years (Brown had not entered her permanent employ until 1851), and she put Colonel Ponsonby to work looking up the historical precedents. 'I foresee troubles,' Ponsonby wrote to his wife. 'If she gives it to Brown and Lohlein—well and good. But if she gives it to the keepers and gillies here, the English well be angry . . .'[110] Princess Alice, with whom Ponsonby conferred, also thought the idea an unfortunate one.

Before the Faithful Service Medal scheme could be put into operation, the O'Connor outrage from which Brown emerged as hero made it imperative that a second, or higher award be created, this latter for service beyond the call of duty. Thus it was that the Devoted Service Medal—sometimes known as 'The Greater Order of Brown'—came into being, this new award carrying with it a £25 annuity for life. So far as I have been able to ascertain, Brown was the sole recipient of this second medal, which lapsed with his death.* The medal itself was a handsome affair in gold designed by Wyon, showing the young Queen Victoria in relief on one side,

---

* Well over a hundred of the silver Faithful Service Medals were awarded during Queen Victoria's lifetime, and the practice has been continued by her successors. The Royal Victoria Medal, as it is now called, is restricted to servants with extremely long service records; thus, at Windsor on July 29, 1967, Elizabeth II presented the medal to a tractor driver with 35 years's ervice, and to a sawmill worker and a woodsman with 34 years' service each.

and on the other a wreath containing within it the words: 'To John Brown, Esq., in recognition of his presence of mind and devotion at Buckingham Palace, February 29, 1872.'

Londoners may have been titillated by the po-faced announcement of Brown's award in the Court Circular, but the Queen's children were not. Brown, they reasoned, had been decorated for doing what, after all, was only his duty, while Prince Arthur, who had knocked the pistol from O'Connor's hand, had received only a tiepin for his pains. This, at any rate, was the burden of complaint from the Prince of Wales, writing to his mother from Rome. The Queen, of course, indignantly denied that Prince Arthur had been slighted. 'The Queen was almost sure that so absurd an idea could not have entered dear Arthur's head', she wrote to her son's tutor, Sir Howard Elphinstone, adding, 'Arthur . . . wore his pin continuously, and repeatedly said how much he liked it.'[83]

How much pressure, if any, Brown exerted on Queen Victoria to honour his services it is difficult to ascertain. What is certain is that Brown in the early 1870s was in a rebellious mood and threatening to quit the Queen's service. This was largely due to boredom with his enforced bachelor existence—Brown was clearly tired of forever playing 'Uncle John' to a growing number of nieces and nephews while the prospect of having bairns of his own dimmed. In November, 1870, a rumour made the rounds that the Highlander had married a Miss Ocklee, one of the maids.* 'I would believe the story unfounded, if I did not think that everything, especially here, may always have a foundation,' Sir Henry Ponsonby wrote from Balmoral to his wife, who had enquired whether the gossip were true. Ponsonby automatically assumed that Brown would leave the Queen's service if he had married, but thought that this would be a great pity. 'Here he is,' Sir Henry pursued, 'we have the best and worst of him . . . But a new man may be anything

* Miss Ocklee, who was Princess Beatrice's personal maid, married a steward named Lawson early in 1873.

and may if he gets the same power not be so harmless.'[110]

Others took it for granted that the Queen and her attendant would part company in the event that the latter married, for Her Majesty demanded single-minded devotion from those who served her. It was partly her dislike of change which caused the Queen to oppose members of her Household getting married, but the Queen also believed that no man could serve two Mistresses, which is the same tortured reasoning advanced by the Roman Catholic Church in imposing celibacy on its priests. 'A man always told his wife everything, and therefore all her private affairs would get known all over London,' Queen Victoria argued with Frederick Ponsonby, Sir Henry's son, whose marriage she succeeded in delaying for three years while he served as her Assistant Private Secretary.[113] She used the same line of reasoning in a vain effort to stop Sir James Reid, her physician, from marrying her Maid of Honour, the Hon. Susan Baring. The Queen banished the good doctor from her presence after he became engaged ('If I had been younger I would have let him go,' she told the Princess Royal), but relented when Sir James crossed his heart and solemnly promised never to do it again.[79]

The prospect of losing John Brown, who was showing signs of mutiny, spurred Queen Victoria to think up other ways of showing her gratitude to him. Ennoblement, of course, was out of the question, but the Queen could and did revive the ancient title of 'Esquire', and bestowed it upon the Highlander. Queen Victoria intended 'Esquire' to convey its original meaning of shield-bearer, someone of gentle birth who attends a knight, and who is, in fact, next in degree below a knight. 'You will see in this,' she wrote to Brown concerning his new title, 'the gtest anxiety to show more & more what you are to me . . . Every one hears me say you are my friend & most confidential servant.' The Queen's intention miscarried, however, and far from adding lustre to Brown's name, 'Esquire' served merely to expose this Sancho Panza to ridicule.

Brown's elevation to Esquirehood carried with it other changes. Beginning in 1873, *Whitaker's Almanack* listed Brown as a member of Her Majesty's Household, along with the Master of the Horse, the Grand Falconer, the Equerries in Ordinary. 'John Brown, Her Majesty's Personal Servant,' followed immediately after the names of Count Albert Edward Gleichen and the other Pages of Honour. Of more immediate interest to Brown, his salary was increased to £400, which brought it on a par with that of a Page of the Back Stairs. No Page ever enjoyed Brown's privileges, however. The Highlander not only had his own personal servant (usually one who doubled as a piper), but his own sumptuous apartment in each of the Royal residences.

Colonel Ponsonby was kept busy looking up historical precedents to reinforce Brown's shooting privileges ('I have been employed all afternoon writing an Apologia for Brown's shooting . . . a long paper about Servants who shot at Windsor in former times,' Ponsonby informed his wife in November, 1874).[110] And not only at Balmoral and Windsor, but at Osborne the well-stocked covers were completely under Brown's dominion. Prince Christian, the Queen's son-in-law, was vexed on more than one occasion to find, upon going out for a day's sport, that Brown had been before him and cleaned the woods of pheasant. As for salmon fishing in the Dee, Ponsonby gives us this picture of Brown's overlordship: 'At 6 in the morning Brown sends up to find out how the fish are. If he hears a bad report he does not go out & the Queen then offers it to Dr Marshall. In the evening the usual song at dinner is, "Poor Dr Marshall never catches anything." '[110]

On Sunday, November 3, 1873, Queen Victoria took what she regarded as an important step in her spiritual development: she received Communion for the first time in the tiny Presbyterian church at Crathie, among the humble servants and tenants on her Balmoral estate. Her action profoundly shocked those members of the Royal Household who, like

Sir Thomas Biddulph, were staunch Anglicans and who suspected the Queen of a Machiavellian plot to deal ritualism a blow. This, however, was not the main reason she decided to take the Scottish Sacrament.

The truth was that she had been contemplating this step for two years, and that she had even taken the precaution of sounding out her spiritual advisers on the subject. None of the ecclesiastics she consulted approved, but none had the courage to say no. The Dean of Windsor, Dr Gerald Wellesley, thought the Queen's action might strengthen the case of the disestablishers, but ended lamely by saying that he could see no harm in the Queen taking the Scottish Sacrament if it was a comfort to her. The Dean of Westminster could find nothing in the Coronation Oath which forbade the practice. As for the Archbishop of Canterbury, he waffled so much that in the end it sounded almost as though he desired inter-Communion.[110] But, as a precaution against the Queen's action being publicized, the Household was warned not to discuss it among themselves (they referred to it only as 'The Event of Last Sunday'), and, of course, no mention of it appeared in the Court Circular.

From her earlier description of Communion Sunday we know what it was like when Queen Victoria arrived at the kirk on that Sunday in November, 1873, to find the interior transformed. In the cross seats facing the pulpit were two long tables covered with snowy linen. The seating arrangement itself was different on this Sunday, for, instead of taking their places behind the Queen in the gallery, John Brown and the other Highland servants were seated below among those who were taking the sacrament at the 'first table'. From her gallery vantage point the Queen could take in all 'these simple good people', the men in their best plaids, the women with tartan shawls. Directly below Her Majesty sat John Brown's parents—his father, eighty-three, and very much bent, his mother wearing the high, muslin 'mutch' of older times, and with a sprig of thyme, the Highland woman's scent bottle, in her Bible. In another part of the kirk the Queen could spot Brown's uncle, Francis Leys, who was one of the elders.

When Dr Malcolm Taylor, the preacher, invited 'all true penitents to receive Communion, the hardened sinner alone to abstain', Queen Victoria descended the stairs and took her place at one of the tables. But when the silver cup was passed to her the Queen, evidently overcome by emotion, nearly spilt the wine, so badly did her hand shake.

After 1873 Queen Victoria took the Sacrament regularly at Crathie kirk. She was a Presbyterian at heart; the Shorter Catechism appealed to her while the subtleties of High Anglicanism filled her with deep distrust. Partaking of the Scottish sacrament did something more than satisfy the Queen's instinct for religious simplicity. It drew her closer to the humble Highlanders on her estate, notably, to the Brown family—the brothers and sisters-in-law of her faithful Highland attendant—whose charmed circle she was thus permitted to enter. From this period dates the Queen's intense interest in the burials, christenings and marriages among the Brown clansmen. It was as though, in descending from her manse pew in the gallery to the tables to partake of the Lord's Feast, Her Majesty had somehow entered into a new, more intimate union with John Brown, himself. It was her way of saying 'Thy people shall be my people.'

At the same time the Queen resented it when members of the Household tried to get on friendly terms with the Browns. Mindful of the Queen's reproaches that she neglected the 'poor cottars', Anne, the Duchess of Athole, dropped in for tea on the William Browns at Bush Farm, and while there sketched the couple and their bairns. Far from being pleased the Queen was furious. Through Ponsonby she let it be known that 'the Household have no right to force themselves into people's houses and take possession of their rooms for tea . . . this is wrong and must not be repeated.'[110] However, when two small boys drowned in a burn near Balmoral that same summer the Queen, herself, rushed to Bush Farm to warn Mrs Brown 'never to let dear little Albert run about alone, or near the burn.'[146]

Queen Victoria showed favouritism to the Brown clan not only at Balmoral, but also when she was in residence in the south. Thus, in December, 1873, she prevailed upon the Dean of Windsor to baptize the month-old daughter of Archie Brown, John's youngest brother, there being no Presbyterian minister available. The Queen herself drove to Archie's house in Windsor to attend the christening, the baby being named Victoria in her honour. However, Her Majesty disapproved strongly of upper-class Scots having their children baptized by Anglican ministers, as she told the Duke of Argyll, suspecting that the intention was to use this as a 'stepping stone to their becoming Episcopalians.'

When John Brown's father died in October, 1875, in his eighty-sixth year, Queen Victoria not only attended the simple funeral service, held in Micras cottage, but commanded the greater part of her Household to do likewise. (They stood outside, as the cottage was too small to hold more than a dozen mourners). Afterwards the Queen remained in her carriage as the funeral cortège slowly wound its way down to the cemetery below the kirk. 'The sons were there, whom I distinguished easily from their being near good Brown, who wore his kilt walking near the hearse', she wrote in her journal. 'I went back to the house, and tried to soothe and comfort dear old Mrs Brown, and gave her a mourning brooch with a little bit of her husband's hair which had been cut off yesterday . . . Saw my good Brown at a little before two. He said all had gone off well, but he seemed very sad . . .'[146]

Mention was made earlier of the physical changes in Brown which had surprised reporters when he appeared in the witness box against O'Connor. He had grown 'grizzled and grey in the Queen's service', as one newspaper expressed it, meaning that there were patches of white in among the kinky, ginger-coloured hair, although Brown, himself, had not yet turned fifty. More significantly, he had lost his leanness which, combined with his height, had made him a striking figure in his native costume. The 'whipcord thews' and the 'feline cleanness of build' which were requisite to the graceful wearing of the kilt, according to Emily Crawford, were now totally absent in Brown's case. Indeed, from photographs of him taken in the mid-1870s, he appears to have experienced some difficulty in buttoning his jacket over his expanding girth.

It is from this period that Brown began to have trouble with his legs. Earlier Queen Victoria had complained of 'my poor Brown' being run off his feet by the Equerries in demanding that he carry their 'trifling messages . . . He is often so tired from being constantly on his legs that he goes to bed with swollen feet and can't sleep from fatigue,' the Queen wrote indignantly to Lady Biddulph, obviously intending that the latter should pass the word along. 'He must not be made "a man of all work", ' she concluded; 'besides it loses his position . . .'[78] Brown had some cause to complain of overwork in the 1870s for, in addition to his attendance upon the Queen, he had been delegated many of the duties of the Royal almoner. It was Brown who received the doctors' reports when the Queen's servants were ill, and who made arrangements with the undertaker when they died. He also advised the Queen on such abstruse matters as whether she should replace at her own expense the *HMS Queen Adelaide*, a pleasure barge which she kept at Virginia Water, and which was due to be broken up. (Brown's advice to the Queen was not to 'fule' away her money.)[71]

But this was not the real reason why the Highlander appeared to be always tired and grumbling about being overworked. The truth was that Brown was running out of steam. That 'vigorous, light, elastic tread' which had astonished Queen Victoria when Brown first began to lead her pony had lost its springiness. Instead, Brown apparently unmindful of the weight he had put on, was forever injuring his legs by jumping down from the box of the Queen's carriage. The Queen's Highland journals are full of references to these mishaps, which, the year following Brown's death, became the subject matter of a seventy-seven-page lampoon written by an Irish-American and entitled *John Brown's Legs, or Leaves from a Journal in the Lowlands*.* The pamphlet, which parodies Queen Victoria's literary style, is dedicated 'To the Memory of those extraordinary Legs, poor bruised and scratched darlings', and at one point the Queen commands Lord Tennyson to write a sonnet about Brown's extremities, holding that 'no nobler theme ever inspired the pen of genius'.[105]

Not only did the Highlander's legs bother him but, Brown came out in blotches on one occasion, while at Balmoral, according to Colonel Ponsonby. In fact, Brown's face became so swollen that he was ordered to remain in his room, no doubt as a precaution against contagion, but also possibly because his grotesque appearance might have frightened some of the more sensitive among the Queen's ladies. (Lord Charles Fitzroy was quick to attribute Brown's condition to drink.)[110]

In March, 1876, Queen Victoria postponed by a few days her departure for Germany because Brown's legs had begun to play him up again. Even after the Royal party had embarked aboard the *Victoria and Albert* in Portsmouth Harbour there was some question as to whether the yacht would proceed, owing to Brown's condition. Colonel Ponsonby pictures the agitation among the Queen's ladies aboard. 'Oh, dear, the leg!' cried Lady Ely to Lady Churchill. 'What leg?' asked the latter, who was a little slow in following her companion's thought. 'Oh, the leg is all right, and we shall go, dear!' Lady Ely exclaimed.

And go they did, the Queen travelling incognito as the 'Countess of Rosenau'. The state of Brown's leg did nothing, however, to sweeten his temper during the Queen's stay in Coburg. It was during this visit that the Highlander, after the Queen had murmured disapproval of the violent drum-

* The author was Kenward Phillip, an Irish Land League sympathiser, who also wrote a pamphlet entitled, 'Boycotting: or Avenging Ireland's Wrongs', published in New York in 1881.

M   177

ming which accompanied the Guard whenever they presented arms, walked up to their commanding officer and ordered,
'Nix boom boom!'[110]

It became increasingly apparent that Brown was classicly
prone to accident when on August 11, 1877, while accompanying the Queen on a tour of the dreadnought *HMS
Thunderer,* he fell through an open space inside a gun turret
and severely damaged his shins. (In contrast, the Queen,
who was fifty-eight, clambered up and down ladders like one
of the deck hands—'I have not forgotten my sea legs,' she
boasted in her journal.) But these were no ordinary shin
barks, judging by the length of time it took them to heal. It
was not until September 17, or more than a month after the
gun turret accident, that the Queen could report, 'Brown's
leg though he had to stand so much, did not hurt him, which
I was thankful for, and he has waited at all our meals, made
my coffee in the morning, etc.'[146] Considering how long it
took for Brown to regain the use of his legs, it is apparent
that something more than accident proneness was involved
in his mishaps. That something, in the opinion of Dr Hal
Yarrow, a medical expert I consulted, was almost certainly
recurrent erysipelas.

Dr Yarrow, a Fellow of the Royal Society of Medicine,
has the benefit, of course, of having Brown's entire medical
history, including his terminal illness, spread out before
him. But Dr Yarrow has also had extensive experience in
treating skin diseases, and after studying the references to
Brown's swollen legs which occur in Queen Victoria's
journals, and in the papers of her secretary, Sir Henry
Ponsonby, he is of the opinion: 'The picture presented . . .
is that of a fairly typical case of recurrent cellulitis of the
legs accompanied by recurrent attacks of erysipelas of the
face.' (Here Dr Yarrow is referring to the occasion at
Balmoral when Brown came out in blotches, and to a sub-
sequent occasion when his face swelled to such an extent
that the eyes were shut.)

Erysipelas was variously known in the Middle Ages as

Sacred Fire (*Ignis Sacer*), Hidden Fire, Infernal Fire (*Ignis Infernalis*), Mal de St Marcel, Mal Persique, Mal Gehennal, Feu-Dieu, Mal des Ardents, and St Anthony's Fire, synonyms that are at once suggestive of the febrile nature of the disease, and of the superstition with which it was surrounded in medieval thinking. It is caused by streptococci, which usually enter the body through an abrasion of the skin, and which usually affect the face and head, causing them to swell, although the legs are frequently the locus of the infection. Recurrences are common, according to the medical literature on the subject, as many as forty attacks having been observed, though two or three attacks are more usual. Healthy adults rarely die of the disease, but diabetes, nephritis, or toxaemia are complications which, taken in conjunction with erysipelas, may result in death.

In Brown's case, Dr Yarrow feels that the condition may have dated from 1865 when the Highlander, it will be recalled, cut his legs during an outing, and when one of his limbs became 'so inflamed and swelled so much that he could hardly move', according to Queen Victoria.[146] The London physician has this additional to say: 'It is very likely that the sudden change from the healthy outdoor life formerly led by Brown to that of comparatively soft living as the Queen's personal attendant would make him more prone to recurrent attacks, once the condition had manifested itself.' Finally, Dr Yarrow lists 'chronic alcoholism which, I understand, Brown indulged in towards the end of his life' as foremost among the factors which might have predisposed the gillie to recurrent erysipelas. Brown's medical history has been dealt with at some length because it goes far to explain his increasing surliness and irritability in the 1870s, which caused him to make enemies at every hand.

'The wonder is that these Highlanders are not more often drunk than they are', Sir Thomas Biddulph, himself an abstainer, commented in 1876, after Brown's cousin, Willie

Leys, had been dismissed for drunkenness.* Biddulph was referring, of course, to the crushing boredom of life at Balmoral where all depended upon the whims of the Queen. 'Balmorality' has been coined as a term to describe that unique combination of paternalism plus formal Court etiquette which the Queen superimposed on a people who were naturally free and undisciplined. As their only defence against 'Balmorality', the Highlanders took to drink, downing vast quantities of whisky on every occasion which could conceivably call for a celebration. The fact that a distillery, operated by a Mr Begg, was located on the Balmoral estate did nothing to encourage sobriety; indeed, no Balmoral festivity was complete without a case or two of 'Begg's best'. Nor was Biddulph the only member of the Queen's Household to be concerned about the amount of drinking that went on among the gillies. The Duke of Westminster, Master of the Horse, wrote Queen Victoria a long memorandum on the subject, only to be reminded icily by Her Majesty that this was not part of His Grace's duties.[110]

The Queen's attitude was, of course, decisive, and whether or not it was due to her Hanoverian upbringing, she tolerated a certain amount of drinking among her servants as their prerogative. Early in her reign a drunken footman dropped a lighted lamp on the stairs at Windsor, after which a report on the servant, detailing a long history of alcoholism, went forward to Her Majesty. Instead of ordering the footman's dismissal, the Queen returned the report with the words 'Poor man' pencilled in the margin.[16] When she came to publish her Highland journals the Queen flatly refused to excise the many references to drink with which the journals abound. 'She cannot understand . . . that the mention of drinking the healths of the Royal Family on their home-coming, etc., should be almost entirely omitted

---

* Willie's offence was not that he was drunk, but that he frightened 19-year-old Princess Beatrice, whom he happened to encounter at Balmoral while he was in this condition.

to please the total abstinence movement', Lady Ely pointed out, in returning the corrected proofs of *More Leaves* to Sir Theodore Martin.[118]

Many stories have been told of Brown's behaviour when drunk—of how he would throw tantrums, tear up photographs of himself, burst into tears at the slightest provocation, and how on one occasion, while inebriated, he bought a dozen cheap egg-cups of florid design as a present for his Royal Mistress. (Edith Sitwell relates how, on another occasion, when Brown crashed to the ground while in an alcoholic haze, the Queen tried to cover up by remarking that she had felt a slight earth tremor.)[128] Most of these stories are apocryphal. Some have their origin in harmless episodes which have nothing to do with alcohol. This is not to make Brown out to be a saint, nor to deny that he punished the bottle heavily, but it is just as well to separate truth from fiction. With this in mind, I will confine myself to a single anecdote whose provenance seems reliable. Arthur Ponsonby relates how his father was sent in search of Brown, after the gillie had kept the Queen waiting to go on her afternoon drive. Suspecting what was wrong, Sir Henry Ponsonby went directly to Brown's room, where he found the Highlander lying on his bed dead drunk. After turning the key in the lock, the Queen's secretary went downstairs to the entrance and, without a word to Her Majesty, took Brown's place on the box. 'The Queen knew what it was and knew that he knew,' Arthur Ponsonby claimed. 'But on this and on other occasions she turned a blind eye.'[111]

Alcohol seems to have had a corrosive effect on Brown's character, as well as on his constitution, for in the 1870s when the heavy drinking began he became noticeably more arrogant and rude. Biddulph thought that the deterioration of Brown's character had something to do with the fact that the Highlander was constantly in the Queen's company. 'No man can be always with the Queen without being very much the worse for it,' Biddulph once remarked.[110] But equally ill health may have been the cause both of Brown's bearish behaviour and his increasing inclination towards the bottle.

For whatever reason, Brown now began to quarrel with all comers. On one occasion, when the Queen, on a visit to the Western Highlands made an excursion to Glencoe Pass, Brown became involved in an altercation with the newspaper reporters who trailed Her Majesty at a discreet distance. In fact he nearly came to blows with one of the scribes who was impertinent enough to spy on the Queen with a telescope while she sat sketching the scenery. 'Not even the highest gentleman in England would dare to do what you have done,' Brown told the offending reporter, in ordering him away. When the latter refused to budge, the Highlander threatened to 'give him something more', according to Queen Victoria.[146] Only the timely arrival of some of the journalist's colleagues prevented an exchange of blows. To Ponsonby, who likewise hurried to intervene, Brown boasted, 'By God, I gave them a bit of my mind.'[110]

Another with whom Brown frequently clashed was Superintendent G. P. Neele, of the London and North-Western, in charge of the Queen's train journeys to and from Balmoral. Train travel made Queen Victoria 'fidgety' and she transmitted her complaints through Brown. If it was not the reading lamps ('The Queen says the train shanna stir a fut till the lamps are put in'), it was the train's jolting ('The Queen says the carriage is shaking like the devil') that drew Her Majesty's attention. 'Thus,' Superintendent Neele sorrowfully commented, 'did John Brown's coarse phonograph transmute Her Majesty's gentle complaint.'[100]

It was the military that brought out the worst in Brown, however. In this he appears to have taken his cue from the Queen herself who was inclined to equate the military mentality at its most wooden with John Bullism, a quality which she wished her sons to avoid at all costs. Her Establishment was not to be run as a battleship, as she had told

Prince Alfred. Her sons must avoid the bad manners of
Officers, and show courtesy and consideration to those
below them in rank, she told their tutors. (When Major
Elphinstone took the cavalry officer's side against Archie
Brown, the Queen had reminded him, 'It is not fair to take
the part of the stronger against the weaker.')[83]

Thus it was with the Queen's tacit consent that Brown
challenged the Generals in her entourage. A particular
target was General Sir Henry Lynedoch Gardiner, an
Equerry, who once made the mistake of enquiring of Brown
after the Queen's health. 'The Queen's very well,' Brown
replied haughtily. 'It was only the other day that she said to
me, "There's that domned old fool General Gardiner
coming into waiting, and I know he'll be putting his bloody
nose into everything that doesn't concern him." '[113]

More serious in its consequences was Brown's quarrel
with Major General Sir John M'Neill, another of the Queen's
Equerries, who had been decorated for bravery in the
Maori war. It arose simply enough when Brown came to the
Equerries' Room with a message from the Queen ordering a
carriage to be sent round. Whether Brown leaned against
the General's desk, or looked over the General's shoulder as
he wrote out his reply is not known; anyway, the General
ordered the gillie to wait outside, until he was sent for.
Brown was livid, complained to the Queen that the General
had shouted at him as though he were a private soldier.
That same evening M'Neill received a letter from Her
Majesty asking him whether he would like a command in
India, and specifically naming a small, Godforsaken outpost.
It took all of Sir Henry Ponsonby's diplomacy to put the
matter right; but thereafter General M'Neill's waitings
were so arranged that he never came to Balmoral or Osborne
where the Queen might have to speak to him.[113]

Most serious of all, of course, was the enmity that existed
between the Prince of Wales and Brown. The Prince
smarted under the humiliation of being relegated in favour

of a servant as the male head of his mother's household, and the situation grew so intolerable that Prince Albert Edward very pointedly refused to go to Balmoral one year because of the prominent rôle John Brown was allotted at this Highland retreat. The quarrels between these two—rivals, in a sense, for the Queen's attention—were carried on through third parties, but were no less deadly in intent.

Rightly or wrongly, the Prince of Wales held Brown responsible for the so-called 'Great Pony Row', which dragged on in the '70s until everyone's nerves were frayed. Very likely it was Brown who had complained to the Queen that her dear little mountain ponies were being ridden to death by some of her entourage, notably her German secretary Hermann Sahl, Canon Duckworth, and the sculptor Edgar Boehm (or 'Mr Bum', as Brown called him). The upshot was that these three gentlemen were, by the Queen's orders, severely restricted in the use of her stables, whereupon a first-class dispute broke out. Boehm threatened to leave Balmoral, Duckworth acted as though the Established Church had been impugned, while Sahl confined himself to writing three-page memoranda.* Meanwhile, the Queen's ponies stood in danger of dying from lack of exercise and obesity, according to Ponsonby.[110]

The enmity between the two rivals flared into the open again in 1874 when Brown began to cast covetous eyes at a bit of grouse-land that formed part of the Prince of Wales's Abergeldie estate. 'If this ground was for any of the gentlemen at Balmoral to shoot over, I would most willingly give it', the Prince told Ponsonby. 'But when I know who it is for, I will not give it.'[110] In the end, the disputed bit of land was added to the Queen's shooting, whereupon Prince Albert Edward claimed that he had been tricked out of it. Delegated as peace-maker, Ponsonby began by asking the

---

* Eight years were to transpire before Sahl, in June, 1877, again asked for a pony, and when he did he was 'trembling and blushing', according to Sir Henry Ponsonby, who added, 'I myself had a fit of the giggles . . .'[110]

Prince why he had decided to boycott Balmoral in the coming autumn:

PRINCE: Suppose I refuse to tell you.

PONSONBY: Then I will have to take back that answer, Sir.

PRINCE: Well, I will tell you that there are so many bothers and troubles about the shooting that I don't care about it. Shooting is pleasant when it is free, but the minute it is hampered with this or that regulation it becomes a bore. Then Grant says he can't take orders from Brown and so on. I don't want to enter into all this, but I am actually compelled to do so.

PONSONBY: I don't think it necessary that I should repeat to Her Majesty about Grant and Brown, but I will tell her what you have said about the inconvenience.[110]

'You say you wish the Prince had the pluck to say how he hates JB', Ponsonby wrote to his wife. 'He does say so to me, and that, as he is brought into such prominence at Balmoral, is one of the reasons he hates Balmoral.'

The Queen's children and members of her Household might hate Brown but, in such delicate matters as the breaking of bad news to Queen Victoria, it was usually Brown who was chosen for the task.* The Queen herself acknowledged Brown's unique abilities as a comforter when her baby grandson, Prince Sigismund, had died suddenly in 1866, and again when her favourite preacher, the Rev. Norman Macleod, died in 1872 ('My tears flowed fast, but I . . . thanked good Brown for the very kind way he broke this painful and unexpected news to me').[146] In December, 1878, Brown was once more the bearer of bad tidings to the

---

* Occasionally, the Queen herself employed Brown on errands of this kind. Thus, early in February, 1881, Brown was dispatched to No. 24 Cheyne Row, in Chelsea, to enquire after Mr Thomas Carlyle, only to learn that Carlyle had passed away that very day.

Queen, this time telling of the death of her own daughter, Princess Alice, the Grand Duchess of Hesse.

Princess Alice had come down with diphtheria on December 8, having nursed her five children through this disease and, in the process, having watched the youngest of them die. At first the prognosis was hopeful, according to Sir William Jenner, whom the Queen had dispatched to Darmstadt immediately to assist at her daughter's bedside. But by December 13 the disease had spread to the Princess's windpipe, and she was having difficulty breathing. That night Bertie and Leopold came to their mother's room to calm her fears (she was agitated, but did not overlook the fact that both sons were improperly dressed; they wore 'sort of smoking jackets, for which they made many excuses'.). And so it was that early the following morning Brown appeared with the dreaded news in the form of a telegram from the Queen's son-in-law, Prince Louis of Hesse: 'Poor Mama, poor me, my happiness gone, dear, dear Alice. God's will be done.'[148] It was seventeen years to the day since the Prince Consort had passed away, a coincidence which the Queen was probably not alone in finding 'almost incredible . . . most mysterious'.

Princess Alice was the most intelligent and talented of Queen Victoria's children, with a zeal for sanitary housing reform which would have made her father proud. (It was Her Royal Highness who translated into German Octavia Hill's essays *On the Homes of the London Poor*.)[3] It was said that Princess Alice was an agnostic and that the walls of her sitting-room at the Neue Palais, Darmstadt were covered with framed Positivist mottoes, as well as with William Morris wallpaper; but when Ponsonby visited the Neue Palais after her death the only framed quotation he could find was one hanging above the window where her tiny son, Prince Frederick William, had fallen to his death in 1873, which read: 'Suffer little children to come unto me.'

11

THE OLD FACES FADE

IT was while accompanying Queen Victoria on holiday in Italy that John Brown, in the Spring of 1879, suffered his first severe attack of erysipelas. This time there could be no doubt as to the nature of his illness, for the inflammation affected not only his legs, but quickly spread to his face. Erysipelas of the face is not only painful, but gruesome to behold, for the victim's features swell beyond recognition: the ears thicken as do the lips, blebs form on the eyelids, the eyes themselves are forced shut, and as the swelling reaches the forehead, it advances as a perfectly defined ridge. Fortunately, the attacks are not of long duration, from four to eight days being the average; but Brown's condition, for which Sir William Jenner ordered complete rest, lasted quite long enough to spoil the Queen's holiday.

It was in headlong flight from the memory of Princess Alice's death that Victoria had settled on Italy. By now the Queen had formed the habit of taking a short Spring holiday on the Continent, usually in Germany, before going to Balmoral. But Germany, of course, was out of the question because of its associations with her daughter. ('I could not bear to go there this Spring,' the Queen confided in her journal.) Switzerland was too cold; this left Italy, which 'I have long desired to see', and so it was arranged that Her Majesty should visit Baveno, on Lake Maggiore. But even on the Continent death pursued her. During an overnight stop in Paris, she learned that her grandchild, Vicky's darling boy Prince Waldemar, had passed away, a victim of haemophilia ('this awful disease').

At Baveno it rained most of the time and the Queen was confined indoors at the Villa Clara, which overlooked the lake and the Borromean Islands in the middle of it. However, on those quick sorties which she permitted herself between rain squalls, what impressed Her Majesty the most were the pigs ('such dreadful queer-looking pigs, as thin as greyhounds') and the children ('they know me quite well, and call out "La Regina d'Inghilterra" ').[148] On one occasion Ponsonby hid behind a wall and spied on La Regina as she made her sightseeing rounds of the village. 'Two carabinieri . . . appeared at a slow march, followed by the Anglo-Italian coachman, then by Brown and the Queen and Miss Cadogan (a Maid of Honour), and by Jemmy Machendy, the young piper, whose kilt created the greatest amusement among the old women.'[110]

It was not long after the Queen's arrival at Baveno that Brown came down with erysipelas, and as a precaution against contagion the Highlander was isolated from the Queen and her entourage. This completely upset the Queen's plans to visit Venice, where a palazzo had been placed at her disposal by a wealthy Scottish merchant named Malcolm. (According to one report, Malcolm had planned to dress his gondoliers in kilts so that the Queen would feel at home.) Within a fortnight Brown was well enough to go back on the box, but he remained morose for the balance of the holiday. To protect his head from the sun, he wore a wide-brimmed black hat which gave him the look of 'an English parson on a holiday tour who is not enjoying himself', as Ponsonby wrote to his wife. Not only was the Highlander 'surly beyond measure', according to Ponsonby, but he was determined that the Queen should not enjoy herself. She dare not stop the carriage to admire the scenic beauties for fear of incurring his reproachful looks. 'Today', Ponsonby told his wife, 'we could see Brown all the way—a beautiful drive—with his eyes fixed on the horses' tails, refusing to look up . . . it prevents the Queen seeing anything.'[110]

The Queen laboured under the illusion that with a Highlander on the box, she could travel about Italy incognito

without attracting attention, but an excursion to Milan soon
put this notion to rout. There the Queen, as she visited the
Duomo, was followed by a small army of Italians, and was
soon complaining that there were not enough police to hold
the curiosity-seekers in check. ('If she had gone as Queen we
might have had fifty police', Ponsonby protested.) After
visiting the Duomo, Her Majesty went for a drive in the
surrounding countryside, with Ponsonby and other members
of her entourage following on behind. 'I stopped the
carriage once', Ponsonby related, 'and ran back to tell her
these were San Lorenzo's columns. But this stopping of the
carriage was coldly received and a crowd began to assemble
to see the Highlander, and so we went on—and I didn't
trouble them again.'[110]

May, 1879, marked two milestones in Queen Victoria's life:
she celebrated her sixtieth birthday, and she became a great
grandmother for the first time,* the latter event calling
forth congratulations from Lord Beaconsfield,† who never
overlooked such an occasion. 'He remembers the birth of
the royal "great grandmother" herself', Dizzy, who was
then in his seventy-fifth year, reminisced, 'and little did he
think then that he should be her servant and counsellor.'[148]
Dizzy's days in office as the Queen's First Minister were,
however, drawing to a close. After his triumphal return
from Berlin bringing with him the 'peace with honour' that
had ended the Russo-Turkish hostilities, the old wizard
appeared exhausted, and already his arch-rival Gladstone
was warming up in the wings.

Lord Beaconsfield's failing health highlighted Queen
Victoria's dilemma in her effort to keep the clock hands
frozen at the moment of Albert's death, December 14, 1861.

---

* On May 12 Vicky's eldest daughter, Princess Charlotte of Saxe-
Meiningen, gave birth to a daughter. When Queen Victoria died in
1901 she was survived by thirty-one grandchildren, of whom seventeen were married, and by thirty-seven great grandchildren.

† Disraeli was elevated to the peerage as the Earl of Beaconsfield on
August 12, 1876.

For having refused, as far as possible, to have new faces about her, she was to find herself singularly bereft as the old faces faded away. Already some of the old faces were missing. Sir Thomas Biddulph, the Keeper of the Privy Purse, had passed away, as had John Grant, the Queen's Head Keeper, whose pawky humour the Prince Consort had found so entertaining. They were soon followed by Dr Andrew Robertson, the Queen's Balmoral Factor, who, in his early practice as a country doctor, had brought a whole generation of Crathie parishioners into the world. Queen Victoria now braced herself for the loss of Lord Beaconsfield, who was suffering from a combination of Bright's disease, bronchitis and asthma. (In his last three years Dizzy was kept alive largely through the efforts of a homeopath who prescribed claret, among other unorthodox remedies.)

In April, 1880, although she had threatened to abdicate rather than do so, Queen Victoria was forced to take Gladstone for the second time as her Prime Minister. But the switch made no difference in the Queen's friendship for Disraeli, which grew more intimate, if possible. With little regard for Constitutional niceties, the Queen continued to consult Gladstone's rival on policy matters, and to assure Dizzy that 'what has happened is only a horrid dream.' Quickly dropping the formal third person in her letters to Dizzy, she wrote, 'I often think of you—indeed constantly —and rejoice to see you looking down from the wall after dinner.' (Lord Beaconsfield's portrait by von Angeli hung in the dining-room at Windsor.) Again, she lamented, 'Oh! if only I had you, my kind friend and wise counsellor and strong arm to help and lean on!'[22]

That other strong arm upon whom the Queen was accustomed to lean, John Brown, likewise remained steadfast to Dizzy in his hour of adversity. Brown consoled his hero by sending him salmon freshly caught in the Dee. In writing to thank him for one such 'Leviathan' Dizzy expressed the hope that 'some day you may throw a fly into the humble waters of Hughenden'. After the arrival of still more salmon, Dizzy wrote to the Queen in May, 1880, 'No man has been more faithful to me in my fallen fortunes than the fisherman . . . '[14]

In the few months remaining Lord Beaconsfield continued to haunt the drawing-rooms of the wealthy and the socially powerful, 'moving still, an assiduous mummy from dinner party to dinner party', in Lytton Strachey's phrase.[136] The mummy comparison is an apt one, for Dizzy's face had become like a death mask, with the skin stretched tight, and the pallor accentuated by his hair, dyed coal black. It was shortly after dining with the Prince of Wales at Marlborough House that the elderly statesman caught the chill which hastened his end. Dizzy died quietly at his Curzon Street home on April 19, 1881. Towards the end, when asked if he would like a visit from the Queen, Dizzy showed a flash of his old wit. 'No, it is better not,' he replied. 'She would only ask me to take a message to Albert.'[14]

Brown, who was delegated to break the news of Dizzy's death to Queen Victoria, took the loss almost as badly as did his Royal Mistress, who described it as 'a national calamity'. ('My poor faithful Brown was quite overcome when he had to tell me,' the Queen informed Lord Rowton, Dizzy's secretary and lifelong friend.)[14] When the Highlander had recovered sufficiently he started a subscription among the servants and Royal Household to erect a monument to his hero, only to run into heavy opposition. 'The first person asked to subscribe,' Ponsonby related, 'was Miss Pitt, who flatly refused to give one halfpenny towards perpetuating the memory of Beaconsfield.'[110] The gesture, however, was characteristic of Brown's generosity. He was always the first to pass the hat, whether it was to buy a wedding present for one of the Royal family, or to help out a servant who was down on his luck.

Brown had other positive qualities, including geniality as a host. Lord Ribblesdale's valet told his master of the many pleasant evenings he had spent in Brown's company, while his lordship was being entertained by the Queen. 'He appeared to be a favourite,' Lord Ribblesdale recalled, 'and Mr Brown invited him to his room where, over whisky and tobacco, they went into committee on the state of the nation.'[122] Brown's politics were simplicity itself, his views being coloured largely by the Queen's prejudices. Occasionally, however, he differed sharply from his Royal Mistress on political matters. This happened when the question arose of the Queen's assumption of the title 'Empress of India' by Act of Parliament in May, 1876. Brown held that the Imperial title added nothing to her lustre. It happened again in 1877 when Britain stood in danger of becoming involved in the Russo-Turkish war. Asked by Ponsonby if he favoured war, Brown spluttered, 'Dammit—I beg your pardon—no. I think it would be awful—dreadful deal of fighting, and at the end no one would be better and a' would be worse for it.'[111] One has only to contrast this with some of Queen Victoria's more bellicose utterances of this period ('Oh, if the Queen were a man, she would ... give those Russians ... such a beating!')[22] to see that the Queen and her servant did not see eye to eye on this issue at least.

So much has been written in denigration of Brown that it is pleasant to report an earlier episode where the Highlander's generosity of spirit again contrasted sharply with the attitude of his Royal Mistress. This episode goes back to the terrible winter of 1868-69, when unemployment reached its highest peak in twenty years, with over a million persons on the relief rolls. Queen Victoria might be excused if the plight of this ragged army was not vivid to her mind, for a million is a large number for the mind to comprehend; but 6,000 of the neediest cases were dockyard workers and their families of Portsmouth, Hampshire, which is on the doorstep of the Queen's residence at Osborne. If Her Majesty was aware of their suffering she gave no sign.

Many of the shipwrights and mechanics thrown out of work when the Admiralty shut down the Portsmouth dockyard were forced to sell their furniture in order to feed their families, and they ended by begging in the streets. The *Hampshire Telegraph* gives this description of a typical dwelling that had thus been stripped of every saleable item: 'There was not a chair in the room, nor a spark of fire in the grate, and in a corner sat the mother with her infant a week old, pale and shivering, without food . . .'

It may have been this, or a similar harrowing scene described in the press that caught Brown's eye, and prompted him to take up a collection among the servants at Osborne. The sum thus realized was considerable and was duly acknowledged in a paragraph in *The Times* of February 22, 1869, which I quote in its entirety:

HER MAJESTY'S SERVANTS AND THE DISCHARGED DOCK-YARD WORKERS: The Committee of the Portsmouth Dockyard Discharged Workmen's Relief Association thankfully acknowledges through the medium of *The Times* the receipt of £22.16s.6d. subscribed by Mr John Brown and the Queen's servants at the Royal establishment now at Osborne, and forwarded to the chairman of the committee, Mr S. J. Vine, by Mr Backler, of the Royal yacht.

During the last years of his life, Brown, when at Balmoral, enjoyed the use of an imposing two-storey house of grey Aberdeen stone, which the Queen caused to be built for him in redemption of an earlier promise. Although the Queen christened it *Baile-na-choil* (meaning 'house in the woods'), the house became better known as 'Brown's Wick', an allusion to its owner's close affinity with the House of Brunswick. The Queen intended that the house should be Brown's Patmos in the event she predeceased him, and that it should revert to Brown's relatives in perpetuity following his death, which explains the pencilled notation in her handwriting, 'What does this mean?' opposite the 'Forfeiture & Irritancy' clause in the lease.[78] When completed, this 'princely residence', as the newspapers described it, was elegantly furnished. The chairs and other items of furniture bore the Royal coat of arms, and the walls were adorned with portraits of members of the Royal Family, including a signed portrait of Her Majesty the Queen, dated 1877. It was, as Emily Crawford described it, a house 'any laird might be glad to live in'.[27]

After Brown's death, the more sensational weeklies hinted that *Baile-na-choil* was one vast storehouse of loot that Brown had amassed during his lifetime. *Truth* estimated his fortune at £20,000, adding, 'Brown has certainly feathered his nest well . . . seeing that when he entered the Royal service a "stable gillie" he possessed nothing.' *The World*, on the other hand, claimed that the fortune consisted largely of 'beautiful and costly pieces of plate and articles of jewelry', explaining that, 'Every distinguished visitor to the Court was told that it would be well to remember Brown . . .' Jerrold, in repeating these allegations, goes on to infer that Brown took bribes: 'He (Brown) was said to take large percentages from the tradesmen, and in return would, when possible, give them his help.'[71]

The trouble with Jerrold and his journalistic colleagues is that none of them has bothered to check the facts. Had they done so, they would have discovered that Brown, who died intestate, left an estate valued not at £20,000, but at one-third of that amount—£6,816.9s.11d., to be exact— which consisted largely of bank deposits at Windsor, Ballater, and Braemar (apparently Brown was safeguarding himself against the possibility that one of these banks fail). As for the 'beautiful and costly pieces of plate and articles of jewelry' with which *Baile-na-choil* was said to be stocked, the entire contents of this house, including Brown's personal effects, as assessed by inventory filed in Aberdeen, were valued at no more than £379.19s.6d. George IV did better by his favourite servants, according to the diarist Greville. Holmes, a Page of the Backstairs, had an income of £12,000 a year, thanks to various appointments and perquisites. As for Batchelor, the *valet de chambre*, George IV gave him the Windsor apartment formerly occupied by Nell Gwynne.[56]*

Not one scintilla of evidence has been produced which would link Brown to bribe-taking, or to any other form of influence-peddling for financial reward. To the contrary— Sir Henry Ponsonby, who had ample opportunity to study Brown at close quarters, was convinced of his integrity. 'I believe he was honest', Ponsonby wrote after Brown's death, 'and with all his want of education, his roughness, his prejudices and other faults he was a most excellent servant.'[111] This verdict was echoed by friends and neighbours who had known Brown since he was a stable-lad, and in an in-bred community like Crathie the neighbours were often the best judges of a man's character. Visiting Crathie shortly after Brown's death, F. P. Humphrey talked to one of the cottars about the Queen's Highland servant. 'Favourite servants', the cottar mused, 'as a general thing gain their high places by under-hand practice . . . But John Brown wasn't that kind of man. He was honest to bluntness, spoke his mind right out to high and low.'[65]

Although honest, Brown, like many simple people, was susceptible to flattery, a weakness which Windsor tradesmen undoubtedly learned to use to their advantage. there were lifted eyebrows when a good many local tradesmen who were known to be John Brown's friends were spotted among the guests at Prince Leopold's wedding in St George's Chapel, Windsor, in April 1882.† According to *Truth*, these shopkeepers and purveyors 'were seated on the chairs in front, while Peers and Peeresses and persons well known in 'society' were standing behind'. *The World*

---

* Batchelor died on June 22, 1868, at the age of 83, having served four monarchs, George III, George IV, William IV, and Queen Victoria.

† Prince Leopold, to whom Queen Victoria had given 'Duncan' as one of his names, was considered to be the Scot of the family. Unfortunately, within 18 months of his marriage the Prince was dead, having suffered a brain haemorrhage while on holiday with his wife at Cannes.

added that some of the commercial element were even invited to the wedding *dejeuner* 'thanks to the intervention of their powerful friend.'

No one knew how to play upon Brown's weakness better than Sir John Bennett, watchmaker and jeweller of East Cheap, London, and one-time Sheriff of the City of London. In the former capacity Sir John used to call with his sample case at Windsor Castle on the eve of Royal birthdays or other great occasions, in the hopes that some trinket might take the Queen's fancy. But Her Majesty's taste did not run to jewelry in the matter of gifts, and so Bennett usually went away empty-handed, as far as orders were concerned. Seeing Bennett in a chap-fallen mood after one of these visits, one of the Equerries took pity on him, suggested a way in which the jeweller might redeem his fortunes.

'Brown is hovering about the Stewards' Room where you are to lunch—ask him to lunch with you,' the Equerry suggested. Seeing Bennett's look of bewilderment, he explained, 'If you make much of Brown you will gratify you-know-whom.' Sir John needed no further prompting, but went up to the gillie and introduced himself, saying, 'Mr Brown, I am a great admirer of your part of Scotland. It's a bonnie country, and most so on Deeside.' He then invited the Highlander to share the lunch which the Queen had ordered for him in the Stewards' Room—'it will help my appetite to hear good plain Scotch from the mouth of a Crathie man.' Brown not only accepted the invitation, but produced the keys to the Queen's wine cellar, and the jeweller was treated to a succession of superlative wines that had been put down in the reign of George IV. After lunch Sir John was summoned to an audience with the Queen, who ordered nearly everything he showed her from his sample case, and who thereafter 'remained as good a customer as Sir John could wish'.[27]

Another anecdote of this period presents John Brown in an amiable light, and shows to what celebrity he had attained in the closing years of his life. It concerns a visit which Queen Victoria paid to the Royal Infirmary at Edinburgh in the autumn of 1881. Among those invited to meet the Queen on this occasion was the elderly Lady Ruthven, whom Ponsonby describes as being blind, deaf, and shouting 'like six Sergeant Majors'. During a lull while the assemblage was awaiting the Queen's arrival, Lady Ruthven's voice could be heard booming, 'Tell me, Bailie Mucklewaite, why is she so tardy?' Not hearing the reply, her Ladyship continued relentlessly, 'I love the Queen—I long to see the Queen—but I came here to see John Brown.'[110]

On March 2, 1882, a group of Eton boys, in top hats and tails, were on hand at Windsor station to cheer Queen Victoria when she arrived by train from London at 5.30 p.m. After the train had pulled into the station, John Brown hurried along the platform to open the door of the Queen's railway carriage, while Sir Henry Ponsonby came forward to escort the Queen and Princess Beatrice through the waiting-room to their closed carriage. The carriage, with Brown on the box, had not gone more than fifteen yards when the Queen heard what she thought was an explosion from the locomotive engine, but what was in fact a shot fired at her. It was the seventh and last of the public outrages to which she was subjected, and undoubtedly the most dangerous of them all. This time it was no broken flintlock stuffed with bits of paper that was aimed at her but a loaded, six-chambered revolver capable of rapid fire.

Superintendent George Hayes, of the Windsor police, who was present in an official capacity when the Royal train arrived at Windsor station, heard the explosion at close quarters, and glanced left in time to see a man taking aim with the revolver for a second shot at the Queen's carriage. 'I immediately sprang at him,' Superintendent Hayes later told the examining magistrates. 'I caught him by the collar and neck, and bent down to take his firearm from him.' Just then an Eton boy rushed up and began belabouring the

man with an umbrella (according to some accounts, the
Etonian's umbrella struck the assailant's arm and thus
deflected his aim). On the way to the police station in a
hired cab, the prisoner gave his name to Superintendent
Hayes as Roderick Maclean, said he was a Scottish poet, and
that he was starving, 'otherwise I would not have done
this'.*

Surprisingly, Queen Victoria was not nearly so shaken or
frightened at being fired at with live ammunition as she had
been at the earlier O'Connor outrage, when frankly she had
been terrified. 'Took tea with Beatrice, and telegraphed to
all my children and near relatives,' she recorded in her
journal under date of March 2, 1882. 'Brown came in to say
that the revolver had been found loaded, and one chamber
discharged.'[148]

Mention of Brown raises the question of the Highlander's
whereabouts during the fracas at the railway station. In his
biography of Brown, Tisdall tries to make the Highlander
the hero of the occasion: 'The carriage stopped, Brown
leaped from the rumble and rushed to seize Maclean . . .
Brown, who had torn Maclean from the arms of the others
and grasped him by both wrists, turned his head and shouted
to the Queen, "Get on wid ye." . . . Brown's figure was so
commanding that no one questioned his exclusive right to
the prisoner, until the policeman . . . came running up.'[139]

This account, including the colourful 'Get on wid ye', is
pure invention, as is evident from Superintendent Hayes's
sworn testimony in court. The truth was that Brown, far
from being a commanding figure, was nowhere in the
picture. Not only was he slow in getting down from the
rumble—could his leg have been bothering him?—but the

---

* With prophetic insight *Spectator* pointed out what would have
been the consequences had the Queen's assailant been named Macarthy
instead of Maclean: 'No conceivable evidence would have convinced
the country that the Land Leaguers were not responsible or have
induced them for half-a-century to trust any popular party in Ireland.'
Two months later Irish assassins struck down Lord Frederick Caven-
dish and T. H. Burke in Phoenix Park, Dublin.

Highlander appears to have had difficulty in comprehending what was going on and, according to Queen Victoria, could only repeat, with a 'greatly perplexed' face, 'That man fired at Your Majesty's carriage.'

Clearly Brown had been napping on the box, and in his place a new hero, or rather heroine, emerged—Princess Beatrice. Queen Victoria's journal was full of praise for this youngest daughter, 'my Benjamin', as she called her. 'Nothing', the Queen wrote, 'can exceed dearest Beatrice's courage and calmness, for she saw the whole thing, the man take aim and fire straight into the carriage, but she never said a word, observing that I was not frightened.'[148] In a letter to the Empress Augusta, the Queen also spoke of 'my dear Beatrice (who) appeared very quiet and courageous . . .'[150] Not a word about Brown, except to note his bewildered demeanour.

Roderick Maclean was one of the few poets who have looked to assassination as a means of avenging a rejection slip. For at Maclean's trial for high treason at Reading, Berkshire, police disclosed that they had found in his lodgings some verses dedicated to Her Majesty. Pinned to them was a letter written on Buckingham Palace stationery and reading, 'Lady Biddulph is obliged to return Mr Maclean his verses. The Queen never accepts manuscript poetry.' The Scot was mentally unbalanced, like the majority of Queen Victoria's assailants. He had suffered a brain injury in 1866 as the result of a fall and had been discharged from the Bath and Somerset lunatic asylum less than a year before his attempt on the Queen.

In the Reading courtroom Maclean presented a seedy, destitute appearance. His green great-coat was faded and had a worn velvet collar, and a flowing black tie only partially concealed the frayed edges of his shirt. 'Few who looked upon him had any doubt that insanity had marked him for its own', Montagu Williams, Q.C., who defended him, recalled, adding, 'With a vacant, imbecile expression, he kept glancing hither and thither about the crowded Court.'[63] After listening to eight medical witnesses testify that Maclean was of unsound mind, the jury found him 'not guilty on the ground of insanity', and he was ordered to be detained during Her Majesty's pleasure.*

Queen Victoria, however, left for Mentone before the Maclean case came on for trial. It was her first visit to the French Riviera, later to become a favourite holiday spot. This time Brown, having been caught napping once, nearly drove everyone crazy with his exaggerated concern for the Queen's safety, professing to see Fenians lurking behind every palm tree. Three of the Irish Republican Brotherhood were in fact reported to be heading for Mentone from Paris, but Sir Henry Ponsonby investigated and found the report to be the usual hoax. In thanking Ponsonby for his reassurances, the Queen wrote, 'She trusts Sir Henry will also reassure Brown who was in such a state heightened by his increasing *hatred* of being "abroad" which blinds his admiration of the country even.'[111] The reason Brown detested Mentone, in particular, was that no one there professed to understand English, much less his special brand of Scottish dialect. ('He can communicate with no one when out, nor keep anyone off the carriage, nor the coachman either', the Queen explained.) Another reason why Brown was so miserable was that the huge pith helmet which he wore at Mentone to keep the sun off his face had become 'an object of the greatest interest to all the country people in the neighbourhood of Mentone', according to *The World*. (Word flew around that Brown was in fact the Lord Mayor of London.)

Mention of the Lord Mayor calls to mind that Brown,

---

* Queen Victoria was furious with this verdict. 'If that is the law,' she stormed, 'the law must be altered.' And altered it was by an 1883 Act which substituted 'guilty but insane'. The anomaly thus created (a striking instance of the power the Queen exercised over her Ministers) remained on the statute books for 81 years, until Parliament in July, 1964, acted to restore the original statutory verdict of 'not guilty on the ground of insanity.'

resplendent in his native regalia, was very much in evidence when the Queen drove down the Strand to open the new Law Courts in December, 1882. On this, one of the last occasions that Brown was seen by the larger public, a bystander was overheard to remark, 'Everything considered, he looks well . . . He shows no signs of suffering from his duty.'

Probably the last glimpse the public had of Brown was early in March, 1883, when the Queen was out driving in an open carriage in Windsor and a shower came on. Those who braved the rain to see the Queen were amused by Brown's solicitude. From his elevated perch behind, he opened first the Queen's umbrella and handed it to her without a word being exchanged. He then handed an umbrella each to the ladies riding with the Queen, and motioned for them to hoist the umbrellas without delay.

The Queen, now in her sixties, had not altered her habit of driving about in an open carriage in defiance of the elements. This continual exposure to the raw British climate resulted in crippling rheumatism for Princess Beatrice, the Queen's usual companion on these outings, who was forced to seek treatment in the south of France. It also had a deleterious effect on John Brown's health, already seriously undermined by over-indulgence and lack of exercise. In an ex post facto article, *Lancet* warned of 'the depressing effects of a suddenly or persistently lowered temperature' upon even a robust constitution such as Brown's. 'A somewhat long drive in an open trap on a bleak day, and an hour or two spent standing about in the cold, might prove more than even his hardy frame could bear' the medical journal declared. This was precisely what was now to transpire. That once rugged physique, nurtured on a diet of brose and kail, was to prove no match for the inclemencies of March. That constitution, once sound, was to succumb to the treacherous mist that arises from the Thames at Windsor. Mist, a Fenian scare, a hysterical woman, and a St Bernard dog named Hubert—these sound like the ingredients of a

Sherlock Holmes story. As it happened they were links in the causal chain that was to encompass the death of John Brown, that 'child of nature', as Ponsonby had called him.

12

DEATH OF A HERO

To take the hysterical woman first, Lady Florence Dixie enters this story on March 2, 1883, when, at her Windsor home, The Fishery, she sat down to write Queen Victoria a letter concerning the starving peasants in Western Ireland, a subject on which her ladyship was well informed. Lady Florence, aged twenty-six, was, however, everything that the Queen disliked most in a woman. To begin with, she was a big game huntress, a 'female Nimrod', as she described herself in later years after she had turned against blood sports. Then she was an advocate of sex equality—'this mad, wicked folly', as Queen Victoria had once defined it— and of 'rational dress' reform, which meant the right of women to wear trousers. Of more enduring interest, Lady Florence was the sister of the pugnacious 8th Marquis of Queensberry, and as such Lord Alfred Douglas's aunt. Her marriage in 1875 to Sir Beaumont Dixie seems to have whetted her appetite for travel and adventure, and it was while exploring Patagonia with her husband that Lady Florence captured 'Affums', a jaguar which, transported to England, was soon to prove the terror of Windsor Great Park.

Although they were neighbours at Windsor, so to speak, Queen Victoria had another reason for remembering Lady Florence. In the late 1870s her ladyship had created a stir by appearing at one of the Queen's Drawing-rooms with her hair cropped boyish fashion and minus the required plumes and lace veil, all of which was *lese majesté* in the Queen's eyes. Her Majesty had been brought up to believe that no lady was properly dressed at a Court function unless three white plumes could be seen to be standing erect from the back of her head, and accompanied by lappets or a veil.

When a lady whose hair had fallen out during scarlet fever asked permission to appear at a Drawing-room wearing a Dolly Varden cap with the feathers and lappets pinned to it, the Lord Chamberlain replied that the Queen was 'amused', but 'H.M. says decidedly no'. Similarly those with delicate chest conditions had to apply to the Lord Chamberlain for permisson to appear at Court in high-necked gowns, the low-cut bodices of her girlhood days being favoured by the Queen. (The Lord Chamberlain's files are full of such applications, usually accompanied by a doctor's certificate and frequently with the single word 'Granted' scrawled in the Queen's handwriting on the back.) It is understandable, therefore, that Lady Florence Dixie's breach of etiquette should draw Royal wrath on her shorn head in the form of a sharp reprimand from the Lord Chamberlain's office.

This incident together with her ladyship's reputation as a feminist, no doubt crossed Queen Victoria's mind when Lady Florence's letter concerning the Irish question was brought to Her Majesty's attention. However, the letter, on its own terms, made sense. As the owner of a large estate near Ballina, County Mayo, Lady Florence held enlightened views concerning tenant evictions although she was unalterably opposed to Charles Parnell and his Irish Land League. ('What care Mr Parnell or his whole troop of followers what becomes of the poor starving peasants of the West, so long as they can fill their pockets with much-coveted gold?' she wrote to *The Times*.) Her letter to the Queen, moreover, contained the sensible suggestion that these same starving peasants should be given money grants and set to work reclaiming the land. It was only in subjecting Lady Florence's views to a closer examination that one might detect the note of hysteria which lay behind them, and which Queen Victoria would have done well to heed.

On Monday, March 19, Queen Victoria was coming downstairs to go for her afternoon drive in Windsor Great Park when she missed the last step, and, to save herself from falling, came down hard on one leg, thus twisting her knee. 'I could not move for a moment', she noted in her journal later. 'Then Brown came, and helped me with great difficulty into the carriage.'[148] The Queen would have done well had she re-entered immediately and taken to her bed, for by the time she returned from her drive her knee had swelled so badly that she had to be lifted from the phaeton and carried to her room by Brown and Lockwood, the footman.

Barely three miles away at this moment Lady Florence Dixie was arriving home on foot, and her condition was even more lamentable than that of the Queen. Her clothing was caked with mud and in a state of disarray, her face likewise was mud-streaked, her hands were bleeding from knife wounds through the leather gloves she was wearing—all of this according to the story which Lady Florence later gave to the press. When Lady Florence had taken her dog, Hubert, for a walk earlier in the afternoon in the plantation which skirted her estate, she noticed that she was being followed at a distance by what appeared to be two women, but what later proved to be two men in female disguise, according to her ladyship. At a suitably isolated spot, these two transvestites set upon her with murderous intent. Here is her story as she gave it to a Press Association representative:

'One of them seized me roughly by the neck, pushed me backwards, and threw me to the ground with great violence. The other man, his confederate . . . was standing over me . . . I saw in his hand a sort of dagger . . . I saw a momentary flash of steel, and then I felt the blade go through the upper part of my dress here (*pointing to the spot*). Luckily the blade came in contact with one of the steel stays of my corset and glanced off . . .

. . . the wretch withdrew it, and plunged at me again with the dagger. As it descended I caught hold of the blade with my left hand, and held it for a moment. The weapon cut through my glove, and inflicted a deep but clean cut. (*Here her ladyship showed her hand, and pointed to a strip of sticking plaster covering a cut over an inch in length*). He wrenched the weapon from me, and as it slipped from my left I caught it with my right hand . . .

Then I lost my hold upon the knife . . . He was about to deliver the third (stab attempt) when the dog must have pulled him off . . . Then I became unconscious . . . When I regained consciousness I found myself quite alone,'

Lady Florence's story created a sensation, as may well be imagined, but discrepancies in it were not long in coming to light. Notably it was contradicted by a number of eye-witnesses. Lady Florence, it transpired, was under continuous observation from the time she entered the wood until she left it, thanks to the plantation's close proximity to the Maidenhead road, and to the fact that it was but sparsely planted. A passing soldier, Private Bates, of the Scots Guards, had noticed her ladyship because he was 'struck with the beauty of the St Bernard dog which was with her'. But he had seen nothing of her assailants, nor had he heard any cry or noise of any kind. Groves, a gardener on a neighbouring estate, who had been working not more than thirty yards from the plantation, likewise had heard nothing. The most damaging statement of all, however, came from an Eton College master, who happened to be gathering primroses near the plantation at the hour when the assault allegedly took place. The schoolmaster said that he had kept Lady Florence within his sight the whole of the time, and that he had seen her walk quietly off in the direction of The Fishery.

Meanwhile Scotland Yard's forensic experts had examined her clothing and found that the cuts in her ladyship's outer garments did not correspond with the incisions made in her underclothing. Nor was there the slightest trace of mud on the back of her dress, as would have been the case had she been thrown to the ground violently, as she claimed. L'Affaire Dixie was officially closed on March 30 when the Home Secretary, Sir William Harcourt, in reply to a question in the House of Commons, told Members that the police had discovered nothing to corroborate Lady Florence Dixie's statements.

Charitably, the *Daily News* suggested that Lady Florence had been beset by 'sturdy beggars', and that bomb outrages and other Irish terrorist activities had combined 'to affect her imagination, and to colour (of course, unconsciously) her narrative of events'. More to the point, the *British Medical Journal* dug up examples of hallucination that had come to the notice of Professor Legrand du Saulle, of the Salpêtrière hospital in Paris, where female hysterics 'laboured under the belief that they have been struck or stabbed by others, even after having inflicted blows and wounds upon themselves'. A simpler explanation was advanced by Louisa, the Countess of Antrim, who in her memoirs hinted that Lady Florence was under the influence of alcohol at the time of her 'misadventure'. According to this source, Sir Beaumont and Lady Florence Dixie were more familiarly known as 'Sir Sometimes and Lady Always Tipsy'.[7] The Countess of Antrim, who liked her gossip spiced with malice, is not the most reliable of witnesses.

Sunday, March 18, was a bitterly cold day in which the vernal promise that had driven an Eton master to seek primroses near the riverside at Windsor had vanished, swallowed up by a return of winter. Despite the sudden drop in temperature, John Brown chose to drive to The Fishery in an open dog-cart, with no protection from the elements other than his usual kilt and thin, broadcloth jacket. Brown had come at the Queen's request to carry out his own investigation of the crime, which was said to have been the work of Irish terrorists. 'We have reason to believe that the Invincibles have transferred the scene of their deeds from

Ireland to England,' declared *The Morning Post* in a leading article. News that a gang of Irish cut-throats was operating in the shadow of Windsor Castle (for it was thus that the story was given out by the press) had, of course, filled Queen Victoria with alarm—all the more so as she lay help-less with a wrenched knee.*

Sir Henry Ponsonby had called upon Lady Florence earlier, and was still at The Fishery when Brown arrived as reinforcement from Windsor Castle. Doubtless both were pleased to note that her ladyship appeared none the worse for her recent ordeal. 'Little minding the wounds in her hands she made tea for her guests as though nothing had occurred,' according to a reporter from *The Morning Post*, who was also present. 'Hubert,' the reporter added, 'was rolling himself in the grass outside the cottage and evidently enjoying . . . the caresses of Mr John Brown.' When Lady Florence invited Brown inside to join the others at tea, the Highlander was loud in his commiserations. 'What an infernal thing to do', the Queen's attendant exclaimed, glowering as though he would like to punch the heads of a dozen Irish Invincibles. When told that it was the St Bernard that had saved Lady Florence's life, Brown insisted that he must have a photograph of Hubert. 'If you don't have it made, Lady Florence, I'll have it made myself and pay the photographer,' he offered.

Brown had been sent to The Fishery not to palaver with the gentlefolk, but to conduct an on-the-spot investiga-tion of the crime; therefore, excusing himself, he drove to the plantation where Lady Florence had allegedly been stabbed. The Sherlock Holmes rôle was one that would have filled Brown's soul with delight. One can picture him combing the plantation for clues, examining every broken twig and

* As an indication of how nervous the Queen had been made by recent Irish outrages, including an explosion in Whitehall, she had earlier asked Scotland Yard to investigate a house near the castle where mysterious digging was in progress in the garden. The owner, as it turned out, was merely installing an ornamental fountain.

every trampled blade of grass in the hopes that it might yield the identity of Lady Florence's assailants. One can imagine, too, his disappointment in coming away empty-handed. 'The whole case so puzzled Mr Brown,' according to a Central News Agency report, 'that he spent considerable time in the open air making his inquiries, thus exposing himself to the bitter cold . . .' Most likely, too, Brown got his clothing wet in tramping about in the underbrush. The drive back to Windsor Castle in the open dog-cart did nothing to improve matters, so that by the time he arrived at his room in the Clarence Tower, Brown was thoroughly chilled, and coming down with a nasty cold.

Despite his cold, Brown refused to take to his bed, for his steadying hand was needed by the Queen just at this time. The swollen knee had been succeeded by painful rheumatic attacks, not unlike the 'flying gout' she had experienced in '71 as an aftermath of her illness. By Saturday, March 24, however, the Queen felt well enough for a drive in the open, and Brown and Lockwood, the footman, carried her down to the little pony-chair, which she had not used since 1865. What memories of those earlier days must have come flooding back to the Queen as, cocooned in wraps, she started out; for then, as now, she had been convalescent, not having recovered from the shock of Albert's death. The pony-chair had happier associations, for it was linked in the Queen's mind with Brown coming south to act as her permanent attendant. Pony-chair outings at Osborne, with Brown keeping up a steady stream of cheerful talk as he walked alongside her—this was what the Queen's physician had prescribed to renew Her Majesty's interest in life, and the experiment had succeeded beyond expectation. Now without warning, the Queen was to be deprived of this never-failing source of comfort.

On Saturday evening Brown was seen in Windsor, 'apparently in fair health, although still suffering from a cold', according to the Press Association. But later his cold grew worse and Sir William Jenner was summoned. By the following morning erysipelas had appeared on one side of Brown's face, and the swelling rapidly spread over his entire head, accompanied by high fever. It was Easter Sunday, but the joyous festival evoked no response in the Queen who wrote querulously in her journal, 'Had not a good night. Vexed that Brown could not attend me, not being at all well, with a swollen face, which it is feared is erysipelas.'[148] By Easter Monday Brown had become delirious.

Judging by her actions, Queen Victoria still had not grasped the seriousness of Brown's condition. With the aid of Lockwood and a cane, she managed to attend the christening of Prince Leopold's daughter in the private chapel at Windsor, and afterwards she listened to a Guards' band play the 'Alice of Albany' waltz composed specially in honour of her newly-baptized granddaughter. That afternoon she went for a drive in the Castle grounds with Princess Beatrice walking alongside the pony-chair. According to *The Times*, the swelling in the Queen's knee joint was 'gradually disappearing', but the knee was 'still rather stiff'. That night the Prince of Wales took his family to Her Majesty's Theatre in the Haymarket to see *A Trip to The Moon*, thereby inaugurating a flurry of theatre-going on the part of the Royal Family.

By Tuesday afternoon Brown had sunk into a coma from which he never regained consciousness. At 10.40 that night, the hour when the Prince of Wales and his suite were emerging from a performance of Offenbach's *Belle Lurette* at the Royal Avenue Theatre, Brown passed away, his brothers William and Archibald being at his bedside at the time. 'Erysipelas, 4 days', was given as the cause of death by James Reid, M.D., who signed his Death Certificate, but, unwittingly, a sentence from the obituary which Queen Victoria helped to compose sums it up better: 'During the last eighteen years and a half, he served Her Majesty constantly, and never once absented himself from his duty for a single day.'

'Weep with me for we all have lost the best, the truest heart that ever beat . . .' This wild, passionate outburst was addressed to those who had loved John Brown best, for it was to his relatives that Queen Victoria now turned for solace. 'As for me', she wrote to Jessie McHardy Brown, the wife of Hugh Brown, 'my grief is unbounded, dreadful, and I know not how to bear it, or how to believe it possible.'* Recalling how when she had left Balmoral the previous autumn 'we parted all so well and happy', the Queen poured out her heart: 'Dear, dear John—my dearest best friend to whom I could say everything and who always protected me so kindly and who thought of everything—was well and strong and hearty not 3 or 4 days before. And my accident worried him. He never took proper care, would not go out the whole time (a week) I was shut up and would not go to bed when he was ill.' She then fell back on that stoical resignation which had helped her to bear the deaths of her mother, her husband, and her daughter Alice. ' "The Lord gave—The Lord hath taken away. Blessed be the name of the Lord." . . . Dear excellent upright warm-hearted strong John' was already among the elect 'happy, blessing us and pitying us while we weep.' The letter to Jessie Brown ended on a note of envy. 'You', she concluded, 'have your husband—your support, but I have no strong arm now.'

The grief into which Queen Victoria was now plunged was nearly as great as that occasioned by the loss of the Prince Consort. She herself drew the parallel in a note to Sir Henry Ponsonby in which she described herself as 'utterly crushed'. 'Her life', she wrote, 'has again sustained one of those shocks like in '61 when every link has been shaken and torn . . .' Wherever she turned, 'the loss of the

---

* To appreciate the extent to which Queen Victoria's journals were re-written by Princess Beatrice one has only to compare this outburst with the matter-of-fact entry in the Queen's published journals: 'Am terribly upset by this loss, which removes one who was so devoted and attached to my service, etc.'

strong arm and wise advice, warm heart and cheery original way of saying things and the sympathy in any large and small circumstances—is most cruelly missed.'[111] Into this grief Gladstone now blundered with a letter of condolence which surely must rate as a model of tactlessness even for this most insensitive of Prime Ministers. Having noted that 'Your Majesty has been deprived by a sudden and fatal illness of the service of Mr J. Brown', whom he referred to as a 'domestic', Gladstone then went on to trust that 'Your Majesty may be able to select a good and efficient successor, though it may be too much to hope that anyone, however capable, could at once fill the void.'[57] In contrast to Gladstone's unfeeling attitude, Lord Rowton, who had been Disraeli's secretary, called in person to condole with the Queen over her great loss, as Disraeli would have done, had he been alive. It was just because Brown was irreplaceable that the Queen could not be consoled, and it was a measure of her despair that she should turn to those to whom Brown meant nothing and invite them to share her grief. Thus to her seventeen-year-old grandson, Prince George, the future King George V, she wrote, 'Never forget your poor sorrowing Grandmama's best and truest friend . . .'[78]

As happened to her at other moments of great emotional stress, the Queen temporarily lost the use of her legs, this apparently being the body's way of protecting the mind from the hurt it had sustained. It had occurred in 1861 when, according to Lady Clarendon, the Queen seemed 'hardly able to move one leg before the other'.[152] Again, in 1871, when the Queen had been under steady fire for her refusal to emerge from retirement and to take part in the life of the nation she had conveniently developed 'flying gout'. In the present instance, the Queen's wrenched knee initially made it impossible for her to walk unaided, but when her helplessness persisted after the swelling in her knee had gone down, her doctors concluded that her troubles were at least partly of psychogenic origin. As late as ten months after Brown's death the Queen still could not stand 'beyond a very few minutes', according to the Court Circular of January 21, 1884.

Queen Victoria was extremely sensitive about her semi-invalid state and gave this as her reason for banishing all male members of the Household from her dinner in the weeks immediately following Brown's death. 'How can I see people at dinner in the evening? I can't go walking about all night holding onto the back of a chair,' she complained to Ponsonby.[110] Again, it was the reason for the great secrecy which surrounded her journeys to Osborne and to Balmoral, secrecy which gave rise to all sorts of wild rumours that the Queen had lost her mind, and that the injured knee was being used as a blind to disguise the true state of affairs. But the Queen did not relish being seen by the public as she was carried to her railway carriage in a sort of sedan chair, and on one occasion at Perth a screen of large evergreens was placed around the Queen's railway coach to protect her from prying eyes. 'As if it were pleasant for any lady to be carried in and out of a carriage before crowds of people,' the Queen expostulated in a letter to Sir Theodore Martin.[96]

The state of the Queen's legs also resulted in Sir Henry Ponsonby being deluged by the public with suggested remedies, including one from a Mrs Cash advising that the Queen should ride a tricycle. 'Fancy the Queen on a tricycle,' Ponsonby wrote to his wife.[110]

But to return to the events that transpired immediately following Brown's death, the Highlander lay in state for six days in the Clarence Tower, Windsor, before being given what amounted to a hero's funeral. Meanwhile, the press dutifully published a Court Circular obituary which bore unmistakable signs of the Queen's composition. This 'imperial eulogy', as *The Daily Telegraph* called it, occupied twenty-five lines of the Court Circular of March 29th to inform the public of the 'grievous shock' sustained by the Queen in the loss of this 'honest, faithful, and devoted follower' who had secured for himself her 'real friendship'. One has only to compare this with the five lines which the Court Circular had devoted to the death of Lord Beaconsfield, that 'most valued and devoted friend and counsellor', to appreciate the unique position Brown occupied in the Queen's affections.

In addition, most of the national dailies carried long obituary articles, while the Scottish press resorted to poetry in describing John Brown's virtues. Typical of these poetic effusions is one which appeared in the *People's Journal* of Glasgow, describing in Scottish dialect how the Highlander rescued his 'sonsy Queen' from unnamed perils, and ending with the refrain:

> 'He's gane at length, though lo'ed by a'
> John Brown is deid!'

Another, entitled 'John Brown's Coronach', obviously owed something of its inspiration to Poe:

> 'No more will his bugle be heard in the forest,
> Where oft with the Prince he had wander'd of yore;
> . . . .
> The lively and loving John Brown—Nevermore!'

More like a 'coarse phonograph' than a bugle—this, at any rate, was the way that Railway Superintendent Neele had described Brown's voice.

Brown's death had been the signal for a general exodus on the part of the Royal Family, most of whose members found that they had pressing engagements in other parts. The Prince and Princess of Wales left on Wednesday for Sandringham, where they were to be hosts that week-end to the Prime Minister and the Archbishop of Canterbury. Prince Alfred, the Duke of Edinburgh, likewise departed hastily on Wednesday to open a dog show at Warwick, where Hubert, the saviour of Lady Florence Dixie, was the main attraction. The St Bernard proved to be singularly lethargic despite prods from Prince Alfred's walking-stick, but then 'a dog which has disregarded sharp knives was not likely to take any notice of a mere walking stick', as *The Warwick & Warwickshire Advertiser* pointed out. Prince Alfred managed to get back to London in time for the comic double-bill, *Uncle Dick's Darling* and *Mr Guffin's Elopement*, at Toole's Theatre that evening, bringing his total to the highest number of Royal theatre visits since the onset of Brown's illness. (In the week that elapsed between Brown's death and the funeral service at Windsor, the Duke and Duchess of Edinburgh attended the theatre four times.) Queen Victoria could do nothing, of course, about her own children's lack of respect for the dead, but she could and did see that an atmosphere of mourning was maintained within the precincts of the castle, where, in memory of Brown, the bell in the Curfew Tower was tolled. Also, the pipers were not permitted to play as usual under the Castle walls.

Leaning heavily on Princess Beatrice, and aided by a walking-stick, Queen Victoria crossed to the Clarence Tower, on Tuesday afternoon, April 3, for the brief funeral service conducted by the Reverend Thomas Orr, a Congregational Minister. (There was no Presbyterian Minister at Windsor.) Brown's body had been placed in an inner lead shell, which, in turn, had been lowered into a polished oak coffin, with charcoal packed between the two casings; and the whole now lay open on the bed where Brown had slept. After the service had been read the coffin was first sealed, then removed to the visitor's entrance to Clarence Tower, where a second service was conducted in the presence of a large number of servants and members of the Queen's Household.

The Queen watched from the windows of the Oak Room as the glass-sided hearse bearing Brown's remains drove away from the castle. On top of the coffin was the Queen's wreath of myrtle and choice white flowers, which seemed more suitable for a wedding, but which bore the legend in Her Majesty's hand-writing, 'A tribute of loving, grateful, and everlasting friendship and affection from his truest, best and most faithful friend, Victoria R & I.' Alongside it was a wreath from the Empress Eugenie. Thus, with the tributes of two Empresses to bear him witness, John Brown's remains were drawn through the streets of Windsor on the way to the railway station by horses suitably caparisoned with sable plumes. Most of the shops along the route to the station were shut, their blinds drawn, as a mark of respect to the Queen's favourite.

Nearly five hundred mourners, including parties of Colonel Farquharson's men from Invercauld, and of the Earl of Fife's men from Mar Lodge, attended Brown's funeral in Crathie cemetery on Thursday, April 5. To serve as a pall Queen Victoria had sent the rather faded and worn tartan plaid which had accompanied Her Majesty and her attendant on all their outings at Balmoral. It was removed at the last moment as the coffin was lowered into its grave. In paying her last respects to her friend the Queen had thought of everything, including this scribbled reminder to Hugh Brown, 'To tell Mrs Hugh to place a wreath of flowers in dear Brown's room on his bed on the day.'

There were still patches of snow on the hills above Balmoral when Queen Victoria came north in May, and visited Brown's grave for the first time. She was still feeling terribly depressed. As she wrote to the Empress Augusta before leaving Windsor, 'I miss my faithful, kind friend and constant companion more and more at every turn . . .' She added that she was still lame ('The last few days I have been able to get about my room on two sticks, but I still have to be carried up and down stairs').[150]

Within an hour of her arrival at Balmoral the Queen drove off in her pony-chair to Crathie cemetery to inspect Brown's grave. In a letter to his wife, Sir Henry Ponsonby sets the scene: 'The Deeside looked very pretty with the light green birches and the sun was bright if not warm . . . It was a day that one could easily understand would make the Queen low and she was low.'[110] No headstone had yet been erected, but one had been ordered from Aberdeen, and

the Queen had already agreed upon its inscription, in con-
sultation with Tennyson.* The floral tributes of Princesses,
Empresses, and Ladies-in-Waiting, wreaths now withered
and the colour of bracken, lay strewn over the grave, but the
grave had been stripped by souvenir hunters of everything
else that was portable, including the metal holders for the
wreaths, the parchment labels, and even the bits of string
to which the labels had been attached.

By the time the Queen returned to Balmoral in the
autumn, the headstone, a handsome affair in Aberdeen
granite, with a Scottish thistle design carved on its cornice,
had been put up, and the grave enclosed by an iron railing
to discourage vandals. The wording was that of Queen
Victoria, who loved to occupy herself with such details:

This stone is erected
in affectionate
and grateful remembrance of
JOHN BROWN
The devoted and faithful
personal attendant
and beloved friend of
QUEEN VICTORIA
in whose services he had been
for 34 years
Born at Crathienaird 8 Dec. 1826
Died at Windsor Castle 27 March 1883

There followed the text suggested by Tennyson, and a
quotation from Matthew XXV:21: 'Well done, good and
faithful servant; thou hast been faithful over a few things,
I will make thee ruler over many things: Enter thou into the
joy of the Lord.'†

* The lines suggested by Tennyson are certainly not among his most
felicitous: 'That friend on whose fidelity you count, that friend given
you by circumstances over which you have no control, was God's own
gift.' The last three words have been acclaimed by Spiritualists as
belated acknowledgment of Brown's psychic powers.

† This is the quotation Sir Walter Scott had inscribed on the tomb-

By the autumn of 1883 Brown's grave had already become a tourist mecca, and the coaches and carriages plying between Ballater and Braemar stopped at Crathie regularly to permit their passengers to alight and to pay their respects to the Highlander in the tiny cemetery. As many as a hundred visitors a day made this pilgrimage during August, according to Mrs Campbell, wife of the Crathie Minister. 'You should charge a shilling a head,' the practical Lord Bridport suggested.

At one time Albert memorials had occupied Queen Victoria's attention. Now it was Brown memorials. They ranged from plaster of Paris busts of the gillie to gold tie-pins of Brown's head set in diamonds (Dr Profeit, no friend of Brown, saved himself embarrassment by carrying the Brown tie-pin in a coat pocket, slipping it into his cravat only whenever he had business with the Queen).[113]

Most imposing of all the *memento mori* undoubtedly was the life-size bronze statue of Brown by the Vienna-born sculptor Edgar Boehm. This statue, which quickly turned a bright shade of green, was placed, at the Queen's request, alongside the garden cottage at Balmoral where in fair weather Her Majesty had sat in the open and worked on her despatch boxes while Brown watched over her. Now it was his bronze effigy that stood guard, for it was almost as though the Queen endowed it with a talismanic power to ward off evil. Whether or not it frightened off evil spirits, the statue was so life-like that it scared the old cottar women, who gave it a wide berth in daylight hours and crossed themselves if they were forced to pass it after dark. Nor did it meet with the approval of the strict Calvinists; Lord Erroll, for one, likened it to the graven image which Nebuchadnezzar raised to the pagan idol Bel. Local superstition,

stone of Tom Purdie, his forester, gamekeeper, and general factotum, who lies buried in Melrose Abbey. Purdie and Brown had many traits in common, including a liking for whisky. 'Tom is to be trusted with unlimited gold, but not with unmeasured whisky,' Scott used to say.

however, had nothing to do with the statue's removal after Queen Victoria's death to its present hillside niche. This, as explained earlier, was the work of her enraged son, Edward VII, who sought to banish every reminder of Brown.

A compass and a map are not absolutely essential, but the sightseer would find them helpful in locating Brown's statue today, so carefully is it hidden from view on the hillside behind *Baile-na-choil*. One takes the road past the golf course until one comes to the model dairy which Prince Albert designed; then one turns off on a footpath and climbs until, in rounding a bend, one comes almost face to face with the green giant, screened by fir trees and larches. So secluded was the spot on the day that I visited it that a young hind broke from cover and bounded ahead on the footpath, as though to show me the way. It is a supremely confident-looking John Brown who gazes out on the Dee Valley from this leafy bower. Here, one feels, is a gillie who could not easily be put out of countenance by a Lord-in-Waiting.

Boehm, that 'Landseer in marble', as he was called, has depicted the Highlander bareheaded and in his native costume, with a sly suggestion of a smile playing over his rugged, handsome features. The chest is expanded, the better to display the medals which the Queen awarded to him for services beyond the call of duty. Beneath are carved the enigmatic words, suggested to the Queen by Tennyson:

'Friend more than Servant, Loyal, Truthful, Brave,
Self less than Duty, even to the Grave.'

13

ALONE

'FRIEND more than servant,' yes—but how much more? How intimate was the relationship between the Queen and her servant? Where did the friendship begin, and where did it end? These questions have puzzled all who have studied Queen Victoria's life in any detail. Probably the man best able to answer them was the Reverend Randall T. Davidson, the future Archbishop of Canterbury, who, ironically, entered Queen Victoria's life just as Brown was departing from it. There was a slight overlapping in their periods of influence, for Davidson was summoned to Windsor Castle for his first audience with the Queen on December 9, 1882. 'Was seldom more struck than I have been by his personality,' the Queen recorded as her first impression of Davidson, who was then only thirty-five. Some intuitive feeling prompted her to add, 'I feel that Mr Davidson . . . may be of great use to me . . .'[148] Following her intuition the Queen named Davidson to fill the office of Dean of Windsor when the Deanery unexpectedly fell vacant in May, 1883, but by that time the young cleric's 'great use' had become apparent.

Randall T. Davidson had a number of important attributes to recommend him to Her Majesty. For one thing, he was a pure-blooded Scot, born in Edinburgh of Presbyterian parents. For another, he had the right social and religious connections, having married Archbishop Tait's daughter, as well as having served that prelate as chaplain-secretary at Lambeth Palace. Then again, Dean Davidson was of 'singularly pleasing' appearance, as Queen Victoria, always responsive to masculine good looks, was quick to note. He was clean-shaven, and had the domed forehead and intense blue eyes that betoken the intellectual, but his smile the

Queen found wholly disarming. Neither was his youth an 'insurmountable obstacle' in her eyes. It was, as she remarked, 'a fault which recedes quickly . . .'[10]

Dean Davidson, for his part, was awestruck by Queen Victoria from the beginning, and even more so by the responsibility that had suddenly been thrust upon him. Of an interview with the Queen which took place less than two months after Brown's death, he wrote in his diary, 'Most touching, solemn and interesting, but terribly difficult.' He then invoked the Almighty, 'Oh God give me guidance and grace if I am to be called on thus to counsel and strengthen in spiritual things.'[10] The Dean was to need all the Divine guidance and grace he could muster in months to come, for nothing in his previous experience at Lambeth Palace had prepared him for the seemingly mad caprices of the Sovereign he now served.

In preparation for the memorial service at the Royal Mausoleum, Frogmore, on December 14, 1883, the twenty-second anniversary of Prince Albert's death, the Queen commanded Davidson to draw up a special prayer which would bracket the Prince Consort with John Brown, and at the same time dwell upon the death of Davidson's predecessor, Dean Wellesley, and upon the travels of Prince Arthur, the Duke of Connaught, who was at that moment in India. 'A very difficult task', he noted in his diary, 'but it must be done.'[10] Gradually the Dean was introduced to the weird cult Queen Victoria consecrated to the dead, a cult which decreed that Prince Albert's room at Windsor should remain exactly as he had left it, with his hats, gloves and canes lying about, and that even Brown's room in the Clarence Tower should be sealed off. One day shortly after his appointment the Dean was startled to observe a footman bring hot shaving water to Prince Albert's dressing-room at Osborne at about the hour the Prince Consort had been accustomed to dress for dinner. He was told that this ritual had occurred daily ever since the Prince's death. ('I have again and again had talks with the Queen there before dinner with the hot water actually steaming', Davidson later recalled.)[10] The Dean's greatest shock, however, came in March, 1884, when he learned that the Queen had written a memoir of John Brown, which she intended to publish, together with excerpts from Brown's diaries.

In February Queen Victoria, without much fanfare, had published *More Leaves from the Journal of a Life in the Highlands,* which she had dedicated to Brown (his name seemed to pop up on nearly every page). Gladstone, to whom the Queen had sent an advance copy, thought the book 'innocence itself'; but the Queen's family were acid in their comments, the Prince of Wales complaining that his name had not been mentioned once (it had occurred five times, his mother corrected him). Whatever the Royal family might think of *More Leaves,* the public gave the book a warm reception ('few sovereigns and fewer people have been so kindly spoken of as herself', she wrote to Sir Theodore Martin). This success gave Her Majesty the idea of embarking upon a Life of Brown, which she intended for private publication in the first instance, though few of her advisers doubted that the book would be long in reaching the larger public.

News of this latest undertaking burst like a bombshell upon the Household, sending its various members scurrying for the nearest cover. Sir Theodore Martin, who was approached for help in editing the memoir, begged off on the grounds that his wife's delicate health required his constant attention. Ponsonby, whom the Queen next sounded out, referred her to the Bishop of Ripon and to Dr Cameron Lees, of St Giles's, Edinburgh, as being more competent in literary matters. These good clerics, though appalled at the thought that the Brown memoir and the diaries might see light of day, ducked a direct confrontation with the Queen. This left Dean Davidson, the 'new boy', as designee to brave Her Majesty on this delicate subject. Davidson's advice, literary or otherwise, had not been sought by the Queen, but as soon as he had read the Brown memoir in rough draft the Dean determined that its publication must be stopped at all costs, even if it meant resigning his office. Accordingly, in thanking the Queen for a presentation copy of *More Leaves*, Davidson seized the opportunity to hint that a further instalment of the Queen's Highland journals would be inadvisable. Many among the humbler classes had not shown themselves worthy of the Queen's 'gracious confidences so frankly given', to judge by the criticism that had appeared in certain journals. In calling this to Her Majesty's attention he hoped that he would not be deemed presumptious, the Dean concluded.[10]

Presumptuous was exactly what Queen Victoria thought of the Dean's intervention, and she lost no time in letting it be known that she intended to publish the Brown memoir despite his objections, whereupon the Dean declared, in a second letter, that he felt duty bound to use every means of persuasion, so strongly did he feel on the subject. The Queen, through Lady Ely, asked Davidson to withdraw his remarks, or at least to apologise for the pain they had caused her. The Dean was willing to apologise for the pain, 'but as to the suggested book . . . I must adhere to everything that I have said'.[10] Having stood his ground, the Dean then offered to resign.

Unaccustomed to such opposition, the Queen banished Dean Davidson from her sight. His place in the pulpit on Sunday was taken by another cleric. Then, as suddenly as it had blown up, the quarrel was over. Summoned to her presence on an entirely different matter, Davidson found the Queen 'more friendly than ever', in his own words. 'My belief is that she liked and trusted best those who occasionally incurred her wrath.'[10] As for the Queen's Life of Brown and the excerpts from the gillie's diaries, we have Arthur Ponsonby's word for it that his father, Sir Henry, burned them.*[11]

* The Spiritualists gleefully hail this bonfire as proof that Brown's diaries contained records of seances which the Queen held with the Highlander acting as her medium.

What could the Brown memoir have contained to throw the Queen's Household into such an uproar, and to cause the Dean of Windsor to threaten to resign? Judging from the Queen's published Highland journals, the mixture would have been much the same as before—more humorous anecdotes in which Brown figured as Sancho Panza, more of his 'cheery, original way of saying things', as the Queen expressed it. (Brown once described as 'hell and hot water' the relationship existing between the Duchess of Roxburghe and the Hon. Horatia Stopford, both Women of the Bedchamber, who were not on speaking terms.)[113] That in addition to this arcana the memoir contained matter which her advisers considered explosive is made all too clear in a letter from Sir Henry Ponsonby to the Queen in which, in advising against publication of the memoir, he refers to 'Your Majesty's innermost and most sacred feelings . . . passages which will be misunderstood if read by strangers . . .'[114]

Just how sacred her feelings for Brown were, and how open to misconstruction they would have been, became evident to me when in the course of my research I came upon an extract from the Queen's journals which escaped the bonfire. The extract was copied out by the Queen after Brown's death, and sent in the form of a letter to his brother Hugh, presumably for perusal by the entire Brown clan. It is worthwhile recalling the incident to which the Queen refers in her letter. In June, 1866, Queen Victoria lost a grandson, Prince Sigismund, the Princess Royal's youngest son, who died of a cerebral haemorrhage. This sudden death seems to have constituted a moment of truth for the Queen in revealing to her, as she turned to Brown for comfort, that her own grief for Prince Albert had diminished. The letter to Hugh Brown, which is undated, reads as follows:*

'I found these words in an old Diary or Journal of mine.

* This letter is now in the possession of Brown's great-niece, Mrs Hilda Harris, of Stockport, Cheshire.

I was in great trouble about the Princess Royal who had
lost her child in '66 and dear John said to me: "I wish to
take care of my dear good mistress till I die. You'll never
have an honester servant" I took and held his dear
kind hand and I said I hoped he might long be spared to
comfort me and he answered, "But we all must die."
'Afterwards my beloved John would say: "You haven't
a more devoted servant than Brown"—and oh! how I
felt that!
'Afterwards so often I told him no one loved him more
than I did or had a better friend than me: and he answered "Nor you—than me." "No one loves you more".'
(The under-lining is the Queen's own.)

It is possible, indeed probable, that Queen Victoria's
journals contained other protestations of a similar nature,
and that these formed a substantial part of the projected
memoir. In the circumstances, it is understandable that the
Dean of Windsor should risk his future career in order to
prevent publication of such a memoir. The amazing thing,
of course, is that Queen Victoria should want to share such
confidences with the world. It is perhaps the most convincing argument that has ever been put forward as to the
innocence of the Queen's love for Brown. Had there been
anything at all immoral about that relationship the Queen,
presumably, would have been at pains to hide it. Far from
trying to conceal it, here was the Queen ready to proclaim
her love for Brown aloud, and only the combined pressure
of her spiritual and temporal advisers prevented her from
doing so. (Lord Rowton, in desperation, suggested that
Brown's diary should be set in type by one confidential man,
who would drag out the job over six months, by which time
'H.M. would see how impossible it was to issue it', according
to Ponsonby.)[78]

But if Queen Victoria's love for Brown was wholly blame-
less, wherein did the Highlander's attraction lie? In the

letter just quoted Brown appears as an unpleasant, Uriah Heep-like creature insisting over much upon his own worth ('You'll never have an honester servant, etc.') What could the Queen possibly see in him?

The answer lies in Queen Victoria's isolation—'alone on that terrible height', as Tennyson expressed it. With the exception of Brown, Queen Victoria was never able to form a deep, personal friendship with any of her subjects. Some engrained professional instinct—perhaps it was the fear of showing favouritism—prevented her from becoming truly intimate, even with Bedchamber women like Jane Lady Churchill and Anne Duchess of Athole, who had devoted their lives to her service. The Queen herself bemoaned the lack of a woman in whom she could confide ('a woman requires woman's society and sympathy sometimes, as men do men's', she had written to her Uncle Leopold while Albert was still alive). Undoubtedly this was what Dean Davidson had in mind when he deplored the fact that Her Majesty had no one 'on the appropriate terms with her for friendly remonstrance or even raillery of a kindly sort.'[10]

Friendly remonstrance, raillery—this was the rôle that Brown filled to perfection. Brown was in the tradition of the great Court jesters of Tudor and Stuart times. He was in line with Will Somers, Henry VIII's fool, who 'pain'd the devil' with the truth, and who mocked Cardinal Wolsey to his face. Brown's prototype was Archy Armstrong, 'the foul-mouthed Scot', who started life as a sheep-stealer, but who lived to find favour with James I. As Laurence Housman remarks, 'The special function of Mr John Brown is not to be a Courtier . . . his way is to tread heavily on the border-line which divides familiarity from respect.'[64]

Viewed in this light, Queen Victoria's submission to Brown's rough ministrations, her toleration of him addressing her as 'wumman', become understandable. As Lytton Strachey points out, 'it is no uncommon thing for an autocratic dowager to allow some trusted indispensable servant to adopt towards her an attitude of authority which is jealously forbidden to relatives or friends . . .'[136]

In accepting such a symbiotic relationship as the mirror image for Queen Victoria's attachment to Brown there are various inconsistencies to be accommodated, contradictions to be reconciled. Would Strachey's dowager have addressed her trusted servant as 'darling one', for example? I came across this expression in an otherwise businesslike letter which Queen Victoria wrote to Brown in October, 1874, urging him to send for his brother, Hugh, then in New Zealand, because their mother's health was failing. 'I hope, darling one, you will do this', the Queen concluded—the ease with which the expression slips out would seem to indicate that it was an habitual term of endearment. Would Strachey's dowager, too, have sent lacey valentines to her favourite butler or chauffeur? Lady Longford, in researching her biography of Queen Victoria, managed to unearth at Windsor a handful of greeting cards, some in lace-like frames, which the Queen had addressed to Brown.[78] One such card seemed to betoken a quarrel for its illuminated verse read, 'Forgive & Ye shall be Forgiven. St. Luke vi.37.' Another, dated January 1, 1877, showed a saucy serving-maid, with a verse which commanded Brown to 'Smile on her and smile on me, and let your answer loving be' and was inscribed, 'To my best friend JB from his best friend, V.R.I.' It was exactly the sort of valentine a tweeny might send to the under footman with whom she was walking out.

In fairness, it should be pointed out that Queen Victoria sent valentines to Disraeli as well (in acknowledging one such Dizzy speaks of 'the pretty picture that fell from a rosy cloud this morn').[148] In retrospect, these valentines acquire a certain period charm—could it lie in the reflection that the preoccupation of a tweeny might also be that of a Queen? If the Queen chose to place her Prime Minister and her personal servant on the same footing as recipients of this gracious custom, who was there to question the wisdom of her choice?

It was Queen Victoria's way of doing things, and to her it seemed wholly natural, just as it seemed natural to order the Dean of Windsor to bracket Prince Albert and John Brown in the same memorial prayer.

Truth seldom catches up the lie, and nowhere is this more apparent than in the case of Monarchs, who are ready-made subjects for mythomania. (The willingness to attribute insanity to members of Royalty who are perfectly sane is a case in point. Perhaps a form of sympathetic magic is involved. Perhaps he who mythologizes about a Monarch is in the position of the primitive mother who, in the hopes of averting the eyes of jealous gods, loudly denigrates her child, bewailing its ugliness, its bad temper and so on. No such genial motive, however, can be ascribed to the author of a libellous pamphlet which appeared in 1873 alleging, with some show of circumstantial evidence, that Queen Victoria was the morganatic wife of John Brown, and that she had borne him a child. The pamphlet, which enjoyed a wide vogue, was the work of one Alexander Robertson, a native of Doundounadine, near Dunkeld, in the Eastern Highlands, who was a republican of deepest hue, and who had a bee in his bonnet concerning the toll bridge which the Dukes of Athole operated across the river Tay at Dunkeld. For years Robertson had carried on a half-insane agitation to have the bridge toll repealed, going so far as to petition the Lord Chancellor to remove the 7th Duke of Athole from the magistrate's bench for having embezzled public funds.* The Queen's name was dragged into this bizarre dispute,

---

* This explains the prolix title of the pamphlet, *John Brown, A Correspondence with the Lord Chancellor, Regarding a Charge of Fraud and Embezzlement Preferred Against His Grace the Duke of Athole, K.T.* It was published at 37a Clerkenwell Green, London, which now houses the Marx Memorial Library, and which has working-class associations dating back two centuries. It was here that the first Socialist press in Britain was founded, by William Morris in 1893. It was here that Lenin, for a brief period in 1902, edited *Iskra*, the organ of the Russian Social Democrats.

presumably because Anne Duchess of Athole was one of her Ladies-in-Waiting. Had he confined himself to the allegation that the Queen had been secretly married to Brown in the Presbyterian church, with the Duchess of Roxburghe as her witness, Robertson would have made himself appear ridiculous enough. By asserting that the Queen had travelled to Lausanne, Switzerland in great secrecy in order to give birth to Brown's child, the pamphleteer was plainly indulging in the wildest sort of fantasy.

It was Lucerne, not Lausanne, that Queen Victoria visited in August, 1868, the only time she ever set foot on Swiss soil, and far from being kept secret, her visit had all the fanfare, and many of the logistical problems, of a travelling circus. Apart from Prince Leopold and her two daughters, Beatrice and Louise, the Queen was accompanied by an entourage which included a Lady-in-Waiting, a German secretary to handle her correspondence with her German relatives, the Keeper of the Privy Purse, and her own personal chaplain, plus the usual complement of cooks, wardrobe maids and menservants. In addition, her bed and her carriage and horses travelled with the Queen.

The charming Pension Wallis, overlooking Mont Pilatus and the Rigi, threatened to burst at the seams with so many supernumeraries, so that when Prince Arthur announced his intention to join his mother, the Queen begged him to reconsider. 'We have no room to spare for a mouse', she wrote.[83] But the truth, as stated earlier, is the tortoise in the race to overtake the lie, and the Robertson libel has been repeated many times over by those who have not bothered, or perhaps did not want to ascertain its veracity.* There was no question of bringing the pamphleteer to justice, for, as Earl Granville wrote to the Lord Chancellor at the time,

* The Dowager Duchess of Roxburghe, who was named in the pamphlet as a witness of the Queen's morganatic marriage, laughed at the suggestion when Frederick Ponsonby questioned her many years later. The Duchess herself was the victim of a similarly cruel slander in 1880 when *Vanity Fair* reported that she was about to marry the factor on her Scottish estate.

'The evils of a discussion on such a subject in a Court of Law, or of an attempt to punish the offender without full discussion appear to me immense.'[118]

Even had Queen Victoria been inclined to stoop to folly, there were always her ladies, most of them pious and given to good works, to stand Cerberus-like between Her Majesty and any such inclination. Bedchamber women like Jane Lady Churchill, Jane Marchioness of Ely, and the Hon. Horatia Stopford, with her strong High Church views—these were the best guarantors of the Queen's innocence, as far as any irregular union was concerned. The Countess of Erroll, whom Dean Davidson described as a 'hot Evangelical', alone was enough to underwrite the purity of the Court. When in waiting Lady Erroll divided her time between handing out temperance tracts and campaigning against Windsor theatricals, which she considered to be 'works of the devil'. (Lady Erroll once begged the Queen to close Kew Gardens to the public on Sundays so that the Lord's Day might not be defiled by people who took their ease there.)[91] These good ladies had the opportunity to observe Queen Victoria from day to day, and had there been the slightest hint of impropriety in her relationship with Brown, they would have found excuses to retire from Court.

The Queen, however, had no need of her ladies to protect her from moral turpitude, for her own sense of right and wrong was sufficiently strong. She was, in fact, a deeply religious woman, as all who knew her intimately have testified. Her religion was strictly practical—she did not hesitate to label as 'twaddle' the sentiments expressed by the clergyman who wrote to her after Prince Albert's death, 'Henceforth you must remember that Christ Himself will be your husband'—but it was nonetheless deeply felt.

We have seen how in moments of great emotional stress the Queen's instinct was always to seek spiritual counsel. After the Prince Consort's death it was to the Rev. Norman Macleod ('How I loved to talk to him . . . to speak to him of my sorrows and anxieties')[146] that the Queen had turned, and this big, jovial ecclesiastic read Robert Burns aloud to her while she discovered the therapeutic value of the spinning-wheel. Then, in 1866, troubled because her grief for Albert had begun to wane, the Queen had turned to tender-hearted Dean Wellesley, to be reassured that 'a settled mournful resignation' was a state to be desired.[78] Seventeen years later the pain of her parting from Brown drove the Queen to unburden herself to Wellesley's successor, Dean Davidson, even though the 'Boy Dean', as he was called, was a comparative stranger to her at that time.

Dean Davidson, who was to remain Queen Victoria's friend for the rest of her days, was impressed by the 'religious basis' of her life, 'her genuine and prayerful anxiety to do right at every juncture', as he expressed it.[10] Many years after the Queen's death, and after he himself had been elevated to the See of Canterbury, Archbishop Davidson confided to Hector Bolitho that he thought the Queen's friendship with Brown to be 'unwise'. 'One had only to know the Queen personally to realise how innocent it was', the archbishop added.[15]

Most of the misunderstandings concerning Queen Victoria have arisen from trying to judge her by ordinary standards when she was, by virtue both of her position and of her character, an extraordinary being. Even Strachey's auto-cratic dowager, as we have seen, is an over-simplification, for Queen Victoria does not fit easily into any category. She was a highly complex personality, made vivid by her con-tradictions, and capable of emotions that were startling in their range and depth. Her denigrators have insisted upon juxtaposing her love for John Brown with her love for Prince Albert, as though they were the same in degree and kind, and as though the one cancelled out the other. Noth-ing could have been further from the truth. The spectrum of the Queen's love was broad enough to accommodate at opposite ends the cold, priggish, unhappy Coburger who was her consort, and the simple, warm-hearted Highlander whom her husband had chosen to lead her pony. Somewhere in between there was room for Lord Beaconsfield, to whom the Queen sent valentines of cupid basking on cloud banks, and for the sly, ingratiating, faintly sinister Munshi from Agra, Abdul Karim, who was to follow on as Brown's successor. The Queen saw nothing incongruous in such a hugger-mugger arrangement; to her it seemed the natural order of things, as natural as her belief, amounting to a certainty, that she would be reunited with her loved ones after death, and that they would resume relations where they had left off.

Speculation concerning life after death bulked large in those intimate discussions which the Queen held with Dean Davidson in what had been Albert's dressing-room at Osborne, with the steam rising from his shaving-water. Her grief for Brown still being fresh, the Queen was concerned in those early tête-a-têtes with the prospect of meeting the Highlander again in the great beyond; but in general she liked allusions to life beyond the grave to be made in sermons, as well as in conversation. Dean Davidson was surprised by the definiteness of the Queen's beliefs on the subject. 'It did not correspond with the sort of common sense test which she liked to apply to theological teachings,' he explained.[10] He was even more astonished by the hieratic order which the Queen's eschatology sought to impose upon the hereafter.

Nowhere is this hieratic order better expressed than in the Queen's last will and testament which is dated October 25, 1897, and which is deserving of attention as a social document in its own right. The Queen's will, which Lady Longford unearthed during her researches at Windsor, reads:

'I die in peace with all fully aware of my many faults relying with confidence on the love, mercy and goodness of my Heavenly Father and His Blessed Son & earnestly trusting to be reunited to my beloved Husband, my dearest Mother, my beloved Children and 3 dear sons-in-law.—And all who have been very near & dear to me on earth.

Also I hope to meet those who have so faithfully & so devotedly served me especially good John Brown and good Annie Macdonald who I trusted would help to lay my remains in my coffin & to see me placed next to my dearly loved Husband in the mausoleum at Frogmore.'[78]

The remarkable thing about this document is not, of course, that it associates her trusted servants with members of the Queen's family—that was Queen Victoria's way—but that it relegates these servants to a secondary plane, or substratum of the Victorian Valhalla. In those first dark days after Brown's death, the Queen had written agonizingly to her grandson, Prince George of Wales, 'I have lost my dearest best friend who no-one in this world can ever replace.'[78] But by 1897, when the Queen came to make out her will, Brown had been paired off with Annie Macdonald as a devoted and faithful retainer.* It had taken the Queen nearly fifteen years to disentangle her emotions from the chaotic state in which Brown's death had left them, but she had at last got her priorities right.

Further evidence of this new order of priorities may be found in the sepulchral rounds, her version of the Stations of the Cross, which Queen Victoria made when at Balmoral. Her first thought naturally was for the Prince Consort, the Alpha of her existence; and no sooner did she arrive each autumn than she had herself driven to Craig Lowrigan, where Prince Albert's cairn towered over the others like Cheops over the lesser pyramids of Giza. Often the first snow lay on the ground before the Queen got around to John Brown, Her Majesty postponing until just before her departure for Windsor her visit to Brown's grave. Marie

* Annie Macdonald, the Queen's wardrobe maid, died in June, 1897, after having served her mistress for forty-one years. Annie it was who lifted the Queen dry-eyed and lifeless, and put her to bed on the night that Prince Albert died.

Mallet, a Woman of the Bedchamber, gives us a glimpse of Queen Victoria, aged seventy-seven and crippled by gout, on such a pious errand in 1896. 'I have been walking with the Queen this morning,' Mrs Mallet wrote to her husband on November 5, 1896, 'and we went to the Church to wreathe the tombs of various Browns. H.M. got out of her chair and laid a bunch of fresh flowers on John Brown's grave with her own hands . . . it is really very curious, but do not mention the curious fact.'[91]

Overlooked by those who insist that Queen Victoria and John Brown were lovers is the fact that from the moment of his death the Queen honoured Prince Albert's memory, until her own death intervened. Either her grief for Albert was sincere, or it made a mockery of death, and made of Victoria the arch-humbug of the age to which she lent her name. As honesty—what Dean Davidson called her 'absolute truthfulness and simplicity'—was perhaps Queen Victoria's outstanding virtue, the second hypothesis may be ruled out. But one need not take the Dean's word for it. One has only to examine the published extracts from Queen Victoria's journals, in which the Queen's most intimate thoughts are recorded to see that, although time blunted the keen edge of her grief, it never left her. To select but one example from among many, the Queen's journal entry for August 20, 1867, pictures her feeling of desolation upon arriving at Floors, the Duchess of Roxburghe's estate, near the Scottish border. 'The feeling of loneliness,' she wrote, 'when I saw no room for my darling, and felt I was indeed alone and a widow, overcame me very sadly . . . I thought so much of all dearest Albert would have done and said, and how he would have wandered about everywhere, admired everything, looked at everything—and now! Oh! must it ever, ever be so?'[146] In August, 1867, the 'Mrs Brown' scandal, it will be recalled, was at its height, with the Queen's name linked to that of her gillie by a dozen different rumours, each more outrageous than the other, and Brown himself pictured leaning against

the Throne in the pages of *Tomahawk*. A year later, in opening the Glassalt Shiel, the hunting lodge which Queen
Victoria built overlooking Loch Muich, she noted, 'The sad
thought struck me that it was the first widow's house, not
built by him or hallowed to his memory. But I am sure his
blessing does rest on it, and on those who live in it.'[146]

Queen Victoria had only one husband, and her place was
beside him in the magnificent mausoleum at Frogmore, as is
made plain by her will. In time the Frogmore mausoleum
became a sort of pantheon, with busts and monuments to
the Queen's children who preceded her in death, and to her
sons-in-law who likewise predeceased her. Even in this
holy-of-holies a place was made for Brown, but it was not
beneath the great dome where sun shafts beat down on the
marble effigy of the Prince Consort sculptured by Marochetti. Brown was consigned to the ambulatory which en-
closes the inner sanctum, like one of the outer circles of
purgatory that ring paradise in Dante's *Divine Comedy*.
There beneath a funeral urn a modest tablet was erected
to Brown's memory.

Looking through the Brown memorabilia that are now the
property of his great-nephew, Mr Hugh Lamond, I came
across more than one token of Queen Victoria's high esteem
for her Highland servant. Here, it was a gold watch, which
the Queen had given to Brown for Christmas, 1875; there,
it was a sterling silver pipe case with 'VRI Christmas 1880'
engraved on it, and with a handsome meershaum pipe
inside. There was even a volume of poems in Scottish dialect
after the manner of Burns with the inscription, 'To Her
Faithful Attendant John Brown from his true friend VR,
Balmoral, June 7, 1869.'

But the most touching of all these gifts, to my way of
thinking, was a leather-bound Bible, which bore the inscription in the Queen's handwriting on its fly-leaf, 'To John
Brown from his faithful friend VRI, Osborne, Feb. 10, 1878.'
The tenth of February was the most sacred day in Queen

Victoria's calendar, for it was her wedding anniversary. Here, it would seem, was another overwhelming proof of the innocence of her relationship with Brown, for what widow of taste and sensibility would make her lover the present of a Bible on such an occasion? But there was more to it than that. Dean Davidson had marvelled at the sweeping nature of the Queen's affections, which had sought to encompass within a single prayer the Prince Consort, John Brown, and his own predecessor, Dean Wellesley, while sparing a thought for the safety of the Queen's son, Prince Arthur, in his travels. How much greater was the love expressed in this simple gift on the Queen's thirty-eighth wedding anniversary, by means of which her trusted servant and friend was made to share at once in the happiness of her married life, and in her grief at her husband's passing. The synthesis thus achieved, like certain Vedic chants, seemed almost breath-taking in its beauty and simplicity.

SELECT BIBLIOGRAPHY

(*Note:* The numbers in the text refer to sources listed in the Bibliography below).

1. Airlie, Mabell Countess of. *Thatched with Gold.* London: Hutchinson, 1962.
2. Albert. *The Prince Consort and His Brother: Two Hundred New Letters.* H. Bolitho (Ed.). London: Cobden, Sanderson, 1933.
3. Alice, Grand Duchess of Hesse. *Letters to Her Majesty the Queen.* London: John Murray, 1885.
4. Allan, Oswald. *The Vacant Throne.* (Pamphlet). London: E. Head, 1877.
5. Allan, Oswald. *Worthy a Crown?* (Pamphlet). London: Head and Meek, 1876.
6. Amberley, John Viscount. *The Amberley Papers,* 2 vols. Bertrand and Patricia Russell (Eds.). London: L. and V. Woolf, 1937.
7. Antrim, Louisa Countess of. *Recollections.* London, 1937.
8. *The Annual Register.*
9. *Appleton's Magazine.* 'Queen Victoria's Private Character.' November 28, 1874.
10. Bell, G. K. A. *Randall Davidson.* London: Oxford University Press, 1938.
11. Benson, E. F. *As We Were: A Victorian Peep-Show.* London: Longmans, 1930.
12. Benson, E. F. *Queen Victoria.* London: Longmans, 1935.
13. Behrman, S. N. *Conversation With Max.* London: Hamish Hamilton, 1960.
14. Blake, Robert. *Disraeli.* London: Eyre and Spottiswoode, 1966.

15. Bolitho, Hector. *Victoria the Widow and Her Son.* London: Cobden-Sanderson, 1934.
16. Bolitho, Hector. *The Reign of Queen Victoria.* London: Collins, 1949.
17. Bradlaugh, Charles. *The Impeachment of the House of Brunswick.* (Pamphlet). London: Austin, 1873.
18. Bright, John. *The Diaries of John Bright.* R. A. J. Walling (Ed.) London: Cassell, 1930.
19. British Medical Journal. *Porphyria—A Royal Malady.* By Ida MacAlpine, M.D., M.R.C.P., Richard Hunter, M.D., M.R.C.P., D.P.M., Professor C. Rimington, and others. London: British Medical Association, 1968.
20. Broadhurst, Henry. *From a Stonemason's Bench to the Treasury Bench.* London: Hutchinson, 1901.
21. Brown, Ivor. *Balmoral.* London: Collins, 1955.
22. Buckle, G. E. and Monypenny, W. F. *The Life of Benjamin Disraeli, Earl of Beaconsfield,* 2 vols. London: John Murray, 1929.
23. Clarendon. *Life and Letters of George William Frederick, Fourth Earl of Clarendon,* 2 vols. Sir Herbert Maxwell (Ed.). London: Edward Arnold, 1913.
24. Conway, Moncure D. Autobiography: *Memories and Experiences.* London: Cassell, 1904.
25. Corti, Egon. *The Downfall of Three Dynasties,* London: Methuen, 1934.
26. Corti, Egon. *The British Empress.* London: Cassell, 1957.
27. Crawford, Emily. *Victoria, Queen and Ruler.* London: Simpkin, Marshall, 1903.
28. Creston, Dormer. *The Youthful Victoria.* London: Macmillan, 1952.
29. Crewe, the Marquess of. *Lord Rosebery.* London: John Murray, 1931.
30. Cust, Sir Lionel. *King Edward VII and His Court: Some Reminiscences.* London: John Murray, 1930.
31. Dasent, Arthur I. *John Thadeus Delane: His Life and Correspondence.* London: John Murray, 1908.

32. Davidson, E. Morrison. *Eminent Radicals in and out of Parliament*. London: E. J. Francis, 1880.
33. *The Derby Papers.*
34. Disraeli, Benjamin. *The Letters of Disraeli to Lady Bradford and Lady Chesterfield*, 2 vols. The Marquis of Zetland (Ed.). London: Ernest Benn, 1929.
35. *Dod's Parliamentary Companion.*
36. Dowty, A. A. *The Coming K———*. (Pamphlet). London: Ward, Lock and Tyler, 1872.
37. Dowty, A. A. *Edward the Seventh*. (Pamphlet). London: 1876.
38. Dowty, A. A. *Jon Duan* (Pamphlet). London: Weldon, 1874.
39. Duff, David. *Hessian Tapestry*. London: Muller, 1968.
40. Duff, David. *The Shy Princess*. London: Evans Brothers, 1958.
41. Emden, Paul H. *Behind the Throne*. London: Hodder and Stoughton, 1934.
42. Ernest II. *Memoirs of Ernest II, Duke of Saxe-Coburg-Gotha*, 4 vols. London: Remington, 1888-1890.
43. Esher, Viscount. *Journals and Letters of Reginald, Viscount Esher*. Maurice V. Brett (Ed.). London: I. Nicholson and Watson, 1934.
44. Findlater, Richard. *Banned! A Review of Theatrical Censorship in Britain*. London: MacGibbon and Kee, 1967.
45. *Fraser's Magazine*. 'English Republicanism.' By Thomas Wright. June, 1871.
46. Fulford, Roger. *Queen Victoria*. London: Collins, 1951.
47. Gardiner, A. G. *The Life of Sir William Harcourt*, 2 vols. London: Constable, 1923.
48. Garvin, J. L. *The Life of Joseph Chamberlain*, 3 vols. London: Macmillan, 1932.
49. Gathorne-Hardy, the Hon. Alfred E. *Gathorne Hardy, First Earl of Cranbrook: A Memoir*, 2 vols. London: Longmans, 1910.
50. Gernsheim, Helmut and Alison. *Queen Victoria: A*

Biography in Word and Picture. London: Longmans, 1959.

51. Gladstone, Herbert J. G. *After Thirty Years.* London: Macmillan, 1928.

52. Gladstone, W. E. *Gladstone to His Wife.* A. Tilney Bassett (Ed.). London: Methuen, 1936.

53. Gladstone, W. E. *Political Correspondence of Mr. Gladstone and Lord Granville,* 1868–86, 4 vols. Agatha Ramm (Ed.). London: The Historical Society of Great Britain, 1952–1962.

54. Gower, Lord Ronald. *My Reminiscences,* 2 vols. London: Kegan Paul, Trench, 1883.

55. Grant, Daniel, M. P. *Royalty at Home.* London: J. S. Virtue, 1894.

56. Greville, Charles. *The Greville Memoirs,* 8 vols. London: Longmans, 1888.

57. Guedalla, Philip. *The Queen and Mr. Gladstone,* 2 vols. London: Hodder and Stoughton, 1933.

58. Gwynn, S. and Tuckwell, G. M. *The Life of the Rt. Hon. Sir Charles W. Dilke, Bart., M.P.,* 2 vols. London: John Murray, 1917.

59. Hardie, Frank. *The Political Influence of Queen Victoria.* London: Oxford University Press, 1935.

60. *Harper's Magazine.* 'Queen Victoria's Highland Home.' By J. R. Hunter. October, 1895.

61. Harrison, Royden. *Before the Socialists.* London: Routledge and Kegan Paul, 1965.

62. Helps, E. A. *The Correspondence of Sir Arthur Helps.* London: John Lane, The Bodley Head, 1917.

63. Hibbert, Christopher. *The Court at Windsor.* London: Longmans, 1964.

64. House, Humphry. *All in Due Time.* London: Rupert Hart-Davis, 1955.

65. Housman, Laurence. *Victoria Regina.* London: Jonathan Cape, 1934.

66. Humphrey, F. P. *The Queen at Balmoral.* London: T. F. Unwin, 1893.

67. Huntly, the Marquis of. *Auld Acquaintance*. London: Hutchinson, 1929.

68. Irving, Joseph. *Annals of Our Time, 1837–1891.*

69. James, Robert Rhodes. *Rosebery: A Biography of Archibald Philip, Fifth Earl of Rosebery.* London: Weidenfeld and Nicolson, 1963.

70. Jenkins, Roy. *Sir Charles Dilke: A Victorian Tragedy.* London: Collins, 1958.

71. Jerrold, Clare. *The Widowhood of Queen Victoria.* London: Eveleigh Nash, 1916.

72. Landseer, Sir Edwin. Correspondence transcribed and annotated by R. E. Mitchell. Victoria and Albert Museum.

73. Lee, Sidney. *Queen Victoria: A Biography.* London: Smith, Elder, 1902.

74. Lewis, D. B. Wyndham. *'Good Brown.' The Saturday Book, No. 8.* London: Hutchinson, 1948.

75. Lindsay, Patricia. *Recollections of a Royal Parish.* London: John Murray, 1902.

76. Lockhart, J. G. *Memoirs of the Life of Sir Walter Scott,* 7 vols. Edinburgh, 1937–1838.

77. Longford, Elizabeth. *'Queen Victoria's Doctors.'* (Essay). *A Century of Conflict, 1850–1950.* Martin Gilbert (Ed.). London: Hamish Hamilton, 1966.

78. Longford, Elizabeth. *Victoria R. I.* London: Weidenfeld and Nicolson, 1964.

79. Lytton, Edith Countess of. *Lady Lytton's Court Diary.* Mary Lutyens (Ed.) London: Rupert Hart-Davis, 1961.

80. Lyttleton, Lady. *Correspondence of Sarah Spencer, Lady Lyttleton, 1787–1870.* Mrs Hugh Wyndham (Ed.). London: John Murray, 1912.

81. McCarthy, Justin. *A History of Our Times,* 2 vols. London: Chatto and Windus, 1887.

82. MacCoby, Simon. *English Radicalism, 1853–1886.* London: Allen and Unwin, 1938.

83. McClintock, M. H. *The Queen Thanks Sir Howard.* London: John Murray, 1945.

84. MacConnochie, Alexander. *The Deer and Deer Forests of Scotland.* London: H. F. and G. Witherby, 1923.

85. MacConnochie, Alexander *The Royal Dee.* Aberdeen: W. Jolly and Sons, 1898.

86. MacDonagh, Michael. *The English King.* London: Ernest Benn, 1929.

87. MacLeay, Kenneth. *The Highlanders of Scotland.* London: 1866.

88. MacLeod, Donald. *Memoir of Norman MacLeod, D.D.,* 2 vols. London, 1876.

89. Magnus, Philip. *Gladstone.* London: John Murray, 1954.

90. Magnus, Philip. *King Edward the Seventh.* London: John Murray, 1964.

91. Mallet, Marie. *Life with Queen Victoria: Marie Mallet's Letters from Court,* 1887–1901. Victor Mallet (Ed.) London: John Murray, 1968.

92. Manchester. *My Dear Duchess: Social and Political Letters to the Duchess of Manchester,* 1858—69. A. L. Kennedy (Ed.) London: John Murray, 1956.

93. Marie Louise, Princess. *My Memories of Three Reigns.* London: Evans Brothers, 1956.

94. Martin, Kingsley. *The Crown and the Establishment.* London: Hutchinson, 1962.

95. Martin, Sir Theodore. *The Life of the Prince Consort,* 5 vols. London, 1875-1880.

96. Martin, Sir Theodore. *Queen Victoria as I Knew Her.* Edinburgh: W. Blackwood and Sons, 1901.

97. Michie, John Grant. *Deeside Tales.* Aberdeen: D. Wyllie and Sons, 1908.

98. Morley, John. *Life of W. E. Gladstone,* 3 vols. London: Macmillan, 1903.

99. Morton, J. C. *The Prince Consort's Farms.* London, 1863.

100. Neele, George P. *Railway Reminiscences*. London: McCorquodale, 1904.

101. Newton, Lord. *Lord Lyons: A Record of British Diplomacy*. London: Edward Arnold, 1913.

102. *Notes and Queries*.

103. O'Brien, R. Barry. *The Life of Charles Stewart Parnell*, 2. vols. London: Smith, Elder, 1898.

104. O'Brien, William. *Recollections*. London: Macmillan, 1905.

105. Pamphlet. *John Brown's Legs, or Leaves from a Journal in the Lowlands*. By Kenward Philp (Pseud.). New York: Norman L. Munro, 1884.

106. Pamphlet. *Letter to the Queen on Her Retirement from Public Life*. By One of Her Majesty's Most Loyal Subjects. London, 1875.

107. Pamphlet. *Queen Tresoria and Her People*. London: E. W. Allen, 1881.

108. Pamphlet. *Tracts for the Times, No. 1: What Does She Do With It?* By Solomon Temple, Builder. London: Alfred Book, 1871.

109. Pearson, Hesketh. *Walter Scott: His Life and Personality*. London: Methuen, 1954.

110. *The Ponsonby Papers*.

111. Ponsonby, Arthur. *Henry Ponsonby, Queen Victoria's Private Secretary*. London: Macmillan, 1942.

112. Ponsonby, Sir Frederick. *Letters of the Empress Frederick*. London: Macmillan, 1928.

113. Ponsonby, Sir Frederick. *Recollections of Three Reigns*. London: Eyre and Spottiswoode, 1951.

114. Ponsonby, Sir Frederick. *Sidelights on Queen Victoria*. London: Macmillan, 1930.

115. Ponsonby, Magdalen. *Mary Ponsonby: A Memoir, Some Letters and a Journal*. London: John Murray, 1927.

116. Prebble, John. *Culloden*. London: Secker and Warburg, 1961.

117. Prebble, John. *The Highland Clearances.* London: Secker and Warburg, 1963.
118. *Public Record Office:* Home Office Papers.
119. *Public Record Office:* Lord Chamberlain's Department.
120. *The Quarterly Review.* 'The Character of Queen Victoria.' April, 1901.
121. Read, Donald and Glasgow, Eric. *Feargus O'Connor: Irishman and Chartist.* London: Edward Arnold, 1961.
122. Ribblesdale, Lord. *Impressions and Memories.* London: Cassell, 1927.
123. Russell, W. H. *The War: From the Landing at Gallipoli to the Death of Lord Raglan.* London, 1855.
124. Ryan, Desmond. *The Phoenix Flame: A Study of Fenianism and John Devoy.* London: Authur Barker, 1937.
125. St. Aubyn, Giles. *The Royal George.* London: Constable, 1963.
126. Scott-Moncrieff, George. '*Balmorality,*' Essay in *Scotland in Quest of its Youth.* David Cleghorn Thomson (Ed.). Edinburgh: Oliver and Boyd, 1932.
127. Scrope, William. *The Art of Deer-Stalking.* London, 1838.
128. Sitwell, Edith. *Victoria of England.* London: Faber and Faber, 1936.
129. Sitwell, Sir Osbert. *Left Hand, Right Hand! An Autobiography.* London: Macmillan, 1945.
130. Stanley, the Hon. Eleanor. *Twenty Years at Court.* Mrs. Steuart Erskine (Ed.). London: Nisbet, 1916.
131. Stanley, Lady Augusta. *Letters of Lady Augusta Stanley.* H. Bolitho and A. V. Baillie (Eds.). London: Gerald Howe, 1927.
132. Stanley, Lady Augusta. *Later Letters of Lady Augusta Stanley.* H. Bolitho and A. V. Baillie (Eds.). London: Jonathan Cape, 1929.
133. Stendahl. *Love.* (Gilbert and Suzanne Sale, Translators). London: The Merlin Press, 1957.

134. Stirton, John. *Crathie and Braemar*. Aberdeen: Milne and Hutchinson, 1925.

135. Stockmar, Baron von E. *Memoirs of Baron Stockmar*, 2 vols. London: Longmans, Green, 1872.

136. Strachey, Lytton. *Queen Victoria*. London: Chatto and Windus, 1921.

137. Thompson, E. P. *William Morris: Romantic to Revolutionary*. London: Lawrence and Wishart, 1955.

138. *Tinsley's Magazine*. 'English Photographs by an American.' October, 1968.

139. Tisdall, E. E. P. *Queen Victoria's John Brown*. London: Stanley Paul, 1938.

140. Tisdall, E. E. P. *Queen Victoria's Private Life*. London: Jarrolds, 1961.

141. Tooley, Sarah A. *The Personal Life of Queen Victoria*. London: Hodder and Stoughton, 1896.

142. Tynan, P. J. P. *The Irish National Invincibles*. London: Chatham, 1894.

143. Victoria. *The Private Life of the Queen*. By One of Her Servants. London: C. Arthur Pearson, 1897.

144. *Victoria's Golden Reign: A Record of Sixty Years as Maid, Mother and Ruler*. By a Lady of the Court. London: R. E. King, 1897.

145. Victoria. *Leaves from the Journal of Our Life in the Highlands from 1848 to 1861*. Arthur Helps (Ed.). London: Smith, Elder, 1868.

146. Victoria. *More Leaves from the Journal of a Life in the Highlands from 1862 to 1882*. London: Smith, Elder, 1884.

147. Victoria. *The Letters of Queen Victoria*, First Series, 1837–1861, 3 vols. A. C. Benson and Viscount Esher (Eds.). London: John Murray, 1907.

148. Victoria. *The Letters of Queen Victoria*, Second Series, 1862–1885, 3 vols. G. E. Buckle (Ed.). London: John Murray, 1926.

149. Victoria. *The Letters of Queen Victoria*, Third Series,

1886–1901. 3 vols. G. E. Buckle (Ed.). London: John Murray, 1930.

150. Victoria. *Further Letters of Queen Victoria: From the Archives of the House of Brandenburg-Prussia.* H. Bolitho (Ed.). London: Thornton Butterworth, 1938.

151. Victoria. *Dearest Child: Letters between Queen Victoria and the Princess Royal,* 1858–1861. Roger Fulford (Ed.). London: Evans Brothers, 1964.

152. Victoria. *Dearest Mama: Letters between Queen Victoria and the Crown Princess of Prussia* 1861–1864. Roger Fulford (Ed.). London: Evans Brothers, 1968.

153. Waddington, Mary. *My First Years as a Frenchwoman,* 1876–1879. London: Smith, Elder, 1914.

154. Watson, Vera. *A Queen at Home.* London: W. H. Allen, 1952.

155. Welsford, Enid. *The Fool: His Social and Literary History.* London: Faber and Faber, 1935.

156. West, Sir Algernon. *Recollections,* 1832–1886, 2 vols. London: Smith, Elder, 1899.

157. Whibley, Charles. *Lord John Manners and His Friends,* 2 vols. London: W. Blackwood and Sons, 1925.

158. *Whitaker's Almanack.*

159. White, Terence de Vere. *The Road to Excess.* Dublin: Browne and Nolan, 1946.

160. *Who Was Who.*

161. Williams, Henry L. *Life and Biography of John Brown, Esq.,* London: E. Smith, 1883.

162. Williams, Montague. *Leaves of a Life.* London: Macmillan, 1890.

163. Williams, Montague. *Later Leaves.* London: Macmillan, 1891.

164. Wright, Thomas. *Our New Masters.* London: Strahan, 1873.

Watts, G. F., 147
Wellesley, Gerald, Dean of Wind-
    sor, 93–4, 173, 175, 221, 231,
    236
Westminster, Duke of, 180
Whistler, J. A. McNeill, 100
Wilhelm, Kaiser, 60
William IV, 28, 195, 215
Williams, Montagu, Q.C., 199
Windsor, 11, 19, 28, 36, 60, 71, 74,
    125, 137, 172, 175, 180, 194,

197, 201, 203, 204–5, 208,
    209, 217, 218, 220, 227
Wolsey, Cardinal, 224
World, The, 18, 51, 79, 194, 195,
    200
Wright, Thomas, 158
Wyattville, Sir Jeffrey, 113
Wyndham Lewis, D. B., 26
Wyon, 169

Yarrow, Dr Hal, 12, 178–9